Prior to his retirement, the Honourable Sir Oliver Popplewell was a distinguished High Court judge for nearly twenty years and was involved in a number of celebrated cases over the course of his long career. He subsequently returned to university to take a degree in PPE at Harris Manchester College as Oxford's oldest undergraduate. The second volume of his memoirs, *Hallmark: A Judge's Life at Oxford* is also published by I.B.Tauris.

'[A] delightful book... Here is a life of integrity, intelligence, decency, diligence and public service retold in a clear and self-depricating style that captures the reader from the first paragraph to the last.'
– From the Foreword by Stephen Fry

'I commend *Benchmark* to anyone who likes to read of distinguished men who lead honest and interesting lives, but are not too pompous to recall the time they drank the last of the milk during rationing.'
– Rachel Johnson, *Sunday Times*

Benchmark

A Life in the Law

Oliver Popplewell

Best wishes

Oliver Popplewell

I.B. TAURIS

LONDON · NEW YORK

Published in 2009 by I.B.Tauris & Co Ltd
6 Salem Road, London W2 4BU
175 Fifth Avenue, New York NY 10010
www.ibtauris.com

Distributed in the United States and Canada Exclusively by Palgrave
Macmillan, 175 Fifth Avenue, New York NY 10010

ISBN 978 1 84511 932 4

A full CIP record for this book is available from the British Library
A full CIP record for this book is available from the Library of Congress
Library of Congress catalog card: available

Typeset in Baskerville by Dexter Haven Associates, London
Printed and bound in India by Thomson Press India Ltd

Contents

Illustrations

Illustrations

Hêraclîtus

They told me, Hêraclîtus, they told me you were dead;
They brought me bitter news to hear and bitter tears to shed.
I wept, as I remember'd, how often you and I
Had tired the sun with talking and sent him down the sky.

And now that thou art lying, my dear old Carian guest,
A handful of grey ashes, long, long ago at rest,
Still are thy pleasant voices, thy nightingales, awake,
For Death, he taketh all away, but them he cannot take.

William Cory

For my beloved Margaret

Foreword
Stephen Fry

Perhaps the most stupid word I ever uttered was spoken in Friday Cottage, Little Walsingham, Norfolk, a charming little house of which you will learn more in the body of this delightful book. The word was 'no', an innocent little monosyllable, more often than not the most sensible sound ever to leave a person's lips. Context, however, is all.

I was perched on a low chair by the fire in the sitting room of the cottage, talking about cricket with the hero of these ensuing pages and the conversation went something like this.

'Stephen, would you like me to put you up for membership of the MCC?'

'Oh. Wow. That's awfully kind...thank you, but...no.'

No? I sometimes wake up sweating and screaming when my dreams replay the naked idiocy of this reply. I suppose it was a kind of shyness, an attempt to show independence, or perhaps even a polite reluctance to put anyone to trouble. Who knows the workings of the adolescent mind? In any event, there followed a conversation some four or five years later in the same room:

'Um. You remember asking me if I wanted to be a member of the MCC...well I think perhaps I would quite like it after all.'

'Ah...I'm sorry to say that since I asked you there's been an extraordinary run on membership. I'm afraid the waiting list is now seventeen or eighteen years. At the time it was more or less instant...still, if you'd like me to...?'

'Oh. Oh I see. Oh well. Never mind.'

At the age of 20 it never occurred to me that 17 years would ever pass, or that if they did any single institution would remain in place, unaltered. If I had assented that second time I would now be a member of some 11 or 12 years' standing.

I suppose it is in rather poor taste to begin an introduction to another man's life story with regret from one's own, but with a life so multi-faceted as Oliver Popplewell's, one point of entry is as valuable, I think, as another.

On the surface our hero might be thought to have led a charmed life, the kind of life for which *Telegraph* obituaries are so avidly scoured these days. To combine a brilliant career at the bar, crowned by appointment as a High Court judge (not to mention the ultimate accolade of seeing his obiter dicta parodied in *Private Eye* as Mr Justice Popplecarrot: 'And with the time approaching a disturbing twenty to two, I think we might safely adjourn ... ') with a life in cricket culminating in the presidency of that very Marylebone Cricket Club would certainly be enough for most.

Charterhouse, Cambridge, the bar, the bench, the MCC ... it all sounds very safe, very establishment, very cosy. Certainly Oliver cannot, and does not, pretend to have grown up in a slum fighting his way to success, kicking against insuperable odds. Nonetheless, although he was educated privately and raised by the obligatory beloved Nanny, everything Oliver achieved he achieved by a peculiarly English blend of effort, charm and talent. His upbringing was more Betjeman Metroland than Wodehouse Mayfair, and his success has been entirely his own. Most of his contemporaries, after all, many from wealthier, better-connected families, have done far less.

It is certainly true, nonetheless, that Oliver did benefit from being a member of the legendary Charterhouse eleven, including the great P.B.H.May and immortalised by the writer Simon Raven, England's naughtiest post-war novelist. For those familiar with Raven's *Alms for Oblivion* sequence, Oliver is represented (in my imagination, at least, for I believe Oliver denies it) by the character of Blessington. Every now and then, schools produce a generation of characters who influence and force each other forwards, instilling an invaluable quality of confidence each in the other. Shrewsbury's Ingrams, Booker, Foot and Rushton are a famous example; the Carthusian sodality of William Rees-Mogg, Jim Prior, Simon Raven, Peter May and Oliver Popplewell is another. The rich cocktail of intellectual grandeur, solid acumen, louche brilliance, chivalric splendour and breezy good nature represented by that quintet does not come together often, and I suspect no one member of that group would have been quite the man they were without the influence of the others.

A greater influence by far, of course, was to come into Oliver's life at Cambridge in the shape of Margaret Storey. Margaret's intellect, perception, acuity, determination and – towards the end – physical courage inspired all who knew her. Her marriage to Oliver and the family they produced together remains, of course, the greatest legacy.

The Popplewell Report on the tragic Bradford stadium fire and its far-reaching recommendations, the Jonathan Aitken case, the hilarity of the 'Linford's lunchbox' episode during Christie vs McVicar and *Spike* magazine, provide wonderful anecdotal and judicial insights into the workings of British society at many different levels. Oliver's unique position in cricket allows the reader to see just how contingent and precarious the destiny of the game has been – held dangerously in the balance have been the conflicting impulses of international politics, finance and sport.

But enough from me ... I have been proud to know the Popplewell family all my life; I was born just a week or so after Nigel, the eldest son, and Popplewells in one form of another (right down to Andrew's acting daughters) have crossed my path regularly ever since. Don't be fooled by the disarming modesty of the man. Here is a life of integrity, intelligence, decency, diligence and public service retold in a clear and self-deprecating style that captures the reader from the first paragraph to the last. Of all the sentences that Oliver has ever handed down, perhaps these will prove the most enduring.

Stephen Fry

Prelude

'I'll Move it, Guv'nor'

I was appointed a judge in January 1983. In the autumn of 1983 I went to sit at Reading. My cases there were mainly drugs cases. A good number of those who were accused ended up in the local prison. The most famous occupant of Reading Jail was Oscar Wilde. When I was shown around by the prison governor, like every other visitor I asked him which had been Oscar Wilde's cell. The governor identified one cell as being his. However, he made it clear that they really had no idea but as the question was asked so many times they had fixed on a cell to satisfy the interest of the visitors.

On my visit the governor invited me to the carol service which is held annually in the prison. I demurred somewhat, taking the view that a good number of those present would not have quite the same feeling of good will to all men if they knew that the judge who had put them there was at their service. The governor explained that it was customary for the High Court judge to attend, and also the High Sheriff of Berkshire – Ian Pilkington, together with his charming wife Penny. Accordingly, with some apprehension and a good deal of doubt I set off for Reading Jail to attend the carol service. It was a cold, wet December evening. I arrived to be greeted by the governor and taken to the gym, where the service was to be held.

The hall was divided, with the inmates on the left-hand side guarded by the prison officers. On the right-hand side were the governor's guests, relatives, visitors and VIPs. There was, as always on these sort of occasions, a good deal of talk among the visitors, shuffling of feet and

1

noisy exchanges between the prisoners. Eventually the hubbub died down. The governor got to his feet to welcome us all. His first message, however, did not relate to Christmas but to something much more mundane. He announced that there was a car (and he gave the registration number) blocking the entrance to the prison. He suggested that the owner should now go and remove it from its position so that traffic could go in and out of the prison.

This announcement was greeted with a good deal of amusement by the prisoners but nobody among the visitors got up to acknowledge that it was in fact their car. After a period of some embarrassed silence one of the prisoners stood up and said to the governor, 'Governor, if you would like to give me the keys of the car I'd be happy to move it'. This exchange was greeted with a good deal of laughter which set the tone for the rest of the service.

The next thing that happened was that the parson, having welcomed the congregation, gave us some bidding prayers. Among them he said this: 'Let us give thanks to Almighty God for our presence here tonight.' No doubt this had a lot of meaning for the visitors but fell on fairly deaf ears among the prisoners.

The service continued with a number of hymns, some sung by the choir, and there were five lessons from the Bible. Four of them were read by members of the staff or visitors. The fifth was read by one of the prisoners. He had clearly not got a first-class degree in English but he had been in the prison sufficiently long to acquaint himself with the subject which he was reading. He worked his way slowly and with some difficulty through the reading. When he finally got to the end, he raised his arms in a football salute, clenching his fists above his head and was received by his fellow prisoners with a loud round of applause.

The hilarity continued with the announcement by the governor that he hoped that all the gentlemen, by which he meant the prisoners, would now move quietly to their quarters, whereupon the prison officers took up position around the prisoners and with cries of 'Come on you f— lot look sharp', shepherded them out of the hall back to their cells.

1

Childhood

My father was 47 when I was born and my mother was 38. We lived in Northwood, which was then really a village in north Middlesex which eventually became one of the suburbs on the Metropolitan line so beloved by John Betjeman. It had its own identity. It was a small enough community for us to know a large number of people in the village, and to know and to be known by the shopkeepers.

My sister was nearly three years older than me but we enjoyed a very happy relationship which lasted until her death. Because our parents were somewhat elderly, we were very close. She was a very practical person, fairly laid back but wholly unwilling to be pressurised by our mother. Academically she did not achieve many honours, but when the war came she blossomed. She joined the FANYs and did coding at Grendon Underwood. She was always reluctant to talk about her work and I don't think I ever learnt a great deal about it.

In 1943 she was sent out to Ceylon, as it then was, to do the same work for Force 136 which involved agents operating against Japan. She had a great social life at Mount Lavinia and during her time in India she met and fell in love with her husband, Keith. They married in 1949, but sadly divorced in 1953 – he went off with another woman.

She much wanted to be a doctor but it was not to be and instead she trained as an orthoptist, a job she did with great skill and charm. When she died of a heart attack in 1963 I wept copiously – she had been a very close friend and a happy and amusing companion.

Because of the age of our parents and the fact that my mother was really not interested in small children, we were brought up by a nanny. She was enormously calm and very kind. She was old fashioned in her ways but ensured that we had a fairly strict upbringing and a high standard of behaviour, which she enforced. She stayed with the family from 1924 when my sister was born until the 1950s when she was caring for my niece. We lived in a comfortable detached house with neighbours on either side. Their children were of course close friends with whom we played regularly.

I went first to a little nursery school in Northwood and then to a prep school at Pinner – St Johns, which has now moved to Northwood. It was a daily bus ride. I was equipped with sixpence for the journey, tuppence each way from Northwood to Pinner and a penny each way for the bus up from Pinner to the school. If I chose to walk I could buy myself 10 Mickey Mouse toffees.

My father was in the Civil Service, in the Board of Trade, as it then was, and commuted regularly to London. In those days they worked on Saturday mornings. Our great joy as children was to meet him off the train on a Saturday lunchtime and persuade him that he would like to go to the cinema that had recently opened in what became Northwood Hills. This was a suburban development in the country between Northwood and Pinner, which is now one concrete mass.

My father came from a north-country background, and the Popplewell family came from Bury in Lancashire. He was one of a number of brothers. I never knew his parents but he himself went to Manchester Grammar School. He then got a scholarship to Oxford which he was unable to take up because the family did not have enough money. Instead he went to Manchester University, where he was a scientist. He was also a not undistinguished classical scholar. He had had a broad education. During the Boer War he had been at Leipzig University. There was a protest by the Germans about the conduct of the British in South Africa. A notice was put up in the student common room saying that there would be a meeting in the Zoo Garden to protest against the way the British were behaving, with the exhortation that everyone should attend. My father wrote at the bottom of the notice that the Zoo Garden was a very appropriate place for holding that sort of meeting. He was sent for by the university authorities to explain himself and was then expelled.

He was a quiet, deeply thinking man who had no particular religious beliefs but had a great many christian virtues. He was devoted to children and to the family, hard-working, conscientious and full of dry humour. My mother always complained that he had no ambition and that if he had pushed himself he would have risen much higher in the hierarchy of the Civil Service. I think he spent a good deal of his life resisting my mother's attempts to push him. So did the rest of the family when she tried to push them. Sometime before the war I know that he was earning £1200. I found a copy of *Whitakers Almanac* in which the pay of each civil servant was set out. This seemed to me an enormous sum at the time.

My mother had been born in Sydney but came to England at an early age. She came from a large family with quarrelsome sisters. She was quite the opposite in temperament to my father. She was highly ambitious, poor at personal relations and a great believer that if you made enough fuss you got your own way. I confess that at an early age I found her tiresome. Nothing that happened during my adult life changed that view. They had met when she was in the Civil Service. She had been a Suffragette, though she confessed later that her part had been somewhat minimal. Mrs Pankhurst had been very keen that her young ladies, as she called them, should not involve themselves in any sort of violence, because she was anxious that they should not get sent to prison. Women's rights were part of my mother's mission in life and she never missed an opportunity to complain about how badly women were treated. She worked in the women's movement all her life and contributed substantially to the Fawcett Society and the National Council of Women. Equal pay was a subject about which she felt strongly and to which she devoted much energy.

When she married my father it was the rule then that married women in the Civil Service had to resign. In 1922 when they got married my father was aged 42. They had gone on a walking holiday – heavily chaperoned of course, by his sister – through Bavaria. He proposed; she accepted. On his return he was summoned by my grandmother (my mother's mother) and asked to explain to her what his prospects were and whether he would be able to keep her daughter in the style to which she was then accustomed. He was then eight years off retirement.

My chief recollection of childhood at Northwood was one of peace and harmony. Nanny would generally look after us. We would go on cycle rides on Sunday mornings before breakfast. There were few cars around and we would often go out to Moor Park and have a picnic there. My sister entered small gymkhanas. There were children's parties in the village. I remember on one occasion my sister coming back from a party which she had obviously enjoyed in some distress. When my mother enquired why, she said, 'I said thank you very much for having me but they never said come again soon'. There were visits to Boots to change library books and there was constant playing with friends. When the cinema was built at Northwood Hills it became a frequent source of entertainment.

One of my earliest recollections is going to a party at what was then the Chateau de Madrid in Oxhey Woods. It was a large, as it appeared to me then, glittery hotel which was taken over during the war as the headquarters of Coastal Command. It became famous during the Falklands as the headquarters from which the war was fought. Oxhey Woods used to be full of bluebells. Sadly, they no longer exist. The large houses which once filled the surrounding area have been converted into flats or divided up into small parcels of land on which hundreds of little houses have been built. It is now suburbia *par excellence*.

Our summer holidays followed a distinctive pattern. My parents would go abroad when we were at school. Nanny would take us on summer holidays. To begin with we went to Birchington, then a small seaside resort near Margate and Ramsgate. Our parents used to come and visit us from time to time but the seaside was not their scene. Then for a number of years we went to Totland Bay in the Isle of Wight with Nanny, where we had many happy days. There was the excitement of travelling on a train to London, across London to Waterloo, then down to Lymington, finally catching the ferry across from Lymington to Yarmouth. We took the bus to Totland, where we walked to the boarding house in which we stayed.

In the waters between the Isle of Wight and the mainland there was a constant procession of transatlantic liners. The beaches were clean but we were never allowed to swim after a meal until an hour had passed. It was thought we would get cramp and drown. The swell from the liners caused great excitement when swimming. There were visits to Hirst Castle to see where Charles I was incarcerated, to Carisbrooke Castle in Newport to see the donkeys turning the wheel, and from time

1. O.B.P. aged eight years.

to time the Yarmouth lifeboat came out to rescue some luckless sailor who had trouble negotiating the Needles.

We went on trips around the island to Tennyson's House and to collect coloured sand at Alum Bay. We played cricket on the beach, went shrimping among the rocks and even put our pocket money into amusement machines. Tea came out of a thermos with bakelite mugs and sandwiches of fish paste or raspberry jam, which always seemed to be full of sand. In retrospect it seemed carefree and idyllic, and I dare say that it was.

We were taken abroad twice: to Montreux in 1937 and to Normandy in 1939. My recollection of the journey to Montreux was that we sat up in the train all night and played a game called 'coffee pots'. I suspect this is now totally out of fashion. The object of the game was to think of a word which had two meanings; the guesser then had to ask a question and the other person answered using the words 'coffee pot' in place of the hidden word. It was a comparatively simple game and its novelty soon wore off, as we found, after eight hours in a train.

We stayed in a hotel in Montreux overlooking the lake. The chief pleasure, however, that my sister and I had was in occupying the lift or pressing the button, much to the fury of elderly residents in the hotel who were about to use the lift. We went up into the mountains by the railway, we rowed on the lake, we went to the League of Nations Building at Geneva and we ended up with a weekend in Paris. The Champs Elysées and the Arc de Triomphe were of course very exciting sights for youngsters. We resolved the difficulty of Paris traffic by taking a taxi across the Champs Elysées to the Arc de Triomphe.

Our next holiday in France was somewhat more fraught. We were in Rivabella in 1939, which is a seaside resort a few miles from Ouistreham and Caen. My first impression of France was decidedly unpleasant. I had spent my pocket money on a French éclair only to find that what I thought was cream inside turned out to be a custard-like substance. My view of éclairs has been coloured ever since. We spent hours on the sandy beaches. We went to the casino, and of course much admired the cathedrals in Caen. It was a fine summer and we were oblivious of the threat that was about to come.

But at some time in August the Russians signed a non-aggression pact with the Germans, which threw the grown-ups into a considerable panic because of the very real danger of war. The owner of the hotel told us that she had lost her husband in the First World War and now she would be losing her son in the second war. It was decided that my mother and my aunt should go back to England by train while my father drove my sister and me up from Rivabella across the Seine at Codabec and on to Dieppe. While it did not compare with the Americans getting out of Vietnam, it was nevertheless a journey of some excitement. We crossed the Seine by ferry and arrived at Dieppe to go across to Newhaven. We were one of thousands of English families who had decided that the time had come to return home. We had to sit up on the boat all night and leave the car on the quay at Dieppe.

Those were the days when car travel was organised by the AA (Automobile Association). It was a morning's work to get a carnet and various other documents. Cars had to be winched on and off boats. I was naive enough to believe that my school clothes which were in the trunk in the car would remain in France; thus, I would be unable to return to school. This belief was rudely shattered some week later when the AA rang up to say that they had brought the car back from Dieppe and it was sitting in Newhaven. Rivabella was one of the beaches where troops landed on D-day in 1944. Ouistreham was the scene of some very heavy and important fighting, and Caen was of course battered and besieged for several months.

When I was aged 10 my parents decided that I should leave St Johns at Pinner, which was a day school, and go off to boarding school. My excitement was intense and, while I was frequently homesick, I confess that I much enjoyed it. It is now commonplace to deride boarding schools and to see them as nasty bullying places where some uncaring parents dump their children to get them off their hands. I have to say I found Winchester House School at Brackley very great fun.

Among my contemporaries there was Gerald Priestland, now sadly dead, who has written unkindly about his time at the school, in particular about the headmaster, Mr Hayman. He was a master of the old school, tough but in many ways kind-hearted towards the boys and anxious that the boys should learn. I have no doubt he was something of a martinet and a prize-chaser. Every year the school won some nine or ten scholarships. In the Easter holidays he would take four or five of the scholarship candidates and give them extra coaching in a pub in Amersham. In my year he was very successful. Gerald Priestland, I and George Ray all got scholarships to Charterhouse. There were frequent Winchester scholarships, and the school had a high academic reputation.

However, it was not only at schoolwork that the school excelled. Drama had an important place; there were annual productions of Shakespeare; there was the Mermaid Society, at which plays were read every Sunday. There was great emphasis on games. There were no heated indoor swimming pools in those days. We had a large outdoor concrete pool used throughout the summer term and much enjoyed. We also had the early morning cold plunge in the summer, which was less agreeable but was no doubt part of the philosophy of a 'healthy mind in a healthy body'. Chapel was part of the everyday school life.

Another experience for the senior boys was the telling of ghost stories by Mr Hayman on Sunday nights. This was in fact a very frightening experience; I dare say that child psychologists would now wholly disapprove of it. A dozen of us would sit in what was then the library in darkness round an enormous blazing fire, while Mr Hayman would tell us terrifying stories. It would then be necessary for us to walk to the Upper Lodge or Lower Lodge, some three or four hundred yards in the dark. I often wonder why we didn't find ourselves scarred for life.

We played all local prep schools, the Dragons, Summerfields, Bilton, Maidwell Hall, Swanbourne and others, and gave a good account of ourselves both at rugger and cricket. The match against Swanbourne was cancelled one year: our scorer, who shall be nameless, but who I think subsequently became a very senior army officer, thought it would be amusing to remove the cream from the cakes provided at tea for the Swanbourne team and fill them with mustard. It was no doubt the ability in dealing with the enemy which led him to such great heights in the Army.

They were in truth very happy days. The school was then under a triumvirate of Mr Hayman, Ronald Davies and Stuart Meikle. Ronald Davies had taken holy orders and taught mathematics, Stuart Meikle had married the housekeeper and taught French, and Hayman and Michael Llewelyn (who subsequently became headmaster) taught the classics. The drama and English were in the capable hands of Hope Gill, and Mattinson too taught French. There was carpentry and a school model railway, and there were scouting ventures, film shows and trips of all sorts. One memorable occasion was seeing Prince Obolensky playing rugger at Oxford for the university.

The outbreak of war had only a marginal impact on the boys. There was rationing of course; the windows were covered with what seemed to be large quantities of sticky paper, there were sandbags put up and there was the blackout. But life seemed to go on in much the same way until the fall of France in 1940. We had had some idea of the disaster which had overtaken the country because for a whole week convoys of soldiers in obviously poor shape had passed along the road at the front of the school. This was part of the army that had been evacuated from Dunkirk. The headmaster took some of the boys down to his room to listen to the radio when France fell. The impact of that event has remained firmly in my mind ever since. It happened that I took my scholarship while the evacuation of Dunkirk was taking place; the results came through shortly after the announcement that the evacuation had been completed. It all seemed very exciting to a 12-year-old, but the full significance of that summer, glorious in its continuous sunshine, did not impinge on our minds for some years.

Of my contemporaries at school, Gerald Priestland is probably the best known. He was even then a most distinguished boy, and his writings were admired both by the staff and by the other boys. When another boy came to the school, called Lee, with as many freckles as I had, Priestland wrote a little poem in the school magazine which went something like this:

> There was a time when I alone
> did sit upon my glorious throne
> of freckledom, but now alas
> my freckled glory has to pass
> for now the school has taken in
> a rival who, with freckled grin
> says you have freckles look at mine
> but there is one thing that he doth lack
> cos I've got freckles on my back.

George Ray became a respected master at Eton; Richard Ellingworth, regarded as one of the brightest boys we had, went off into the Diplomatic Service; there were two very clever pairs of brothers – the Hindley and the Bolton brothers – who were outstanding scholars. Whatever happened to them thereafter I never knew. Richard Davis became a close friend – he married one of Clement Attlee's daughters and subsequently became a master of the Clothworker's Company. Another contemporary was John Winington Ingram. He became founder of the *Mail on Sunday* – of him more anon. All in all it was a happy time where we were lucky to be well taught, to be able to play lots of sport, and to make a large number of friends.

2

Growing Up

My parents had chosen Charterhouse because they knew a relation of one of the masters there. I had sat the scholarship at Winchester House and had therefore never been to Charterhouse before I went as a new boy. Because of the bombing the new boys were allowed to go back early in 1940. Driving up to the school, my first recollection is of a very tall, rather shy man coming out and taking the trunk off the back of the car. This was the headmaster, Robert Birley, who subsequently had such a distinguished career in Germany, South Africa and at Eton. It was his shyness which I chiefly remember. Some years later my father and I went to see him in his study to discuss my future after I had left Charterhouse. My father was a man of few words. So too was Birley. I sat there between them wondering how on earth to get the conversation started. I am still not sure how any dialogue took place.

I went into a house called 'Robinites', of which the housemaster was Aubrey Scott. He was a bachelor, small and red-faced. It was said that he had been gassed in the war. He was a man of unpredictable mood. If the house won a match there would be much rejoicing, if they lost there would be great sulking. He was a man of many favourites of which I happened not to be one. The house itself had been a large private house at some time and converted into accommodation for about fifty boys. It could be scarcely described as modern. No doubt if it had been a state school it would long since have been condemned.

The housemaster's control of the house was fairly limited. The head of the house and the head of the Long Room (the common room)

12

held sway. For new boys it was all somewhat frightening. Fagging took place throughout my time at the school. It did not strike us at the time as in anyway undesirable, nor does it now. It was an inconvenience to be shouted for when there was work to be done. It gave to some boys a delusion of power, some of which no doubt was exercised improperly. But life is a series of ups and downs. Thus, to leave a prep school as head boy and captain of games and to be relegated to the lowest of the low at public school was very salutary. Likewise, for those who had held power at the top of a public school to find themselves, as they did shortly afterwards, as privates in the Army was good for the soul.

My fellow scholars were, even then, I thought, a pretty clever lot. George Engle was top scholar later to become Chief Parliamentary Counsel and David Raeburn became headmaster of Whitgift. Gerald Priestland, George Ray and Conrad Dehn, a distinguished QC, were subsequently joined by Simon Raven and by Dick Taverne, now Lord Taverne QC. Dick had arrived in England from Holland in 1940 scarcely speaking a word of English. I remember him as a boy who seemed constantly to be covered in ink; he was bright enough at the end of his school career to get a major scholarship to Oxford. It is easier to predict the future success of boys in their teens than it is at an earlier age. But all of them were clearly going to make their mark in life.

William Rees Mogg, now Lord Rees Mogg, was another contemporary of mine. I first came across him in the cricket world. I had been twelfth man and scorer for the under-16 side one year when we had played Wellington. A close analysis of the score book carried out after the match showed that although we appeared to have won by one run, we were in fact still two runs short. The following year, when I was captain of the under-16 we went to Wellington. Rees Mogg was the scorer. Again we won by the narrowest of margins, but on the return journey it was clear that the events of the year before had been repeated. I can only think that we were not very good at addition at Charterhouse.

Charterhouse during the war was a fairly dull place. The masters were elderly, and were fairly uninspiring. The food was unattractive. I found life comparatively uncongenial. Apart from one serious air-raid on the school, when a bomb dropped within feet of a crowded block house, Charterhouse escaped unscathed during the war. There were exceptions to the rule about dull masters. There was a classics master called Gibson, whose son became Lord Justice Gibson. He was an inspired teacher and instilled a great liking of the classics in all whom he taught. There was a French master called Iredale, whom other masters regarded as a communist. He may have been, but he provoked thought in teenage boys and challenged the conventional view of middle-class conservative boys.

The games at which I did not shine were soccer in the winter and hockey in the Easter term. It was at cricket that I flourished. The eleven was run by Mr Timms, who had played for Northamptonshire. He was a kindly, rather uninspiring cricket master, but had a good knowledge of the game. George Geary, the old England and Leicester player, was the cricket coach. Of George it is not possible to speak except with tremendous admiration. He was not only an immensely able cricketer himself, but had the ability to communicate his knowledge to anyone remotely interested in the game. He had enormous enthusiasm for the game; he had the knack of being able to pick out the strength and weakness of the boy in front of him and improve him. The story of his seeing Peter May as a young boy in the nets and immediately observing that he was a future England player is now too well-known to be repeated, but I have no doubt that his encouragement and coaching stood Peter in very good stead throughout his cricketing career.

George was also an amusing story teller. The Charterhouse Friars, who were the old boys, used to have a fortnight's cricket tour at the end of term. Among our opponents was a team of old Wellingtonians. It was customary during a two-day match for us to entertain the opposing team in Brooke Hall, which was the masters' common room. We tried to entertain the visiting sides in some style and in particular tried to ensure that their ablest performers were especially cared for. Overnight one of the 'not out' batsmen was a young Wellingtonian who had just left school. He was a cricketer of some promise and we ensured that he enjoyed his evening fully. Next morning when it was time for him to come out and continue his innings he was nowhere to be found. This caused a good deal of concern among the Wellingtonians and eventually a search party was sent out to see what had happened to him. He was found lying full length in the long-jump pit on the athletics field, where he had obviously spent the night very much the worse for drink. The Wellingtonians naturally sent him home and debarred him from returning to Charterhouse for a number of years.

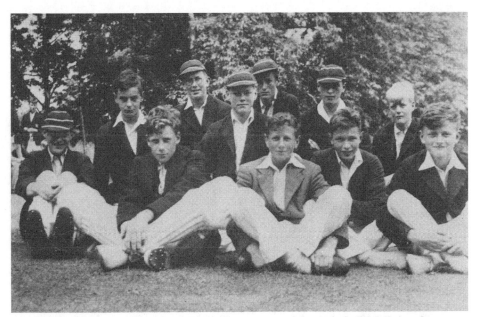

2. Charterhouse under-16. O.B.P. front, second from left; J.M.Prior front, third from left; S.A.N.Raven back, second from left; P.B.H.May middle, left.

About five years later he returned to play for the Wellingtonians. It was customary for George to umpire the matches, and when this young man came out to bat he took guard. George gave him middle and leg and then looked up and said, 'Feeling better now sir?'

My year as captain of the under-16 coincided with the arrival of young May. He was obviously immensely talented and it was no surprise the following year that he was playing for the first eleven and making a hundred against Harrow. My first recollection of serious cricket was being required to keep wicket for the old boys against the school at the age of 15, because they were one short. Raymond Robertson Glasgow, the well-known cricket writer and raconteur, was one of the bowlers. He had played for Oxford University and Somerset. He was by any standards quick and he also swung the ball some considerable distance. I was not used to this. Playing with experienced adults was distinctly frightening. When I stood back about 25 yards at the beginning of the first over I was summoned by Robertson Glasgow bellowing from the far end to stand up and not act as a long stop. I think there have been few more frightening moments in my cricketing life.

The cricket eleven at Charterhouse in 1945 was a memorable one, not only because at regular intervals a photograph of the team appears

3. Charterhouse eleven, summer 1945. Back row, from left: I. W. Lynch, J. H. Perry, H. Le Bas, J. L. Harvey, J. M. L. Prior, J. B. Spargo, T. J. Aitcheson. Front row, from left: O. B. Popplewell, P. B. H. May, A. J. Rimell (capt.), R. L. Whitby, S. A. N. Raven.

in some newspaper showing Peter May, Jim Prior (now Lord Prior) and Simon Raven, but also because it was in fact a well-balanced side with some fine players. Tony Rimell, who subsequently played at Cambridge, was a good all-rounder who was also a very good captain. Of Peter May it is not necessary to say anything more. In Bob Whitby, who subsequently became Prince Charles's housemaster at Gordonstoun, we had a bowler with a classical action; he was also no mean batsman. Jim Prior was, as can be imagined, a solid performer both on the cricket and football fields, though his subsequent political career outshone his cricketing ability.

Simon Raven's career at Charterhouse came to an abrupt end when he was asked to leave because of seducing other boys. He wrote a number of very amusing books about Charterhouse, both fiction and non-fiction, and there was considerable anxiety amongst his contemporaries when it was learnt that yet another book was to be published. Happily he seemed to regard me as a friend, as I did him, and I found him very engaging company.

After a somewhat turbulent career in the Army he went up to Cambridge to Kings, where he got a scholarship. He led a wild life up there and ran into considerable debt. I did not have any money to lend him, although he never ceased to ask. His sexual activities did not reduce during his time as an undergraduate. He was once heard to say about a bride and groom when he went to their wedding, 'Bless the dears, I slept with both of them'. Subsequently he was a distinguished author and novelist, and spent the remaining years of his life as a brother at the old Charterhouse. The old Charterhouse, a charitable foundation, provided a home to a number of elderly, single or widowed gentlemen, where they could live for the rest of their lives. They were known as 'brothers'. There I met him on occasions. He spent his time reading classics.

There was one meeting which epitomised everything about Simon's charm. I went into the bar of the Long Room at Lords to find Simon and a number of his cronies drinking. We exchanged the usual pleasantries and vowed eternal friendship. He asked what I would like to drink, and fetched my drink for me. After a conversation of about half an hour he said he must go and we agreed to see each other again. Off he and his cronies went. The barman then turned to me and said, 'Excuse me sir, that will be £12 4s 10d'. It was typical Simon, but the next time I saw him I could not be angry with him. He was so full of charm and personality and highly intelligent, but somewhere along the line his genius was never fulfilled.

We had one memorable victory over Winchester, during which Bob Whitby took a lot of wickets. Peter May was dropped at cover when he had only scored a few in a low-scoring match. This caused Field Marshal Montgomery, who happened to be watching the game, to observe that in every contest there was a decisive moment, and that was it. It was indeed so. Whitby, Rimell and May all played in the public school sides and Rimell, May and I ended up together in the Cambridge side a few years later.

In those days it was possible to sit scholarships for both Oxford and Cambridge, and also to sit for different colleges at different times at both universities. In 1944 I had a shot at Oxford; it involved travelling to Oxford, which was dark and gloomy. The colleges were naturally cold and uninviting. The only redeeming feature was that John Winington Ingram, who I had last seen at Winchester House and who subsequently launched the *Mail on Sunday*, was doing a short course as a naval officer. He entertained me royally for three days, to such good purpose that any prospect I had of getting a scholarship to Oxford disappeared. I have forgiven him because subsequently I got an award at Queens' College, Cambridge, where I met my wife Margaret; we lived, as they say, happily ever after, until she sadly died in April 2002.

3

National Service

The world seemed to come to an end in my last year at Charterhouse. I had been hoping to go into the Fleet Air Arm in what was then called the 'Y Scheme'. However, no more recruits were needed and so in 1946 when I joined the Navy I joined up as DJX740246 Acting Writer Popplewell. A writer is in the secretarial branch, responsible for dealing with the ship's company pay and part of the secretarial team. On board ship the writer acts as the Captain's private secretary. We joined up at Corsham outside Bath, and I found myself accompanied by Tony Vincent, a fellow old Carthusian.

We were, I think, the only members of our group of 18 who had ever been away from home. That first night, the 16 others were blubbing their little hearts out because they were homesick. After some initial training at Corsham we were sent off first of all to Warrington and then to Wetherby. The establishment at Wetherby was then called HMS *Ceres*. It then became a Borstal and now I believe a young offenders institution.

We arrived at the beginning of the terrible winter of 1946, and although it was peace time the conditions could not have been more disagreeable. The huts had no form of heating, the food was quite awful and the clearing of the parade ground of snow, which seemed constantly to fall, was effected by lining up the ship's company and getting them to throw snowballs at each other. We were not allowed, as I remember, to wear greatcoats for this exercise. My view of Yorkshire, with which I was to be more closely concerned when I met Margaret, has always been distinctly coloured by this experience. During the time we were there, there was some form of transport strike. Anyone who was able to drive a lorry was required to volunteer to drive very large and heavily laden lorries round the Yorkshire countryside in conditions of ice and snow which would be too dangerous now even for a tractor. Happily for us the strike came to an end without any substantial harm to man or lorry.

It was not surprising that a wave of 'flu overtook the camp. At any one time a high proportion of the ship's company was in the sick bay. This nightmare was only relieved by trips to Harrogate to visit some relative of Tony's and the occasional leave home. In those days, to get from Wetherby down to Surrey, where we both lived, was like crossing Siberia, both in similarity of terrain and distance.

From Warrington we were at least able to get into Manchester to listen to the Hallé Orchestra or to go to the theatre or even to visit my cousin, who was professor of law at Manchester University. Ray Eastwood was a very learned man. Unhappily at this stage he was somewhat deaf, and marching over the countryside and repeating trivial banalities to him while wearing naval uniform and heavy boots was somewhat disconcerting.

We had a friendly and competent instructor called Franz Muller, whose German ancestry was a constant source of amusement to us; however, he managed to keep us out of too much trouble with the Gunnery petty officers. Our class was a mixed bag: there was a journalist who was a dedicated socialist, young men who had left school at the age of 15 and one or two grammar-school boys. But like all groups serving in the forces, we shared a common dislike of those more senior to us. We found a camaraderie born of the mutual experience of the disagreeable conditions to which we were exposed. Muller managed to get most of the class through their exams – some, I believe, with the naval equivalent of a distinction. We then had the excitement of finding where we had been posted. In my case it was to Portsmouth Barracks. Tony, too, was sent to Portsmouth, but he was posted to another shore establishment close by.

Our friendship had been seriously put at risk when we had been on guard duty at Warrington on the outer perimeter during the night. In the dark, hearing steps approaching, I had started to challenge and raise my rifle with a bayonet at the end, to find it had ended up within a few inches of an advancing Tony, who was patrolling a neighbouring part of the perimeter. Our days at Warrington had been much enlivened by the antics of the recruit chosen to be right marker. It was by the right marker that we all fell in – we were required to march in concert with his step and pace. However, he was one of those people who were wholly unco-ordinated. The result was that his right arm went forward at the same time as his right leg and the same thing happened with his left arm and left leg. The parade ground, like a church, is sometimes the catalyst for gales of laughter at trivial events. Every time we marched about the parade ground, our class and the other classes on parade were consumed by the antics of our right marker. It took the petty officer in charge of us about a fortnight to discover what it was that made us such an ungainly force. Dad's Army would have recognised the symptoms.

I don't think Portsmouth Barracks had been altered for about 200 years. It was vast and impersonal. The secret of a quiet existence was to look as though you were doing something official, and then nobody took any notice of you. I came across my old friend John Winnington Ingram again as I was quietly carrying some piece of paper across the vast parade ground. I had seen an officer advancing towards me at a considerable distance away dressed in a sub-lieutenant's uniform. At my prep school, for obvious reasons, he had been known as Pooh. As he got closer I recognised him. I said 'Good God Pooh, what are you doing here?' He stood to attention, said 'It is customary for ratings to salute officers in this establishment', and walked off. I have told this story to his embarrassment on many occasions. He claims it is untrue.

Portsmouth itself was an agreeable place to be stationed at that time. I lived at Guildford and therefore at weekends I could easily go home. It was possible to keep civilian clothes in a locker in the YMCA and therefore to walk around Portsmouth in comparative comfort. There was an exceedingly good NAAFI, plenty of cinemas and other entertainment. I had an office which I shared where I could work. I had by this time joined the Inner Temple and had started reading for the bar by way of a correspondence course. The games were well organised. There were duty-free tins of tobacco which were exceedingly cheap, and the food was not too bad.

It was my first experience of sleeping in a hammock. It may well be nostalgia but I still retain the most friendly recollections of its comfort. It required a degree of care in its slinging so as to get the right angle;

it required pieces of wood at head and tail to keep the sides apart and it required a certain dexterity to get into it, particularly in a crowded mess deck. The disadvantage, which was not the fault of the hammock, was the closeness of other bodies and the general crowding into a small building. The smell of barracks at night remains unforgettable to this day. I do not believe that anyone who has ever slept in a hammock would prefer to sleep in a bunk in a ship at sea, certainly not in any sort of storm.

There were plenty of organised games at Portsmouth and I soon found that the ability to play some hockey and some cricket was an immense advantage in the duties to which I was assigned. I came across John Dewes while playing for a Navy side. He was a sub-lieutenant and had already played cricket for England in the Victory Test in 1946. He was to achieve even greater fame for England, Cambridge and Middlesex. He was very critical of the set-up in Navy cricket. Because of his status and the fact that he was not a regular, he was able to get away with criticism which would have earned others a reprimand. We met again at Cambridge and have been firm friends since.

Another good cricketer was Peter Nicholas, with whom I had many enjoyable moments. He was a fine games player, and we kept up our friendship after being demobilised. Sadly, he was to die young. His son Mark was clearly destined to be a successful cricketer. I was able to get him to the Easter coaching classes at Lords and followed his career with especial pleasure. He and my son Nigel played school cricket against each other, and they then joined Hampshire Cricket Club at the same time. For a while they shared a flat, causing a good deal of distress to their landlady by letting the bath overflow, among other mishaps. The Mini which Margaret had lent Nigel was stolen, then subsequently recovered; I think it was for the general benefit of the neighbourhood that Nigel took himself off to play for Somerset. They frequently met on the cricket circuit, and I think honours were about even when they battled against each other.

In the summer of 1947, while I was at Portsmouth barracks, I went on the first of three cricket tours to Germany with the Butterflies Cricket Club. The Butterflies Cricket Club is made up of old boys from various schools: Eton, Rugby, Harrow, Charterhouse, Westminster and Winchester. It was my first introduction to playing on matting. Sometimes the matting was on top of concrete, sometimes it was on rolled cinders and sometimes on top of grass. If the surface below was comparatively firm it enabled leg-spinners to turn the ball prodigiously and get substantial lift. Medium-pace bowlers came on to the bat comfortably, and on the whole it was a surface on which it was a joy to bat.

The sides we played against varied, but at their best were exceedingly good. We played service sides, the control commission and sometimes a combined side. The presence of young professionals doing their national service who were later to play first-class games ensured a competitive game and a severe test to club cricketers. In addition, during the fortnight that we were away, we were exposed to generous hospitality. The entertainment by service sides was usually conducted by those not taking part in the game itself.

Jim Dunbar, secretary of the Butterflies, captained the side and was very much our guide and mentor as well as the chief photographer. He was a fine and accurate medium paced bowler. His wife Sheila came with us and prevented the younger members of the side from doing anything too silly, for which there was ample opportunity, and guided them sensibly in their choice of presents for their girlfriends.

Also included in the side was H. D. Reed, better known as 'Hopper'. Off a three-pace run he was certainly as fast as any bowler in the country; he had played for Essex when he was younger. His mild manner and short run gave no indication of the pace at which the ball would be unleashed. We played on one ground close to the Russian border near Luneberg where the wicket had a concrete base with matting on top. It also had a slope of about one in ten. Hopper bowled downhill, downwind, and his first ball pitched about halfway down the wicket. I was keeping wicket. I stood back about 25 yards. The ball took off like an intercontinental ballistic missile, and only narrowly avoided being six byes. It was rumoured that the Russian radar picked up this missile flying through the sky and scrambled some of its planes.

To last a fortnight, almost every night of which was spent in riotous entertainment, required a strong head, considerable nerve, a good eye and above all a nucleus of good players. In this we were exceedingly lucky. Among those who went on these tours were Peter May, Robin Marlar – shortly to come up to Cambridge and to play for Sussex – John Tanner (who got a Harlequin at Oxford and should have played for the university), Tony Rimell, John May – Peter's brother, who was a fine player – and John Larking, who had some games for Kent and who was probably one of the finest club batsmen at that time. There were also a number of other good club players whose contributions were strong.

No-one who saw the shattered state of Germany's cities shortly after the war could ever forget them, nor the hideously starving faces of their citizens, who stood mutely begging whenever a troop train stopped at a station or along the line. The contrast between the extravagance and richness of food being served to the occupants of the train and their starvation was marked. There was a flourishing black market. Those who could turned their hand to pleasing the occupying forces, and this was never more apparent than in the clubs and restaurants which were opened up for the use of the troops.

We stayed frequently in what had been German Army barracks, and sometimes in houses which had been commandeered from some important official where we were entertained in a great deal of style and comfort. The currency was BAFVs (British Armed Forces Vouchers) – a gin was three BAFVs and a tonic was four BAFVs; it was thus cheaper to buy a double gin than a gin and tonic. Taxis were either free or one BAFV, and the style of living for Army officers and those in the control commission was, I suspect, much akin to that of colonial officials in the 'good old days'.

The contrast between the hopelessness and the poverty of the Germans and the comparative life of luxury of the occupying forces gradually changed during the years that we visited. But even on my last visit in 1953, the comfort enjoyed by the occupying forces was still very much in evidence. The rebuilding of Germany had already started, assisted by monetary reforms introduced by Robert Birley. The Berlin airlift had given Berliners in particular a tremendous sense of confidence, but the topic of war was never entirely absent from conversation. Berlin was in effect an armed city in constant crisis living on its nerves and anxious about a Russian attack.

The journey by train into Berlin in those days was subject to bureaucratic and military control of the Russians. The British zone in West Germany finished short of Berlin. The train which was allowed into Berlin had to be sealed off, so that travellers did not see what was going on in the eastern sector. It was a not-infrequent occurrence that shots would be fired at the train as it went through. The arrival of the train in West Berlin was greeted in a manner something akin to the arrival of the troops relieving Mafeking.

The Russian presence in Berlin was very clear, and deliberately so. The huge war memorial in its sector was not only an enormously impressive reminder of the sacrifices that the Russians had made during the war and the casualties which they had sustained, but equally a monument to the glorification of Mother Russia.

The contrast between life in West Berlin and East Berlin was even then marked. There was no Berlin Wall, but the east was grey, sullen and devoid of any life. Apart from the dramatic war memorial there was little of interest in the Russian part of Berlin. Our hosts were naturally anxious to entertain us in West Berlin and to show us the 'bright lights'. We sampled many of the nightclubs then operating in Berlin. I suspect that not much had changed since the 1930s; there was every variety of nightclub act to cater for different tastes.

At one particular club we went to, each table had a telephone on it. In order to engage one of the girls who sat there, you simply dialled the number of her table. An evening with her, however, turned out to be less than enormous fun, because this was a club where all the women, so beautifully dressed and made up, turned out to be men.

There was another club to which we went, called the Golden Horse Shoe. In the centre of the club was an area of earth and sawdust. Surrounding this area were all the tables at which the spectators sat. Into the arena there emerged a highly spirited horse without a saddle, on which rode a girl clad only in tights. The band struck up some music. A customer was invited to climb on the horse, clutch onto the girl and ride around the arena. The amusement for the spectators was of course that when the customer had climbed on to the horse the band would increase the tempo. The horse would go faster and faster and in smaller and smaller circles. The result was that in due course the rider and the girl would fall to the ground grasping each other. This generated an enormous amount of amusement and excitement among the spectators. It has to be understood that a good deal of drink was consumed during the course of the evening, which may explain why what seemed a pretty harmless exercise should generate such vast excitement.

One evening we all decided that we would visit the Golden Horse Shoe. After watching a number of customers in various degrees of intoxication falling about, we encouraged one of our side, Tony Pelham, to have a go. He needed no second urging, because he was a polo player of some considerable ability. He climbed on to the horse and seized hold of the girl. The music started, it got faster and faster; instead of the accustomed excitement of the rider and girl falling together on each other on the sawdust, there was the most marvellous exhibition of horsemanship, with Pelham going over and under the horse like some wild-west rider.

All this was to the intense fury of the semi-naked girl, who found herself ignored. More importantly, it was also to the intense anger of the owners of the club, who thought that the British were poking fun at their simple entertainment and spoiling the evening for the customers. Eventually the band realised that the sooner they stopped playing the sooner the horse would stop and Tony's gyrations would cease. Eventually they did. Tony stood up on the horse, gave an Army salute and jumped off to the enormous acclaim of his colleagues. We were invited by the establishment to leave on the grounds that our behaviour was not conducive to good relations.

We had parties galore. Our conducting officer, Michael Morton, who subsequently became a solicitor, was then a second lieutenant in one of the Guards regiments. At one party he had the grave misfortune to walk out of a window which he believed was on the ground floor, but found that there was a basement. It was not until about two hours later that we realised that he was missing from the party. Happily, he suffered no more than surface wounds.

We had one member of the cricket team who was enormously deaf and could only hear with his rather elaborate hearing aid. When he was fielding he decided to dispense with this because it impeded his running about. There came a moment when the ball was hit an immense distance towards him, high in the air at mid-wicket. He shouted that it was his. As nobody else had any intention of going for it anyway, he was left to go for it himself. He got within striking distance of it: it did no more than bruise his hands and fall to the ground. For the rest of the day he apologised to anybody who would listen to him for his stupidity in not catching the ball. Nobody had the heart to tell him that a no ball had been called – he was the only person on the field unaware of this.

Tours of this sort were not without some strain between a visiting civilian side and both the kindly organisers of the tour and the German population. One member of the team had been a pilot officer in the war. Whenever we arrived at a station he would point out to anyone who would listen, and they were mostly Germans, that the only reason why that particular station was now running was because he had tried to bomb it and had been wholly unsuccessful.

Our first visit to Hamburg was, I suppose, the most depressing. Not even Berlin suffered as much. Out hosts did their best to make our visit enjoyable, but pointed out that the Reperbahn, the brothel area of Hamburg, was out of bounds to the troops. We took the view that, although we had military status, we could treat ourselves for this purpose as civilians. Accordingly, one evening we set off in order to see whether the reputation of the place was justified. I hasten to add that it was a reconnaissance only. The girls attracted their customers by sitting in the windows of shops in various stages of undress and inviting the customers to come in – then they took them upstairs. Most of the shop windows were deliberately poorly lit in order to prevent the customers appreciating quite how awful the goods on offer were.

However, on one occasion as we walked down the street, we came upon a window where there were no occupants. They had obviously found customers and had vanished upstairs. The opportunity was too good for three of our team. They walked into the shop, sat on the chairs and started beckoning to customers in imitation of the resident ladies. It did not take long before a large crowd had gathered around the shop window. Things began to turn nasty. There was one group of customers who thought this was some transvestite opportunity and that they were being invited to take part in some homosexual orgy. There was another group who did not regard the British attempt at humour as being consistent with the dignity of the arrangements. In the result, our three brave exhibitionists were forced out of the shop and we took to our heels, hotly pursued by irate Germans.

When I look back on the tours now, my chief recollection is the stamina which we showed. These were tiring days in the field, with generous entertainment in the evening and further entertainment throughout the night. Indeed, there were some nights when I can scarcely recollect getting to bed. How we managed to survive a fort-night's cricket playing every day against good opposition can only be attributed to youth, Alka-Seltzer and the strength of my colleagues.

One of the more amusing aspects of my first tour in 1947 was that I had to obtain express permission from the Admiralty to go abroad as a civilian. The memos which must have flowed backwards and forwards from the commander-in-chief at Portsmouth to their lordships of the Admiralty and back would make amusing reading. In order to be properly organised on the tour we were given notional Army ranks. We travelled on a troop ship from Harwich to the Hook of Holland, and then on military trains. We had to be given the status which befitted us: I thus achieved probably the quickest promotion that any writer in the Royal Navy has ever had, and found myself a major during the fortnight of the tour. I was unaccustomed to being able to give orders to officers junior to me in notional rank. It was probably the shortest promotion in memory, because no sooner had I returned to Harwich than I travelled on a naval warrant made out to Writer Popplewell.

There was one other occasion that I achieved senior rank in the armed forces. I went to Germany subsequently on a court-martial, to defend a soldier charged with murder. I found myself being led by David Karmel QC, who was treated as a brigadier. I was awarded the rank of half colonel. As it happened, Karmel had a distinguished war record, and ended the war as quite a senior officer. The court-martial itself was presided over by Field Marshal Lord Carver. He was then, I think, a brigadier. The other officers sitting on the court-martial had been substantially junior in rank to Karmel, and he was treated with enormous respect throughout the whole of the trial.

There was one incident in the course of the trial which was not without amusement. The deceased and our client were private soldiers, and had been drinking in the bar. They had both consumed an enormous amount of drink. During the course of this bout, our client had lost his watch and assumed that the deceased had taken it, so he went up to the deceased's barrack room to sort it out. The deceased had been lying half-asleep in bed. There was then a drunken conversation between them, in which our client accused the deceased of having his watch. The deceased in no uncertain manner told our client exactly what he could do. Our client then produced a knife and started waving it about; unfortunately it ended up in the deceased's stomach, and he died. There was some sort of defence of provocation, and also of lack of intention, but in any event it was going to be either murder or manslaughter.

The court-martial was exceedingly fairly conducted. It involved a good deal of pomp. Each witness was marched in 'left, right, left, right' by the sergeant major and told to halt. During the course of the proceedings there appeared one soldier who had been a witness. He was marched in. He gave his name as 'Private Jones' – pause – 'Sir'. He was then invited by prosecuting officer to recount what he had seen and heard. It went something like this: 'I was standing by the end of the bed. I saw nuffin of what 'appened' – pause – 'Sir. I heard nuffin of what 'appened' – pause – 'Sir.' He was then told by the sergeant major to about turn and was marched out, no doubt feeling thoroughly satisfied that he had remained totally neutral in the dispute between his two colleagues.

After one other court-martial we decided to go and have an evening out in Hamburg, with some of the young officers, who kindly drove us. At about five o'clock in the morning, after an entertaining evening, we were driving back, with the other occupants of the car – apart from the driver – asleep. I suddenly realised that the traffic coming towards us seemed to be passing us very close on the *autobahn*: the driver was driving the wrong way down it!

The judge advocate was meticulous in his directions and in his conduct of the case, as indeed were the court-martial officers themselves. It seemed to me then, and it still does, that court-martial proceedings were essentially fair. They were naturally conducted in a military style, but then everyone involved was used to that and conversant with the ways of the military.

The European Court has recently decided that this is not a proper way of proceeding. Like a good deal of interference from Europe, this is ill-conceived. Trials of military matters by civilians are unlikely to be anything like as effective as what is truly a trial by peers. In particular, the penalties imposed by a court-martial are more likely to reflect the proper military view than anything which a civilian court could possibly do. Unlike a civilian court, a military court has to take into account the effect, on morale or otherwise, of a particular action. In the instant case, my recollection is that a seven-year term of imprisonment was imposed. I was told that that it was in order to bring home to the soldiers that taking of drink was greatly to be discouraged, and that it would be very likely that after that sentence had been promulgated a lesser sentence would in fact be affirmed by a higher authority.

Not the least bizarre judgment among many of the European Court of Human Rights was a decision that the court-martial system, which had operated for decades without complaint, was in contravention of

Article 6 of the European Convention of Human Rights. I don't suppose any member of the court had ever witnessed a court-martial in action. They were concerned with Article 6, which provided 'In the determination of any criminal charge against him, everyone is entitled to a fair and public hearing by an independent and impartial tribunal established by law'.

Central to the court-martial system under the Army Act of 1955 was the role of the 'convening officer' who *inter alia* was responsible for convening the court-martial and appointing its members and the prosecuting officer. This person had the final decision on the nature and detail of the charges to be brought, and a plea to a lesser charge could not be accepted from the accused without his or her consent. In certain circumstances, the convening officer could dissolve the court-martial either before or during the trial. Since he or she acted as confirming officer, the court-martial findings were not effective until this officer confirmed them.

In a number of decisions the European Court of Human Rights held that the requirements of independence or impartiality set out by Article 6 (1) were not met in a court-martial, in particular because of the central part played in the prosecution by the convening officer, who was closely linked to the prosecuting authorities, was superior in rank to the members of the court-martial and had the power, albeit in proscribed circumstances, to dissolve the court-martial and to refuse to confirm a decision.

All that sounded like, and was indeed, the high-minded outpourings of academics. In truth it bore no relation to what actually happened in a court-martial. There was never any suggestion that the convening officer in any way abused his of her position, or caused a trial in any way to be unfair. Nobody who attended a court-martial of any sort, whether for a very serious charge or a minor charge, could possibly have been in any doubt as to the fairness of the proceedings.

There was present at any court-martial a judge advocate, whose responsibility it was to guide the members of the court on matters of law, to control the proceedings and to ensure that they were fairly and impartially conducted. The judge advocate's role was essential to the efficient conduct of the trial. If there was the slightest suggestion of impropriety or bias it was open to the confirming authority to intervene. After a conviction and sentence the case would be reviewed by the judge advocate general's department with great thoroughness. In addition there was a right to appeal to the Court of Appeal, Criminal Division, which was yet another avenue down which a legitimate complaint could be pursued and, if proven, corrected. It is this sort of decision by the European Court of Human Rights which has led many to treat its views with something akin to derision. Now that our domestic law of human rights is being considered, it is to be hoped that our judges will adopt a more realistic approach to the problems which arise. It can only be an improvement.

In the summer of 1947, having now returned to the humble status of Writer Popplewell, I was drafted to HMS *St Angelo* in Malta. This was the shore-based depot for the Navy in Valetta. While most of the days I spent in the Navy are clear in my mind, I have scarcely any recollection of the journey to Malta. We left from Liverpool in a troop ship. I was equipped with my hammock, kitbag and small pursers-issue brown suitcase; I had even acquired a holdall which was 'officers, for the use of' only. We left Liverpool in the pouring rain, sailing across the Bay of Biscay in a storm and emerged through the Straits of Gibraltar into glorious sunshine. Malta from the sea was a magnificent sight, and the range of food which was available was quite astonishing. Bananas, vaguely remembered from before the war, were in full supply, and the nasty, dried-up offerings we received in the war became a distant memory. There was no rationing. Chocolate was in ample supply, and the first few days were spent in delicious expenditure on extravagant items of food long-since forgotten.

Malta at that time was still a large naval port, with all that that involved. There were ample facilities for recreation of all sorts. The Gut, more properly called Strait Street, well known to generations of sailors because of the women plying their trade, was much visited. The dhaisas, not unlike Venetian gondolas, were in great demand, ferrying sailors round Grand Harbour and Sliema. One abiding gastronomic memory was the texture of the drinking water, which seemed to bear a thin trace of oil. Whether this was because the water was brought in by boat from the Italian mainland or whether something was added to deter the sailors' natural ardour, I know not.

I had been at Malta for about two months doing routine secretarial work when I was drafted to HMS *Virago*. *Virago* was a V-class destroyer with a complement of about 180 and was part of the third destroyer flotilla made up of *Virago, Verulam, Volage* and *Venus.* The skipper, who was a lieutenant commander, was the junior captain in the flotilla and therefore *Virago* was allocated all the dreary and dirty jobs. The Fleet was still in a state of some shock and anger resulting from the incident in the Corfu Channel. Corfu is now associated with package holidays, sunshine and bare bodies. Then it had only one meaning – namely, the mining of two destroyers with considerable loss of life. We were always led to believe that *Virago* was intended to be one of the ships that was to go up the Corfu Channel but was replaced because of engine trouble. Whether this was true or not I never found out.

In the result, *Volage* and *Saumarez* were sent up the narrow channel between Corfu and the Albanian mainland to demonstrate that these were international waters. *Saumarez* struck a mine. When *Volage* went to its rescue it had its bows blown off. *Volage* was able to tow *Saumarez* to Malta, where it lay in sad state. There was naturally an international incident. Britain took Albania to the International Court of Justice and was awarded substantial damages, which have never been paid. The incident caused a good deal of heart-searching about the wisdom of the action in taking the ships so close to Albania and was an early indication of the attitude of the Eastern Block to the west.

The reason why the destroyers had been going through the Corfu channel at all was because we had both a military and naval presence in Trieste. Trieste had been captured by the New Zealanders and some elements of the British Army. It was a port which had belonged to the Italians and on which the Yugoslavs were now casting covetous eyes. The area surrounding Trieste was occupied by Tito's Army. The Navy was there to ensure that Trieste was kept open as a port and to prevent any sudden strike by Tito at Trieste.

When I joined *Virago* she lay in Sliema Creek, and was already under orders to proceed to Trieste. I confess I had some apprehension at joining: firstly, because I am not by nature a particularly good sailor, secondly, because I had by that time joined the Inner Temple and was doing some bar exams by correspondence course. The facilities for quiet reading were more than adequate in the base at Malta, whereas the likelihood of some privacy on board a crowded destroyer seemed to me to be nil. This apprehension was however counterbalanced by the excitement at the thought of visits to various parts of the Mediterranean at Her Majesty's expense.

It was always said that *Virago* had been designed for Russian convoys and was therefore well insulated against the cold. It had the opposite effect, however, in the Mediterranean sun. It meant that life on the mess decks varied from unpleasant to extremely disagreeable. Such air as was pumped round the ship seemed only to heat it up. The washing facilities for the lower deck – some 170 men – consisted of five basins without hot water and a rather primitive shower. The officers, of which there were some eight or nine, had some four baths between them, and an ample supply of hot water without limitation of use. It was a good example of the gulf that lay between the lower deck and the officers.

My introduction to *Virago* could scarcely have been less auspicious. I was greeted by the Master at Arms as I clambered aboard with the welcome 'Are you the new bloody scribes?' – all writers were called scribes – I acknowledged that indeed I was. 'Well we've f—ing well, bleeding well been waiting for days for you, where the 'ell have you been?' My explanation that I had received my orders only two hours before and had then come by naval transport as quickly as I could fell on deaf ears. The conversation, such as it was, was concluded with the Master at Arms saying to me 'Well, f—ing well get below 'cos we are sailing in an hour'.

Terrified that I should at least be court-martialled if I stayed any longer in the presence of this grim and austere figure, I clutched my hammock, kitbag and brown suitcase and entered the bowels of the ship. For all that I then knew I might have been in the Hampton Court maze. The ship seemed to be a mass of confined and narrow passage-ways, of metal ladders that seemed to lead nowhere and doors that always seemed to open the wrong way with me on the receiving side. Eventually I found a seaman to whom I explained my predicament. He pointed out that the new scribes always messed with the seamen in the after mess deck and directed my faltering footsteps in that direction. So off I set, and eventually found a hatchway with a ladder leading down to the mess deck I sought. As I was descending the metal ladder, clutching my hammock, kitbag and brown suitcase, my foot slipped. At that precise moment one of the seamen from the mess deck was ascending the ladder bearing in front of him a large mess tin full of tomato puree. He had one hand on the rail, the other holding the tin above him as he climbed. My foot and his tin coincided, the seaman fell back in considerable confusion. I had the wit to hang onto the rail and remained poised on the ladder. The mess tin, now detached from the seaman's hand, fell directly on top of him as he lay on the mess-deck floor.

I was sufficiently wise in the ways of the world to appreciate that the expressions of violence now emanating from the mess deck floor were directed at me, and that if I remained they were likely to be put into effect. No-one could have moved faster or with more agility than I did at that moment. I gripped my hammock, kitbag and brown suitcase and vanished to the top of the ladder and into the passageway faster than I believed possible. I allowed some ten minutes or so to elapse before returning. I assumed, rightly as it turned out, that for the seaman the only clue that he would have as to the perpetrator of this outrage on him would be the sight of a pair of navy boots. I descended the ladder with considerable care and presented myself on the mess deck.

There was still considerable turmoil. The outraged seaman had obviously been in full flow for the past ten minutes. It was not merely wounded vanity – his clothes were, to use a culinary phrase, peppered with tomato. His language was full of violence, continuing unabated, including every swear word, for some considerable time. With an air of insouciance I presented myself as the new scribes, enquired whether this was indeed where I was to rest, and with an air of naive curiosity asked what seemed to be going on. The injured seaman explained again in no uncertain terms what had happened and what he would do to the perpetrator. I expressed considerable sympathy with him and hoped indeed that he would catch up with the perpetrator. He was not, however, to be put off by simple expressions of sympathy and continued to rage for a considerable period thereafter.

The mess deck, which was to be my home for the next nine months, housed some 28 men in two messes. It was I suppose about 30 feet square. We sat at two tables, we each had a locker and we slung hammocks in line. We ate there, slept there and lived there. There is no greater contrast between a sailor at sea and the sailor in a shore establishment. Those in shore establishments have little or no loyalty to their fellow sailors or to the establishment itself. They are often there on a temporary basis. Their sole object seems to be to avoid doing any more work than necessary, to keep out of trouble, to indulge in as many rackets as they can without being caught and generally to skive.

The ship's company on board a ship however, is a different breed. No-one living with 13 others day in day out can avoid the communal scrutiny of character. Each has a responsibility to bear in 101 different ways. The skiver is soon detected. Many are the ways of ensuring communal discipline. The distinction between the officers, always known as pigs, and us, the ratings, which was then very strong, tends to cement the community feeling. Living at close quarters day in day out ensures that there is this camaraderie, which never ceased to amaze me.

The arrival of a new member of the crew necessarily caused some excitement. The fact that I spoke with what they regarded as a 'toff's' accent, naturally gave rise to considerable suspicion. In any event they regarded all 'scribes' as something from another world. Additionally, I was there only for a limited period, whereas most of them were regulars. The majority served during the war. They were older both in actual age and in the ways of the world – particularly the naval world. I soon learnt a great deal of naval lore. There were little ways of doing things that avoided official disapproval and yet achieved their object. I quickly learnt which particular petty officer to approach for a problem, who to avoid, how to keep out of trouble and how to get along with people. It was an introduction to a wholly different world which was at once rewarding and at the same time instructive. Those who think that judges have no idea of how the other half live should try living on the lower deck for a year. Nothing could give a better insight into human problems.

We sailed directly from Malta to Trieste. It was then occupied by the Scots Guards. We had not been there more than a week before we were challenged to a game of rugger. I don't suppose there were more than 15 in the ship's company who had even seen a game of rugger, let alone played it. But volunteers were invited in the usual naval manner, 15 of whom were drafted to play. On the basis of having played centre three-quarter some 10 years before at Winchester House School, I was deputed to play fullback. The only ground which appeared to be available was in territory held by Tito's troops. There was at that time apprehension that Tito might move into Trieste and occupy it. What negotiations went on to allow us to play there I know not, but 15 heroic bodies ill-dressed, ill-equipped and singularly ill-prepared for the contest embarked in two lorries, heavily escorted by some fellow sailors armed with guns.

After a journey through the hills we arrived at the ground to be greeted by our opponents, all of whom seemed to be eight feet tall and nine feet wide, and at the peak of fitness. Apart from the sailors guarding us and some soldiers guarding them, there were no other spectators save for two small Yugoslav boys. Where they had come from or what their interest in the game was we never discovered. We lost the toss. They kicked off. The ball sailed over the heads of our forwards but short of me, luckily, and went into touch. The two Yugoslav boys seized hold of the ball. They turned on their heels. They vanished with it into the distance. Nobody had the opportunity to stop them. Luckily no-one had thought to bring a spare ball and that concluded the game. There were certainly 15 very relieved players on our side.

The commander-in-chief's private yacht was moored in Trieste. Not long after we arrived, though I suspect it was purely coincidental, he ordered his motor boat to be lowered, only to find that the ropes which secured it to the yacht had been removed and there was no way that he could use it. There was a flourishing black market in Trieste, as there was wherever we went. Subsequently, when we were in Gibraltar, vast quantities of tins of paint vanished from the bows of the ship. Armed guards were posted to prevent anything movable being taken. No doubt given time most of the fixtures on *Virago* would have vanished altogether.

The occasion of the wedding of the Queen and Prince Phillip in 1947 was celebrated by a parade in which *Virago*'s sailors took part. In addition we were dressed overall – which involved flags and bunting of all shades and hues being flown from every part of the ship – and lit up. It was not until the lights had been switched on in the evening that it was fully appreciated that the letters 'E' and 'F' did not properly represent the initial letters of the princess and the prince. There was naturally a good deal of good-natured ribaldry from other ships and there was also some more formal and ruder communications to the Commanding Officer from the commander-in-chief.

It was the routine of the third destroyer flotilla to move from Trieste to Venice in rotation. This we did in the October and November. I have been to Venice in different conditions on many subsequent occasions, but I confess that I have never had the same thrill as first coming into Venice from the sea. We anchored off the Grand Canal and we lay there or along side a quay for the best part of five to six

4. HMS *Virago*, Grand Canal, 1947.

weeks. Quite what we were doing from a military point of view I never really discovered. It was however a marvellous opportunity for sight-seeing in a city which then had no tourists and was still to some extent recovering from the rigours of the war. The splendidly efficient water boat service was back in place. It was cheap, uncrowded and enabled us to get around.

Everything else was comparatively cheap. Whereas the pound bought 2000 lira in Trieste, it bought 2400 in Venice. It thus provided those who had some financial acumen the opportunity to make something on the turn. There were one or two on our mess deck who invariably managed to get the exchange the wrong way round. Some of the picture galleries had re-opened. The churches were there to be visited and enjoyed without crowds. It naturally made an enormous impression on me. Most of my colleagues thought it dull and boring. They complained about the absence of things to do or see. Beer was in short supply. The women were a constant source of trouble. There were no facilities for games and there was little which interested them. They were happier when we returned to Trieste.

We sailed back to Malta in time for Christmas. Christmas day in the heat somehow seemed unreal but the service in the cathedral in

Valetta was outstanding. The beauty of the service, albeit conducted in a language difficult to follow, was unbelievable. I can seldom remember taking part in a service which combined so much religious fervour with spiritual beauty.

Sometime after Christmas we received orders to go to Gibraltar where we were to go into dry dock. One of the improvements was the instalment in our washroom of four basins with hot water, and a shower which also had hot water. This was a privilege, we were told, which, if abused, would be withdrawn. Quite how we would abuse it was never explained to us, nor how it could be withdrawn. After three days of gale-force winds and high seas, during which I was permanently sick, we arrived in Gibraltar. It was still very much a naval port with dry-dock facilities and a harbour full of shipping of all sorts.

The Admiral in charge of Gibraltar was Rear-Admiral Sir Ernest Archer. His daughters had been at school with my sister. They had been alerted by her to my arrival. When we docked, over the tannoy came the announcement 'Writer Popplewell to report to the gangway'. There parked on the quayside was the Admiral's car, in full view of the ship's company and of most of the officers. Having obtained leave to go ashore, I marched with a swagger down the gangway and climbed into the luxurious limousine. I was given a royal welcome at Admiralty House, where I was a visitor on a number of occasions. Some of the other guests who were young officers in the Army were a little taken aback to find someone from the lower deck as a fellow guest.

I was able to observe to the Admiral, who was to my eyes a terrifying creature, the merits or otherwise of the officers on board *Virago*. But my real moment of glory came when we went to the Ceremony of the Keys. Once a week, at that time at any rate, it was customary for the Army to lay on a parade in which the keys of the town played an important part. Quite what the origin of the ceremony was I never did discover, but it was always well attended and something of a service occasion. For that purpose there was a dais on which there were chairs for VIPs and for the officer taking the salute. Because I was with the Admiral's daughters, we were shown to the front of the dais and took our seats. I had sensibly provided myself with civilian clothes when I had originally come out from England, which I was allowed to wear ashore. Sitting in the row behind us, to their intense chagrin, were a number of the ship's officers, including the Commanding Officer. I had the agreeable experience of introducing them all to the Admiral's daughters with the suggestion – never actually spelt out – that if they treated me right I would put in a good word for them with the Admiral.

The facilities for those whose ship was in dry dock in Gibraltar were horrendous. They consisted of huts in the dockyard area, which one old sailor said had been there since before the First World War; another thought they dated from Nelson's day. The only form of heating was a large metal fire in the centre of the hut, which gave warmth immediately around it but nowhere else. The washing facilities were something 'out of the ark'. As for the heads, even the public lavatories in Gibraltar were better. These conditions we endured for some two very grim months.

The weather in Gibraltar was often very wet. Apart from visiting the well-known sights in Gibraltar, the chief attraction was to go across the frontier into Spain to the small village of La Linea. Those who have only been to Spain in the last 20 years would not have recognised the area. La Linea was then a small village. It had a few shops of no merit and a run-down café or two. The chief attraction for the sailors were the women. There was also a great financial advantage in a visit to Spain: at that time the official rate of exchange between Spain and England was 66 pesetas to the pound. In any bar in Gibraltar you could change a pound note on the black market for 126 pesetas. Visitors to La Linea would spend 60 pesetas on whatever they chose, come back to the frontier with 66 pesetas in their pocket, change it officially and get a pound back. Thus, the evening cost them nothing.

Since then I have frequently discussed with well-known economists the question of who lost on that transaction. Clearly the sailor did not. Equally clearly the bartenders did not, or they would not have continued to trade 126 pesetas for one pound. It is difficult to see how the Spanish Government lost. The most cogent explanation was that nobody lost. Not being an economist, I had to be satisfied with that answer, but I still find it strange that if someone has got 60 pesetas for free, no-one has lost 60 pesetas.

There was precious little for the sailors to do once the ship was in dry dock. Gibraltar is a small place. Alcohol was readily available in the town. There were a number of outbreaks of violence, particularly when inter-service rivalries took over. On one occasion after an evening out one of the ship's company came staggering back into the dockyard. He approached the dry dock, which was 300 or 400 feet long, with a drop of anything up to 100 feet. There was a chain along the top of the dry dock to indicate to anyone who was sober that there was this drop. Beyond the chain there was a ledge which was probably no more than a foot or two wide. This sailor climbed over the chain onto the ledge. He moved along it for some 300 or 400 feet swaying like washing in the wind. He reached the end. He climbed back over the chain. He then walked back into his hut and went to sleep. He had no recollection of the incident the next morning. It was one of the more frightening experiences of my life.

My parents suggested that while I was in Gibraltar I should take the opportunity of going into Spain. They did not have in mind that I should visit the ladies in La Linea, but something more cultural and educational. Accordingly I applied to the Commanding Officer for 10 days' leave. Then, together with a stores assistant named Desmond Lewtas, I set off for a holiday in Spain. Nothing could then have been more different from the present situation. My parents had sent money to a bank in Gibraltar, amounting, I think, to the enormous sum of £20. I obtained a passport in Gibraltar. This was subsequently to be of considerable trouble to me when travelling around Europe. It trans-pired that in Germany and Austria in the 1950s, while a British passport required no visa, anyone armed with a Gibraltar passport did need one. But that problem was to arise later. There were no problems then in going into Spain and so we set off by ferry across the bay to Algeciras.

Algeciras was still a small town. It had escaped the ravages of the Spanish Civil War. It had always been a distinguished resort where Europeans had wintered and the great entertained. We presented ourselves at the Hotel Reina Christina, which had a famous pre-war reputation, and booked in for the night. The cost was minimal, more particularly because we had our highly valuable pesetas. We ordered a bottle of champagne, which cost us the equivalent of 10 pence, enjoyed a hearty dinner and retired to a comfortable bed for the first time for some months.

Lewtas was an enormously agreeable companion. He had been to a public school, though he never did disclose where. He was very well read and highly intelligent. From time to time, however, he fell foul of the naval authorities by taking somewhat too much drink. Thus he would keep his status as chief petty officer for six months of a year; he would then revert to petty officer and sometimes back to ordinary sailor. But he was a lively and entertaining person and an ideal traveller.

We arrived next morning at Algeciras railway station in order to catch the train to Ronda. There was a line which ran all the way from Algeciras to Madrid. It had been built by British engineers. Algeciras Station resembled nothing so much as a crowded marketplace, containing what looked like the entire population of Southern Spain. By dint of pushing and shoving we managed to get to the ticket office. I then booked two first-class tickets to Ronda in the only Spanish I knew. This was a wise precaution, because the rest of the compartments looked as though they were carrying the last refugees out of Saigon. The train climbed its way slowly and gradually though the mountains on a picturesque journey. It stopped at various intervals. The stops were clearly unscheduled, but they enabled the driver to dismount and visit either various friends or his girlfriend or both.

When we arrived at Ronda we found our way to the Hotel Reina Victoria. The hotel had been built in the nineteenth century to house the engineers who were building the railway. It was almost totally deserted. It seemed to us to be luxury itself. Life was extremely cheap, not only because of the rate of exchange but also because the Spanish economy then was a peasant economy. The hotel itself commanded a fine view over the mountains and the surrounding countryside, where one could observe peasants tilling the fields with tools straight from the Middle Ages. It was very hot during the day, but sufficiently cold in the evenings for there to be a fire in the hotel.

We got up late, enjoyed a large breakfast and then set out for the day with a packed lunch. Ronda itself was and still is a picturesque town set up high in the mountains with the oldest bullring in Spain. It contained many medieval houses but its centrepiece was a magnificent bridge over a large gorge. It had, I suspect, remained unchanged over hundreds of years. There was little or no motor traffic, donkeys and bicycles being the main modes of transport.

As we were to discover, there were still remnants of the Republican forces who now lived the life of bandits up in the hills. We were quietly walking one day in the hills when we heard shots from below. We saw three members of the civil guard; they were firing their guns. We naturally assumed that they were having a go at some wild birds, only to realise, as we saw the rocks beside us fragmenting, that we were in fact the target. We rushed down the hill with our arms in the air shouting 'Inglesé' which we supposed was Spanish for Englishmen. We explained to the bewildered policeman that we were English tourists who were out walking perfectly peacefully in the hills. As we had no other Spanish and they spoke no English, communication was exceedingly difficult. Our passports were of little value because they couldn't understand them. However we did a mime show. Eventually and with much reluctance they allowed us to go free.

Our next experience of this sort was on a bus trip to Malaga. Malaga is now so much part of the Costa Brava that it is difficult to appreciate that in 1948 it was a small fishing port with no other claim to fame than it had been used during the Civil War for ferrying arms to the combatants. The bus in which we travelled must have been built sometime in the nineteenth century. Its progress was like that of the old English stagecoach, in that the bus stopped at every village, everyone got out, we went to the local pub where a glass of sherry and some food was produced, and then all climbed back on board. We sat in the front as befitted the holders of a first-class ticket, which I think cost the equivalent of two pence. The rest of the bus was full of noisy Spaniards jam-packed in with luggage, children and animals of all sorts.

We had only been going about ten minutes when we stopped at the roadside to pick up a diminutive Spanish soldier armed with a gun. He sat beside us. We were only able to communicate by gestures, but we managed to understand from him that his presence on the bus was due to the fact that at regular intervals the bandits came down from the hills. They had a habit of stopping buses, taking all the valuables from the passengers and either pushing the bus with the passengers over the side of the mountains or else just simply shooting the passengers. The role of this rather unkempt diminutive soldier was to protect us against these bandits. He gave an impressive and voluble demonstration of how he would use his gun. Happily, he was never put to the test. I have some doubts as to whether we should have survived if he had been.

The other hazard was that at that time the route from Ronda to Malaga was down a narrow winding road through the mountains, with a sheer drop on one side. There now exists a beautifully cambered, well-made road which makes the journey down from Ronda to Malaga comparatively easy. In those days it was a twisty winding road of uncertain surface and treacherous bends. Our driver had indulged as we had at each hostelry. Additionally, it was his practice to turn round and exchange pleasantries and views of the day with the passengers he was carrying, who were obviously old friends. The bus itself did not always seem to react immediately to the turn of the wheel. Thus, the combination of the threat of the bandits, the state of the driver and the nature of the road and the route were all such as to induce complete panic into otherwise intrepid Englishmen. Once we had reached Malaga we had to contemplate the return journey, which had the additional hazard of being conducted in the dark.

We had a happy day in Malaga itself, wandering around this small village. We sat on the beach and swam. There was no-one else about, save for a few weary-looking inhabitants. If only we had known what we know now, we could no doubt have bought the entire frontage of Malaga for a few pounds. Of the journey back I have only the haziest recollection. Desmond and I decided that the only sensible way to prepare ourselves for the journey was to drink enough so that we would return in a state of total euphoria. He apparently sang throughout the entire journey. I happily fell asleep.

We had 10 extremely agreeable days. We lived like lords. On the middle weekend one of the ship's officers and his wife came up for two or three days' stay. As we were virtually the only guests in the place it was a somewhat incongruous and embarrassing situation. It was made more particularly so when we discovered after they had left that there appeared in the bar two bottles of duty-free whisky, which Ronda had not seen since before the war. It was of course a total coincidence that they should appear so soon after the departure of the officer. It was no doubt unrelated. Desmond felt honour-bound to do justice to them.

Our return journey took us back by the railway, where we fell in with an English couple who were in the cork business. They took us to their home in Algeciras and entertained us royally, with the result that we arrived back on board some three or four hours late. This resulted in our being brought before the same officer who had been to Ronda. We were deprived of a day's pay and had to do an hour's extra duty. Our mouths were closed on the question of the whisky.

We finally set sail from Gibraltar with our new washing facilities. We managed to avoid abusing them and returned to Malta. One of the principle duties of the destroyer flotilla in the Mediterranean was to prevent what were regarded as illegal immigrants landing in Palestine as it was then called. It was a task which everyone found disagreeable. The small boats in which the immigrants sailed would leave some port, generally in Italy, grossly overcrowded, in conditions of great squalor and discomfort. They hoped to reach the Palestine coast at night, usually Haifa, run onto the beach, disembark and scatter before they could be apprehended. It was our task to prevent that happening and to this end we would patrol the coast. Once the boat was within the three-mile limit we would order it to stop, a boarding party would be put on board and it would be then taken in tow, usually to Cyprus.

Sometimes the boats had come all the way from Germany. They were full of people who had been displaced, were refugees or concentration-camp victims. Most had suffered terribly during the war at the hands of the Germans, and what they wanted more than anything was to settle in Palestine and be left alone. Palestine at that time was administered by the British Government, and was in a state of turmoil by reason of the activities of the Stern Gang, Haganna and other terrorist organisations. The blowing up of the King David Hotel and the taking of two service-men as hostages and their execution had certainly not increased the popularity of the inhabitants with the British forces generally.

It was, however, a quite appalling situation, in which women and children were herded like cattle into small boats within a mile or two of freedom and sent to yet another camp. To board some of the small boats was not a difficult problem. Some of the bigger boats, however, like the *Empire Warfield*, presented a very real problem, and there were often running battles. No-one pretended to enjoy it or to find it other than extremely disagreeable.

Being the Captain's secretary, I was privy to the advance information with which we were provided about the departure of various boats, their size, their contents and their time of arrival in our area. Thus, each boat could be readily identified and its arrival anticipated, even without the use of aircraft which regularly flew on patrols. Even if the approach to Palestine was made at night, they were likely to be picked up on the radar. From time to time there were misreadings of the radar screen. Signals would fly from Army HQ to Naval HQ com-plaining that a boat had escaped the watchful eye of the Navy. The rights and wrongs of immigration were heatedly debated on the lower deck. The arguments fell short of being intellectual, and the Balfour declaration was certainly not at the forefront of discussion.

5. HMS *Virago*: preparing to board an immigrant ship, 1948.

As we lay offshore in the glorious sunshine, with the smell of the orange blossom wafting across, it was easy to be oblivious to the fact that onshore Army patrols were being attacked, ammunition dumps blown up and soldiers killed. The American support of the immigrants, together with the adverse publicity from our boarding of these immigrant boats and the consequential human suffering, led eventually to the establishment of Israel as an independent nation sometime after I had left the area. Some of the leaders of the terrorist gangs subsequently became national figures in the political life of the country. It made their complaints about terrorism against their own country somewhat less compelling.

None of the problems which subsequently affected Cyprus – such as the campaign of terrorism by Eoka or the occupation by Turkey – existed at this time. When we took the immigrant boats with their cargo to Cyprus, we had the opportunity to lie offshore and enjoy the beaches on the island, the beautiful countryside and the hospitality of the towns. One Sunday morning, with *Virago* lying a mile offshore, a liberty boat took a party of sailors ashore for swimming and relaxation. By the end of the morning, one or two of the sailors had had a good deal too much to drink. One boasted that he would have no difficulty in swimming out to *Virago*. He stripped off ready to do so; his mates told him that there was no chance of his doing it, whereupon he leapt in the water and struck out from the shore. No-one took much notice of him for a while until it was apparent that about 150 yards off shore he was in some distress. A boat was launched and he was fished out of the water more dead than alive, and lay spluttering in the boat.

When he had recovered, one of his mates told him in no uncertain terms with a good deal of swearing that he knew that he was chicken and that he never could have reached *Virago*. Thus addressed, the swimmer stood up, leapt up over the side of the boat and started yet again to swim off to *Virago*. This time good sense prevailed, the boat kept track of him and when within a few hundred yards, it was obvious that he was likely to sink, he was fished out and his tormentors were forbidden to say anything further to him.

We must have done four or five of these illegal-immigrant patrols. They were generally extremely boring if nothing happened, particularly as at night we had to be blacked out. We did not put into harbour for lengthy periods of time. The only advantage of that was that as no post could reach the ship there was precious little work for me to do. I found therefore that I had plenty of time to continue with my legal studies – part one of the bar exam by correspondence course. I remember that I was equipped with a number of books somewhat out of date and the series of 'Questions and Answers' that were of such value to a whole generation of students. These were questions which had regularly appeared in the papers, together with the model answers. It was a somewhat limited way of learning about the law, though it was undoubtedly an efficient way of enabling a student to pass exams. I did in fact take a number of my part one bar exams while on board.

The chief problem was not so much the nature of the questions for which 'Questions and Answers' had adequately prepared me but the fact that I was required to sit the exam at sea while feeling somewhat seasick. The papers had arrived in my office addressed to the Commanding Officer as all post was. It was a test of moral character that, having recognised the envelope for what it was, I forbore to have a peek and delivered them unopened to the Commanding Officer. Virtue was rewarded when I learnt that I had passed the exams.

On the mess deck one of the chief forms of entertainment was cards. I was introduced to cribbage at an early stage of my life on *Virago*. It was played with great concentration, seriously and with no quarter given, that is it would not have occurred to anyone to point out to an opponent that he had underscored his hand. Because of the audience it was impossible for any cheating to take place, and each hand resulted in a postmortem by the non-players whose expertise was immense. I have always been grateful for the opportunity to learn the game at expert hands. It was never played for money, or rarely so, but almost always for a tot of rum or for some favour.

Those over a certain age, which I think was 20, were entitled to a tot of rum. It was not the sickly-sweet, thin, commercial stuff, but a very strong and sharp spirit. It was diluted with water and distributed at noon, when the pipe 'up spirits' went. There were various portions of the tot for which the game was played. There was 'sippers' which as the name suggests entitled the winner to a sip. This was executed by the winner holding the loser's tot, with the loser's hand poised close to the tot to ensure that nothing more than a sip was drunk and to regain the tot as soon as the winner had had his sip. 'Gulpers' was the next in value in winning, and then finally the whole tot. The issue of rum was very close to the heart of the lower deck, and it was a considerable deprivation to lose your tot. A loser would wander round with a hang-dog look like a small child who has had a toffee taken away from him. It was considered good form even when you won a tot to leave something for the loser, so that his despair was not complete.

It was also customary when there was some form of celebration such as a birthday or promotion, or more particularly when someone was leaving ship, for that person to go round the mess decks and be invited to celebrate with a tot or two in each mess deck. The tot itself was very powerful. Although it was of course quite illegal for this to happen, it occurred with some frequency. With equal frequency the luckless celebrant would find that after a tour of this sort he was quite incapable of controlling himself. Sometimes he would be found totally paralytic, sometimes it had even resulted in death. More usually the celebrant would commit some terrible act of mayhem which would seriously effect his naval career. On one occasion I remember a sailor celebrating his promotion to petty officer in Grand Harbour in the following way. He took the Captain's skimmer, a fast motor boat and drove it in ever-decreasing circles round the fleet to the applause of ships' companies who turned up on the upper deck to cheer him on. Eventually he fell into the sea. His promotion to petty officer was, I fear, short lived.

The tot was also a valuable currency if a favour was sought. In the various ports which we visited, it was possible to buy a number of items which were either not available in England or were much cheaper abroad. The difficulty was getting them home. There were those who, if offered a tot or two, would sew up a parcel by covering it with material. It required a good deal of skill, the right needles, sail thread and sail cloth. But the end result was a shipshape parcel strong enough to endure the worst battering of post offices in a number of different countries.

Once it became known that I was interested in the law, I was asked to adjudicate on a number of small disputes that occurred on the mess deck. I learnt very soon that however just the decision may appear to the adjudicator, there is always one party who feels aggrieved. The other activity in which I was much involved was in helping to write letters from the sailors to their girlfriends or wives. They seemed to think that with my education these women would be more susceptible to the eloquent language with which I was familiar rather than the rather earthy phrases which was broadly the vocabulary of the lower deck. It certainly increased my knowledge, both of the English language generally and the parts of the female body in particular.

It was difficult not to be anxious at what the letters would bring by way of reply. Would they bring a friendly rejoinder? Would the difference of tone and language be noticed? Would the absence of the expressions of what Jack would like to do to the most intimate parts of the female body lead to a certain lessening of desire in the recipient? Would they (in one case) head off what looked like a disastrous split? I have to say with some pride that generally they seemed to get a warmer reception than the previous letters. Indeed in some cases the new style was received with rapture.

There were of course, as one might expect, some failures. Clearly there were still those who liked a discussion on paper about the most intimate details of sex, but on balance I can congratulate myself on having done a reasonably good job. I undoubtedly saved one marriage that seemed to be going adrift. It was certainly of considerable help to me when I was writing to Margaret before we were married, where I adopted what may be described as the more literary than the earthy style. It was also useful to me when I started at the bar in understanding the problems of people faced with the breakup of their marriage.

Beirut was one city that we visited. It was then quite beautiful, with a combination of all that was most attractive in French and Arab culture and architecture. It was a thriving city with a busy port and an American hospital. The war seemed long forgotten and the people appeared happily living in harmony. That was certainly the impression with conveyed itself immediately to an observer.

Our approach to Beirut was by night. It was clear from the red lights which shone from one quarter of the city where most of the sailors would go as soon as we docked. I have to say I managed to resist the invitations to join them. There were however, other entertainments, one of which was a trip some 30–40 miles from Beirut up to the snow-clad hills, where we indulged in some pretty primitive skiing. I think it doubtful if anyone of the ship's company had ever skied in their lives. We had no proper ski boots, only our Navy boots. The skis were old fashioned and elderly. There was no sort of ski lift or facility to climb: if you wanted to climb up on your skis you had to go up crab fashion; if you wanted to stop when skiing, the only way was to sit down.

The weather was exceedingly hot. By the end of the day apart from a few bruised bodies, there was a good deal of sunstroke. It was however, an exciting and exhilarating day and much enjoyed by the ship's company. I remember that at the bottom of the slope, in snow, were bottles of beer. Where they came from I can't now imagine or why we were allowed them. But there were one or two who found the combination of sun and drink and snow too much for them and ended up in some state of disarray.

From Beirut we were back again on Palestine patrol and finally back to Malta. There I found that I was to be sent home and to be released in time to go up to Cambridge in October. I continued with some of my bar exams. I arrived back in England in time to see something of the Australian cricket side. In particular I remember leaving Portsmouth to go home to Guildford, where we now lived, having heard that England were batting at the Oval. But when I arrived home and listened to the radio I was astonished to hear that Bedser was bowling. In the short time that it had taken me to go from Portsmouth to Guildford and home, England had been bowled out for 52.

That summer I had an agreeable time in the barracks at Portsmouth, playing cricket at the United Services ground. There were a lot of very good Navy cricketers at that time with whom I played, though I never got into the representative side. I continued with reading law in preparation for going to Cambridge. I had decided to forego the classics – at which I was never very good – in favour of law, and in October 1948 I went up to Queens' College for three most enjoyable years.

I left the Navy with some sadness. I had learnt a great deal about life in general and sailors in particular. I was appalled at the contrast between the standard of life of the officers and the men. It didn't in the least surprise me that the forces had voted overwhelmingly for the Labour Party in 1945, I was only astonished that the conditions on board ship, which seemed to have remained unchanged for decades, if not centuries, were so readily endured by the lower deck. No-one expects a fighting ship to be like a passenger cruise-liner and necessarily discipline has to be strong, but I still find it astonishing that the appalling conditions which then obtained should have been thought conducive to efficiency. I certainly left the Navy more mature and a more understanding person. No-one could possibly spend a year on the lower deck of a destroyer at sea without understanding and appreciating the very solid qualities that go to make up the English sailor. My experiences certainly served me well when I went to the bar, and eventually to the bench.

4

University

I went up to Cambridge in the autumn of 1948. Nothing that had happened before to me in my life or since has ever been quite so exciting or fulfilling. I look back on the three years at Queens' with unalloyed pleasure. By the time I came down I had acquired a reasonably good degree, I had been called to the bar, I had managed to get a Cricket blue and above all I had met and become engaged to darling Margaret. They were indeed our salad days.

Cambridge in 1948 was not the Cambridge of before the war. It was overcrowded, full of undergraduates who were two or three years older than the norm. Some of them were married, many had distinguished war service and the majority were anxious to get degrees and to start earning a living. But the idea that we had any less fun is quite wrong. Queens' itself was a small college. It was not particularly distinguished either in sport or scholarship, nor did it have any claim to social pretensions.

It was of course a time of austerity. There was rationing of every sort. It was only very gradually that the careful attitudes so long engendered by the war relaxed at all. The totally carefree attitude which was the hallmark of undergraduates before the war and in the generation after us was not immediately apparent. Likewise, a more intense appreciation of life engendered by our service experiences and our age led, I think, to a more mature approach not only to work and our social life but to the sort of discussions and debates that have been the hallmark of undergraduate life for ever.

There was a very strong political feeling in the university. The war itself had instilled in a younger generation a belief that peace must succeed. Thus the advent of the United Nations (UN) and its association were widely supported throughout the university. Russia posed a dilemma for many people. It was necessarily regarded with affection and respect for its heroic efforts during the war, but by 1948 and 1949 its territorial aggression had become manifest. The blockade of Berlin and the Korean War were to cause considerable dismay to a number of those who believed that peace between the great nations could be a reality. Nor were the events in China likely to dispel the anxiety of further problems in the Far East. It is difficult now with *perestroika* and with re-establishment of links with China to appreciate the terrible shadow which the Communist countries cast over several generations. It is true to say that those of us who were up at university shortly after the war lived with the perpetual fear of nuclear war, until quite recently, although we were not perhaps quite so neurotic about it as some Americans who had never been exposed as civilians to war or the threat of air-raids.

I recall that when we were in New York in 1960, there were signs in one theatre advising the audience where the shelters were if the four-minute warning sounded. We had stayed with an American lawyer and his wife in Virginia; he subsequently became a US senator. They had arranged that when the four-minute warning came there was a place in the hills to which they would drive where they had prepared food and other sustenance and a deep shelter for themselves and their family. But although this anxiety pervaded our political consciousness and thinking and talking during our life at university, it was, I think, a time of hope and optimism that our generation at any rate would not repeat the mistakes of our parents' generation and allow dictators and aggressors to seize whatever they wished.

We were naive enough to believe and hopeful enough to expect that the UN would be just that, and that it would act together as a law-enforcing body without fear or favour, and that never again would the world be at risk of a devastating war. The events in Korea were held out to be an example of that unity. As it happened it was only because of the absence of the Russians from the Security Council that the UN Resolution was passed. Those who took part in the war represented a very few nations. The subsequent history of its attempts to maintain the peace in different continents, shows how far below our expectations it fell. Its purpose was praiseworthy, its work conscientious and laudable, but it lacked a political unity to make it effective on any important issue.

Domestically, of course, there was a great deal of political excitement. The Labour Party had now been in power for some three years following the end of the war. Its achievements and difficulties had by this time become apparent. I suppose there is no time when political excitement does not run high at university, but this was certainly a period when the parties on both sides were strongly divided in their views and were flexing their muscles to defeat the other. I was not a member of the Student Union, but the debates were undoubtedly of a high quality, not only from the named speakers and from outside visitors but also from undergraduates, who were able to speak from their own experience of life. It was a time particularly when the midnight hours were spent in earnest discussions about reforming the world, and the hopes and fears of a new generation were confidently expressed as if they had never been expressed before.

Queens' itself was a middle-of-the-road, middle-order sort of college. It had undergraduates from all backgrounds with a variety of ages. It was not dedicated to any particular subject, though it did have a strong bent towards the law. Arthur Armitage, later to become Sir Arthur Armitage and President of Queens', and subsequently vice-chancellor of Manchester University, was our tutor. He had been an outstanding undergraduate and had recently returned from the war. He was in his early thirties and was responsible not only for teaching and supervising us in law, but he was the tutor responsible for our discipline. That he was exceedingly bright, no-one could dispute. He taught us all with a breadth of common sense and good humour so that even the dullest of us was able to understand the simplest principles of law. He implanted in us a desire to seek the principles of justice, not as a dry academic concept but as a real force in the world outside. A criticism of our work or a rebuke as to the quality of an essay was delivered in such agreeable tones that we were ashamed to suffer the reproof. It seldom happened twice.

As the tutor responsible for our discipline, he treated us as adults. He had been sufficiently close to our way of life to appreciate the need from time to time for us to let our hair down. Indeed there were occasions when he joined in and played his part to the full. But he kept a sensible sense of proportion, admonishing us when it was necessary.

He turned a blind eye when others of a less flexible mind would have read the riot act. His voice was easy to mimic, but he was a marvellous enthusiastic teacher and a friend with whom it was possible always to speak on any matter of concern. He pretended on occasions not to be fully aware of what was happening to his undergraduates but this was simply a pose. He had a very clear picture of what was happening in his college and of the quality and ability of his undergraduates.

Queens' in those days (it has been much built on since) consisted of some lovely old rooms, though the sanitation left much to be desired. There were some hideous Victorian buildings close by the chapel and the Fisher Buildings across the river, built before the war, were an eyesore. But the old parts of the college were beautiful as well as tranquil. The President's Lodge in particular was a triumph of exquisite architecture.

I started my undergraduate life sharing a room in a Victorian building. It was designed for one fairly small undergraduate. It housed two of us. I am, I believe, a fairly equable person; so too was my roommate. We were reading different subjects; we came from different backgrounds; we had different friends; we liked different music; we had different working patterns. Indeed, I can think of almost no area where our views coincided. After three weeks of total incompatibility things came to a head. It was entirely my fault. Milk, like every other commodity was severely rationed. I think we got half a pint between us per day – it may even have been less. He had invited his parents for the weekend and asked that I should find myself elsewhere while he entertained them. To this I readily agreed. Indeed, there was no other way of having visitors to the room unless one or other of us went out.

By grave misfortune, on the day that they were due to arrive, totally forgetting that fact, I drank the milk. I then realised to my horror that his parents who were coming to visit their son for the first time, would not be overwhelmed by the luxury of the commissariat. There was no milk to be procured from friends and there was sadly no other source. I made a confession, which not unreasonably was somewhat ill-received. At the end of the weekend we agreed like an unhappy couple that we should part. The division of the spoils, as it were, was happily resolved. He discovered that there was another set of rooms somewhere else that he could have and to which he wanted to go. Thus I was left for the next year occupying these rooms on my own.

The sanitation at Queens' was marginally better than that on *Virago*, but not by much. The food was just about adequate. Because of rationing things like cake and bread were in short supply. Milk was to be treasured. A Dry Fly sherry for some reason was in very great vogue, as was South African Sherry at 12s a bottle. In those days it was not thought a matter of criticism to drink South African. Indeed, if you didn't drink South African there was precious little else to drink. There were still local ladies, known as bedders, who came and cleaned the room. Their efforts were not always immediately apparent. We did not live a life of elegant luxury. The heating was by way of a gas fire; there was none in the bedroom. A bath, which was some 200 yards away, needed to be negotiated, certainly in the winter, with some discretion.

College life was no different, I suppose, to life at Cambridge at any time. There were numerous societies which catered for the widest varieties of tastes. Music, debating, the arts, history, literature – there was almost no subject for which the college did not have some sort of club or society. It was difficult initially not to be swept into a number of clubs by the enthusiasm of the officers and their determination to secure new recruits at the beginning of term. So also did the university societies, which reflected the same interests at university level. At Queens' the dons ranged from the elderly – about whom there were innumerable stories, some true and some untrue – down to recent recruits. I am sure that they played an important part in the college, but for the most part undergraduates did not have much contact with them.

I think the single most shattering experience of my life at Cambridge was my first dinner in hall. Dining was not, I believe, compulsory. However, there was no real alternative which didn't involve cost, and so hall was well attended. After enduring meals on the lower deck for the best part of two years, I had expected the standard of conversation and the tone to be rather elevating and uplifting. Somewhat naively, I suppose, I imagined sitting silent and listening to a latter-day Rupert Brooke soliloquising or some poor man's Bertrand Russell philosophising or even a budding F.E. Smith discoursing wittily on some political or legal problem. Instead I found the subjects of football and women, though not necessarily in that order, to be the predominant topic among my colleagues.

Many, many years later, when we were married, we had a spotty 15-year-old French girl, unattractive both personally and physically, to stay. She was the daughter of some French friends of friends of ours. She came to stay for a week. During the course of it she requested to play on a concert piano. We managed with some difficulty to arrange this, surrounded as we were then with four young children. At the end of the week Margaret asked her if she had enjoyed herself; she drew herself up to her four feet six inches and said, 'I come to learn the English of philosophy. I learn here only the English of the kitchen.' I think my reaction to my first night in hall was not dissimilar.

The initial reaction was gradually dispelled as I came to know and distinguish my colleagues better. Inevitably, we tended to associate with those in our own year irrespective of age and to regard those more senior, if not as gods, certainly akin to them. We tended to treat those who came after us as unworthy of our attention. Likewise, those who were reading law, as I was, necessarily formed a group in the college because we attended tutorials together and also lectures. It was only gradually that my horizons increased, both in relation to friends in college and in the university.

I played hockey for the college, although not with any great success. Once I did find myself playing in a trial for the university – how I came to be picked I know not. I played at inside left. While I quite enjoyed the game it was a total disaster for the outside left, who had university expectations and who scarcely received a pass from me throughout the entire afternoon. I played some Eton fives at university level. I enjoyed squash as a relaxation and once in what was to be my last game, I played rugger for the college. It was for the college third fifteen, which was one short. Like the game in Trieste, I volunteered to play and once again found myself playing full-back. This time I was not so lucky.

Nothing much happened in the first half. I was scarcely called upon to do anything violent, but in the second half there suddenly broke away from a mauling mass in the middle of the field, one of the opposition, who seemed then and still seems to me now to have been eight feet tall and nine feet wide, and to have the pace of an antelope. There was no-one between him and me. There was no place to hide. Indeed, at that age such is the folly of youth that it would never have crossed my mind to do other than to throw myself wholeheartedly at this enormous advancing body. This I did. I understand that I made contract with him. It was not sufficient to prevent him scoring a try. I next remember waking up in Addenbrookes Hospital with a dislocated back and being informed that all my brave efforts had been totally in vain. Thus ended my rather ignominious rugger career.

It has not, however, prevented me when I watch at Twickenham or on the television, from addressing all and sundry who are prepared to listen, on the follies or inadequacies of a particular player. Indeed, I was once invited by Carl Aarvold, who had been recorder of London and a distinguished international rugger player, to be the guest of honour at the annual dinner of the English International Rugger Club. It was only the enormous quantities of drink that had flowed that enabled them, with their vast experience of the game, to view with any amusement my trivial tales of playing full-back at Trieste and Cambridge.

Of cricket I shall have more to say hereafter. Of rowing I can say little. I have to confess I never went down to the river, nor did I ever see any of the bumps. During the time that I was up it was assumed, rightly as it turned out, that Cambridge would always win the boat race, sometimes by a considerable length, and indeed my time at Cambridge included a great day when Oxford sank.

Sadly, the same was not true of university rugger. Oxford seemed to have a preponderance of international players, both home and overseas, and regularly won. The interest in university rugger was then as strong as, if not stronger than, it is today. The presence as undergraduates of those with international experience ensured that the quality of the game was very high, not only in the university match but in the games against the clubs who sent their stronger sides to play the university. Grange Road on a Saturday afternoon was a splendid occasion, followed usually by tea in rooms with friends, a quick supper and a visit to the arts cinema in the evening.

There were a number of distinguished lawyers among my contemporaries. David Widdicombe QC became one of the leading practitioners in local government work and Bill Wedderburn, subsequently Lord Wedderburn QC, was equally distinguished in the employment field. These two used to come up from time to time and tutor us and give us some idea of what life at the bar was like. We viewed them with tremendous awe, partly because they were plainly so much cleverer than we were and partly because they had started on the long trek which then confronted a young barrister. Jimmy Kingham, who became a judge at Luton, was another of my contemporaries, as was Arthur Myerson QC, now a circuit judge in Leeds. A year or two ahead of us were two outstanding lawyers to whom we were always being unfavourably compared: Stephen Brown, recently retired from being president of the Family Division, and Philip Cox QC, who had a distinguished career on the Midland circuit.

We were not to be compared with that great trio of C. B. Fry, F. E. Smith and John Simon, but we were a happy, close-knit lot, as were the other lawyers in the university. There was David Hirst, much in evidence at the union and recently a judge of the Court of Appeal; Murray Stuart-Smith, who also went to the Court of Appeal; Poppy Stanley, who married Tony Jolowitz and became a tutor at Girton; and Eli Lauterpacht, the son of the distinguished professor of international law, and himself an eminent lawyer. Robin Simpson QC, one of the ablest criminal advocates at the bar, was another of my contemporaries. He, I had known at school and in the Navy.

We were I think quite lucky in our law dons – Ellis Lewis at Trinity Hall, Arthur Armitage, Professor Wade, Professor Lauterpacht, Professor Hanson. Professor Wade was the author of Wade & Philips, the leading textbook on constitutional law. Professor Lauterpacht, whom we always referred to as Old Man Lauterpacht to distinguish him from Eli, had written the definitive book on international law. There was a splendid flamboyant barrister-turned-priest called the Reverend Garth Moore, who lectured us on the finer points of evidence. From time to time we attended trials held at Cambridge, took part in moots ourselves, wrote interminable essays and dissected the common law.

My degree course was a two-year course, which was to be followed by an LLB (Bachelor of Laws). In my second year, under the influence of John Vaizey (of whom more anon), I attended economics lectures, which I found absorbing and entertaining. Because we were on a shortened degree course, two years was necessary for the law. But I think that there is much to be said for anyone who wants to read law, for having a broader education at university in addition to law. It is true that the basic concepts of law need to be learnt at an early stage, but I very much regret that I did not have a grounding in, for instance, economics or philosophy, which I know I would have much enjoyed. Going to economics lectures with Joan Robinson was something of an ordeal, because in the middle of her lecture she would suddenly point at one of the audience and ask him or her a question. If you were there simply to learn it was a daunting experience. Joan Robinson was a very distinguished economist, much admired in the faculty and the author of a number of books on economics. Some, such as *The Economics of Imperfect Competition* and *An Introduction to the Theory of Employment*, were standard works for those reading economics. If you wanted to appear really clever, to mention *The Rate of Interest and Other Essays* marked you out as a bit of a swat.

The law lectures were on the whole pretty good, but there were one or two lecturers who simply dished out notes. It was necessary only to ensure that you got a copy of the notes and then to read the textbook. I always thought that the practice which, as my father explained, was adopted at German universities, was a good one – namely that unless the lecture had a set number of people attending, the lecturer not only did not get paid but lost the job as lecturer. It is a marvellous incentive to make the lecture interesting.

I found this out when I came to the bar and started part-time lecturing on law for courses run by the local authorities. Counting the number of the audience on a cold winter's night was a fearfully daunting experience. Being left to wonder whether the lecture would still be on the following week if the numbers were to go down by two or three was sufficient to make even the most boring speaker more entertaining. As this was my sole source of income, for my first few years at the bar, it was not surprising that I applied myself with some determination.

The social life at Queens' was fairly limited. There were no dinner parties in rooms, like parties which had been held before the war. There were invitations to tea, to a drink before a dinner and more particularly coffee and sometimes a drink after dinner, when discussions would go on through the night. These were the days of proctors, when undergraduates had to wear gowns when they went out and about in the city. Cars were in very limited supply, not only because they were frowned on by the authorities for use by undergraduates, but also because there was petrol rationing. Bicycles were absolutely fundamental to any social or indeed any life. They were, unfortunately, regularly borrowed, less regularly returned.

I acquired with some birthday money a small motorcycle which was called a Corgi. It was designed from the folding motorcycles dropped by parachute during the war. It worked on the principle of a stop and start and would go about 30 miles an hour maximum speed downhill and with a fair wind. It did about 70 or 80 miles to a gallon. I had some petrol on my own ration and I obtained some from my parents, who did not use their car much. It had a number of advantages: not the least of those was that when there was a game of hockey or football taking place on Queens' ground, which was about a mile or two out on the Barton Road, I was able to get back ahead of the crowd and have a shower first. The other advantage was that, unlike a bicycle, it could not easily be stolen. It also saved a certain amount of energy.

There were, however, difficulties, not the least of which was that my colleagues thought it amusing and entertaining to dismantle the machine, which could readily be done by unscrewing two or three nuts, and leave it in a folded condition. The other great disadvantage was that I had a girlfriend who lived in a village about eight miles outside Cambridge, whom I used to visit. In the village there was a large alsatian, which was enormously excited by the noise that the engine made. Whenever I started to go through the village, the alsatian would emerge and come bounding after me. The height of the saddle was such that I sat only a few feet off the ground and about level with the jaws of the alsatian. The speed of the alsatian greatly exceeded that of the Corgi. Thus it was always a close-run thing when I entered the village whether I would reach my destination in time without being wildly savaged.

Those were the days too when undergraduates had to be in college by 10pm unless they had got permission to be out or could give an explanation. Arthur Armitage, to whom application had to be made, was always understanding about any legitimate late return. The penalty for being out late without excuse was 'gating', which meant that you were confined to your college, which was extremely tiresome. One alternative was to stay out all night and reappear in the morning. This had considerable disadvantages and was likely to be revealed, because the bedder would notice that the bed had not been used.

The other was to climb in. Queens' itself was, as colleges go, quite an easy college into which to climb. It could be nasty sometimes if too much drink had been taken, because of the spikes and wire, but generally it presented no problem. The 10pm curfew was, however, a problem in visiting other colleges, and more particularly in visiting the ladies' colleges. Girton was so far away, that I confess except for once I never went there. But Newnham was just down the road from

Queens'. Queens' seemed to have some affinity with Newnham. It was there indeed that Margaret was an undergraduate reading history. We were exact contemporaries. She got to know members of the college because the sister of a Queens' man had been a contemporary of hers at school. Thus, at an early stage in her life at Newnham she was introduced to a number of Queens' men, mostly a year ahead of me.

Newnham adopted a very belligerent attitude, as we thought, towards the 10pm curfew. Woe betide anyone who stayed a minute after. There were at the entrance two fearsome ladies who would have done well as wardresses at some concentration camp. They guarded their flock jealously. Margaret always said that it was a great relief for the girls to know that at 10pm that they could wander around the place, safe in the knowledge that there were no men about. There was as always a good deal of boasting among the male undergraduates about how they had slept the night in Newnham or Girton, or had climbed in or climbed out at a late hour. Most of it, I believe, was bravado. I suspect that today's co-educational arrangement has in fact worked to the grave disadvantage of the girls. I know that when our children were at university the girls seemed to spend time washing their boyfriends' clothes in college, whilst the boys complained that they only had half the college available for the rugger side.

Almost every club or society had its annual dance, usually at the Dot – the Dorothy Café. There was the great problem facing undergraduates whether to invite one of the girls from Girton or Newnham, or to import someone from London. At that time the men outnumbered the girls in Cambridge by some 10 to 1. If I am being thoroughly chauvinistic I have to say that some of the girls at university were unwilling or unsuitable to be partners at a dance. The field therefore was fairly narrow. Any girl of character had the opportunity to have a very agreeable time socially without any particular involvement.

Apart from the dances there were of course college dinners. Most clubs had some sort of dinner, of which the Rugger Club and the Rowing Club were the most notorious and the loudest. The food served was marginally better than food in hall. There was a good deal of drink, mostly beer. The speeches were usually terrible. Most undergraduates had no idea how to make a speech, save to repeat rather boringly a number of filthy jokes. The evening usually ended with a lot of singing and rowdiness, which today would go under the description of hooliganism. The damage to the fabric of colleges was regrettably rather serious. From time to time threats were made not to allow a dinner to be held the following year, but by that time the perpetrators of the previous year had gone down and all was forgiven and forgotten.

The worst incident of hooliganism that I experienced was on 5 November. It was customary in Guy Fawkes Week to have a Rag. The purpose of it was to raise money for some charity. It involved people diving into the Cam, bedstead races and the like. But on this occasion it took a rather uglier turn on one particular evening. A very large crowd gathered on Kings Parade. It was an undergraduate and good-humoured crowd, which was simply there to see the fun. It was an example of how easy it is for crowd to turn into a mob and for a mob to be manipulated. There was a cry 'to the police station'. The crowd went in a rush. Outside the police station the mob threw thunder flashes, made various obscene gestures and exchanged pleasantries with the police, but did not do too much physical damage. There was then a cry 'back to Kings Parade', and back to Kings Parade marched the mob. Down Kings Parade there were a series of lamps. At the base of each lamp stood a policeman, there for the specific purpose of preventing damage to the lamp because previous experience had shown that this is what was likely to happen on 5 November.

The crowd occupied the whole of Kings Parade. It was quite impossible for cars to pass down, and any car that did try was stopped, shaken to bits and the occupants terrified. Half a dozen stalwart young men would gather round a lamp-post. They thus prevented the police-man from moving. Meanwhile, someone climbed up and smashed the lamp. This gave rise to loud cheers among the mob. They then surged down Kings Parade destroying the lamps the whole way down. Across the road was the Senate House. It had been constructed in the seven-teenth or eighteenth century. It had old glass in it, and had survived the German attempts to bomb Cambridge. It did not survive the mob's desire to destroy. That evening the glass in the Senate House Building was destroyed. It was a horrendously shameful episode, of which none of the participants could feel other than very ashamed. Hooliganism is not simply a modern phenomenon.

The other events of the winter term were the university rugger match and the soccer match. The rugger match then as now attracted a vast audience on the first Tuesday in December at Twickenham.

The university soccer match was then played at White Hart Lane and attracted a very large crowd. These were the days of amateur soccer, when the Corinthian Casuals still bore a proud and distinguished name and when university soccer players played as amateurs for their country.

While I was up at Cambridge the universities started a soccer side called Pegasus. This is not the place to recount the trials and traumas of its inception, the rivalries between it and the Corinthian Casuals or the unhappy disputes between Oxford and Cambridge about its survival. Suffice it to say that Pegasus was a wholly amateur side consisting of undergraduates and graduates from both Oxford and Cambridge. They had enormous success. They played twice in the Amateur Cup Final at Wembley and won twice. It was a tremendous boost for university football. The club was lucky in that experienced players were available, older both in years and ability than the ordinary undergraduate.

The quality of university rugger and soccer was matched in other sports. In athletics there were Roger Bannister, Chris Chataway and Chris Brasher, and there were oarsmen of international repute. Of the cricketers I will speak at greater length hereafter.

Life at Cambridge in 1948/49 was I suspect not much different from what it was like in 1928/29 or 1968/69 or 1988/89. Each generation thinks that it is doing something new. No doubt those who were there in the sixties were fuller of protest than our generation. But I was struck by one difference between my generation and my children's generation. We were much more politically orientated. We were concerned about the world at large. My children's generation were concerned about immediate problems such as caring for the elderly and looking for a job – politics with a small 'p'. They were generally unmoved by political parties or by wider issues.

I never forget the surprise at finding that my intelligent children seemed wholly unaware that there was a by-election going on at Cambridge during the time they were there. If it had happened in our generation nothing would have stopped us from taking a very active part, believing firmly that only by so doing could we achieve the goals that we had discussed so fervently and at such length. The enthusiasm which prompted John Vaizey and me to join the university Labour Club and bombard poor Ernie Bevin with telegrams saying 'Hands off Greece' was never part of their life. Perhaps on reflection they were unwise. It always seemed to me that unless you were a radical as a young person, life thereafter was going to be very dull.

We were lucky with our entertainment. There was plenty of music for those who enjoyed it, there was theatre and there were numerous cinemas. This was before the age of television. Queens' did have a television set in the junior common room but it gave the impression that there was a storm blowing across whatever picture there was. It was totally unreliable and no-one paid the slightest attention to it. The arts cinema, on the other hand, was an enormous attraction. It is difficult now to remember how great the impact that was made by French and Italian films. It was necessary to book seats for a Saturday night, and the little cinema was always jam packed. The other great source of entertainment apart from the college plays was the Footlights Review. It was good, but not then as distinguished as it was to become in the days of 'Beyond the Fringe' and subsequently in the days of Stephen Fry, Emma Thompson and Hugh Laurie.

5

Cambridge Cricket

When I went up to Cambridge I had played a certain amount of good club cricket. I had played on a Butterfly tour of Germany. While I was in the Navy, I had played at local level and I had also played for the Navy, though not in representative matches. It never for one moment crossed my mind that I would play cricket at anything near university level. I naturally put my name down for nets and took part in the university freshman's trial, where I managed to make 50 not out. Playing in the same side with me was Tony Rimell, who had been my captain at Charterhouse.

Cambridge had been easily defeated in the university match in 1948. There were a small number of old blues remaining – Doug Insole was the captain, John Dewes, who had played for England in the victory tests, and Hubert Doggart, who had made over 200 against Lancashire in his maiden match. There were also a number of others who had not succeeded in getting in the side. A. C. Burnett, known as Tolly, was a rival wicket-keeper. He was not a freshman but made a lot of runs in the trials. Insole had kept wicket for the university the year before. Having got into the final trial, I imagined that was the sum of my achievement.

I was therefore somewhat astonished to be selected to play for the university against Sussex, and thrilled to be playing in the same game with the two Langridge brothers, George Cox, H. T. Bartlett and Charlie Oakes. My first first-class innings was less than distinguished. I was lbw to Charlie Oakes for 2. I did rather better in the second innings, making 23. I caught a couple of catches and much enjoyed myself.

65

I was delighted to be invited to play in the next match, which was against Essex. There was a good deal of excitement generated because John Dewes and Hubert Doggart put on 429 for the second wicket. Poor Bob Morris, who had opened the innings, was out for 8, and at the end of the Saturday Cambridge were 441 for 1. This generated a good deal of publicity because it was a record for the second wicket in England. They needed only 27 more to beat the then world record of 455, set up in India that winter. The previous best English record for the second wicket was 398, by Gunn and Shrewsbury for Nottinghamshire against Sussex in 1890.

Those were the days before the widespread influx of television cameras. However, public interest had been aroused, and a considerable crowd had turned up on the Monday morning to see whether these two would indeed break the world record. Insole had decided in conjunction with Dewes and Doggart to declare and leave the record on one side. What wouldn't the modern generation of university cricketers have given to be able to declare at 441 for 1. It was therefore to a considerably unenthusiastic crowd that we emerged on the Monday morning to come out and field. Insole had to explain to a somewhat hostile press that the batsmen had been asked whether they wished to continue batting and they had replied that they didn't.

The next match was against Yorkshire, in which two young cricketers first appeared for Yorkshire: Brian Close and Freddy Trueman. Wisden described Trueman as a 'promising young off-spinner'. My recollection of the game is of the entire Yorkshire side grumbling throughout the match and making 32 in the second innings. We lost by 9 wickets.

John Warr played his first game for the university in this match. He took 0 for 49 in the first innings and 1 for 59 in the second and dropped a catch. He was only playing in the next match against Lancashire because somebody dropped out. However, in 21 overs he took 6 for 35 and established himself as a permanent member of the side. It led to his going on the MCC tour of Australia, captaining Cambridge in 1951 and playing for and captaining Middlesex. Dewes and Doggart were to have played for the MCC against New Zealand but because Doggart and Barry Pryer, an old blue, were doing exams they were released. It says something for the strength of university cricket.

Tolly Burnett kept wicket in my absence when I was doing exams. I wished him no ill, but was delighted when I found that I was selected

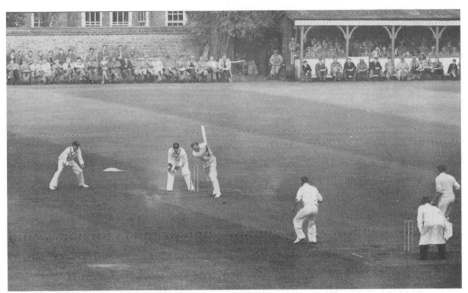

6. Fenners, 1949: Cambridge University vs Yorkshire. M. H. Stevenson batting; O. B. P. non-striker.

to play in the next game. This was against New Zealand, in which we did not distinguish ourselves. On a perfect Fenners wicket we were 45 for 7. I was batting no 9 and was totally unaware of the collapse which had occurred. I was quietly sitting in the dressing room reading a paper, when I became aware that Dick Hawkey, who was batting just above me, was wandering around doing something to his pads. It was not until I realised he was taking them off and not putting them on that I appreciated the dire situation in which we were. Luckily the New Zealanders did not take advantage of the 10-minute rule, and Mike Stevenson and I managed to put on 61.

Nevertheless, a score of 107 on a true Fenners wicket did not seem good enough until, after an hour of batting, New Zealand were 19 for 3. However, Wallace and Reid were each chasing 1000 runs in May, something that was possible in those days, and they then put on 324 for the fourth wicket. Reid was not out for 188 and Wallace, whom I finally caught, made 197. When that wicket fell, who should come out to bat but the great Martin Donnelly. It has always been a great joke between Doggart and myself that Donnelly was caught by me off Doggart's bowling, off a ball which the *Times* described as having turned. My recollection is that Donnelly played for the spin and there was none. Anyway we managed to get rid of him cheaply. But that did not prevent the New Zealanders declaring at 440 for 5. We were beaten by an innings.

Oxford meanwhile had played the New Zealanders. Oxford caught them on a sticky wicket, bowled them out for 110 in the first innings and 126 in the second innings, thus winning by 87 runs. As Oxford had also beaten Yorkshire, the prospects for the university match did not look very promising from our point of view. Meanwhile we played Warwickshire, and Insole and I put on 100 for the ninth wicket, he scoring an unbeaten century.

The next match we played was against the Free Foresters, and I was invited by Insole to play against Oxford. It was of course an enormously exciting moment. Although by now I had thought I had established myself in the side, it simply never occurred to me before I went to Cambridge that I should be playing first-class cricket – certainly not playing cricket in the company of such very distinguished players, let alone get a blue.

Oxford meanwhile had also beaten Sussex by an innings. They were captained by Clive Van Ryneveld the South African and included A. Kardar, who had already played for India. They had a nucleus of a very strong bowling side, including Philip Whitcombe, who had played for the Gents the previous year, and George Chesterton.

Exams now intervened at Cambridge, followed by May Week, after which it was the custom in those days for the university to go on tour. Thus we found ourselves at Horsham playing Sussex for the second time. Among the Sussex players was one David Sheppard, who was to play for and captain Cambridge in the years following. I had the misfortune to be bowled by Jim Parks, normally a wicket-keeper, in what must have been his only wicket in first-class cricket. Oxford meanwhile had beaten Middlesex, admittedly without Edrich and Compton, but nevertheless it was their fifth victory of the summer. Meanwhile, we were yet without a win.

The next excitement was to play the MCC at Lords. To walk through the Long Room onto the field was of course an enormous thrill. The lunches were absolutely delicious. Salmon and strawberries were the sort of fare we undergraduates loved, whereas the old professionals used to complain 'not strawberries again'. I found wicket-keeping at Lords was always a problem because of the slope. It was also not always easy to see the ball against the background of the pavilion, for which the sight screens did very little. The stands themselves sometimes prevented a clear sight of the ball being thrown in from the boundary area. Coincidentally, on that day the combined services, who were playing Gloucester, contained one Writer P. B. H. May, who scored 80 runs in two-and-a-half hours.

Our next trip was to Worcester, where Tony Rimell clinched his place in the side with a score of 160 runs. We were getting dangerously close to the university match, with the necessary problems of selection still unresolved. We set Worcester some 300 runs to win, but were unable to bowl them out in the time available.

Our penultimate game before the university match was against Somerset, where we stayed in private houses. Tony Rimell and I stayed with a fox-hunting gentleman. We were not very popular when Tony explained that in his area they shot the foxes.

We bowled Somerset out for 120 in their first innings and set them nearly 400 to get in their second innings. I managed to make a few runs in our second innings and, with some marvellous fielding by our side, we bowled them out, winning our first game by 140 runs, Doug Insole being the unlikely wicket-taker. This was naturally a tremendous boost and we went off to Guildford to play Surrey in high fettle. We managed to score 426 against a side which included Jim Laker and Eric Bedser, but Jim Laker himself scored 100 against us and we had an exceedingly boring draw. When the Cambridge side was announced Barry Pryer, who was a leg-spinner and an old blue, was left out. This naturally caused a good deal of heart-searching, because he was on the tour with us. We then had a very boring two-day match against the Army. We went to Lords for the university match considerable underdogs, but we totally outplayed Oxford from beginning to end.

When my son Nigel played in the university match in the 1970s, I invited his godfather Richard Davis to come to watch. We agreed to meet. Richard said 'I'll be there at 9.30', and I had to explain to him that the only people watching the game would be the parents of both teams and perhaps the cricket coach. On the Saturday of our match in 1949, by contrast, there were some 15,000 spectators. Cambridge batted all day. I went out to bat at about ten past six. I had instructions to stay there until half past, which I did, although not without some slow hand-clapping from Oxford supporters. By that time we had scored some 339 for the loss of 8 wickets.

7. Oxford vs Cambridge, 1949: Philip Whitcombe
batting; A. C. Burnett slip; J. G. Dewes short leg; O. B. P.
keeping wicket.

Over the weekend we were in an enormously relaxed mood. I was full
of confidence as to how I would follow my instructions to get after the
Oxford bowlers on the morning. Alas, pride goes before a fall. I rushed
down the wicket to Van Ryneveld. I was beaten by the spin, the flight
and almost everything else, and was stumped by yards by my opposite
number, who had not had a very happy day on the Saturday. One thing
I do remember about that innings is that Frank Chester was umpiring.
He was one of the great umpires and immensely fair. One of the Oxford
bowlers, who shall be nameless, was wont to run up to bowl before the
batsman was ready, unwittingly I am quite sure. Frank Chester said to
us to stand aside if it happened and he would no-ball him.

We made Oxford follow on. Murray Hoffmeyer, who batted
throughout the Oxford innings, carried his bat and held them together.
It was, however, a fairly tedious innings, which from our point of view
was much to our advantage. Shortly after tea we bowled them out for
160-odd and they followed on. It was a situation in which we could
never have believed we would find ourselves. It represented some very
good accurate bowling and some good out cricket. But it has to be said
that Oxford's batting was pathetic in the extreme.

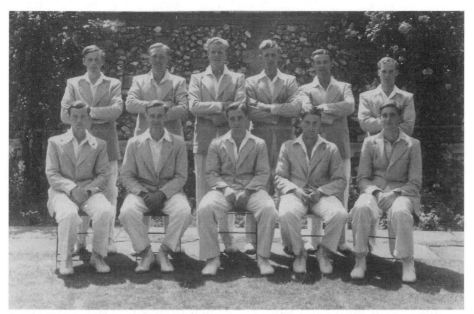

8. Cambridge University Cricket Club, 1949. 'Victorious.' Back, from left: O.B.P., M.H.Stevenson, O.J.Wait, P.J.Hall, A.C.Burnett, A.G.J.Rimell. Front, from left: R.J.Morris, G.H.C.Doggart, D.J.Insole, J.G.Dewes, J.G.Warr.

We gradually tucked away at the Oxford batting. Van Ryneveld had been run out in the first innings; Donald Carr was run out in their second innings. Some good catches were taken. Kardar was caught by Doggart running halfway back to the boundary. When their last pair were in they were 91 on but Chesterton and Wrigley added 40 for the last wicket, and we were left to get 133 in 95 minutes. In the first half hour we made 57, and 102 was scored in the hour. In the result, we won by 7 wickets with a quarter of an hour to spare. It was in any view a team triumph, made more pleasing by the fact that we were underdogs and had scarcely won a match all season, whereas Oxford were a strong side who were much fancied.

The 1950 summer started off with the usual trials. In addition to Rimell and myself from the Charterhouse side of 1946, there were May and Bob Whitby. Bob's bowling and batting gave him the ability to be a useful all-rounder, but unhappily he had a poor game against Essex and did not play for the university again. I was due to take my final exams and therefore decided that I would not play for the university during the term, which almost certainly meant I would not be invited to go on tour. My successor was a young wicket-keeper called Wyn

Denman, who was exceedingly good, and it was a considerable wrench not to be with the team up at Fenners.

Trying to read law and spend six days a week from 10am until 7pm playing cricket at the same time was quite impossible. You could of course take books up to Fenners and try and read them while the side was batting, but truth to tell it was not a very rewarding or successful enterprise. I talked to Doggart about it. He quite understood the situation, but he could not promise in any way that my place would be kept open after exams. Indeed it did not seem right that it should, and provided Wyn Denman had a good summer at Fenners I assumed that was the end for the time being of my first-class cricket career.

The first excitement of the summer was a century scored by Sheppard in his first game for Cambridge. A line-up of Dewes, Sheppard, May and Doggart probably constituted the strongest batting line-up for any university at any time. It could certainly compare favourably with any county side or even a test side, either before or after. True it was that we were able to bat on the true pitch at Fenners with its marvellously fast outfield, but the runs did not decrease when we went on tour. Some idea of this golden year of Cambridge batting can be judged by the scores made against first-class counties.

Against Sussex we made 359 for 5 and declared; against Lancashire 320 for 9 and declared. In the next game we showed just what a powerful side we were. It was against the West Indies, who were to beat England shortly after in the test match at Lords. Dewes and Sheppard put on a first-wicket stand of 343. Ramadin and Valentine, who were to be such thorns in the flesh of England, took no wickets and had nearly 200 runs hit off them. Cambridge declared at 590 for 4, having been 507 for 3 at the end of the first day. It is ironic to think that if a test team scores 507 in two days they think they have done remarkably well. On the first day 129 was scored before lunch, and at tea the score was 301.

The runs were scored in 145 overs at something over 4 an over. If Cambridge thought that they were going to have it all their own way they were sadly disabused. Frank Worrell made 160 and Everton Weekes 304 not out. For poor Wyn Denman the match was a disaster. He never got into bat, which was understandable and he had to field for a day and a half.

However, the real tragedy for him was that when Everton Weekes had made 10 he played at and snicked a ball outside his off-stump from John Wait, which went into Wyn Denman's hands, but which he failed to hold. As Weekes scored another 300 runs and the West Indies themselves made another 400, it might well be regarded as a somewhat expensive miss. When I went down to Fenners to see what had happened I was greeted with cries of 'Come back Popplewell, all is forgiven'. An interesting sidenote is that May bowled for the first time in his first-class career, but without success.

Exams and May Week now intervened, and I was restored back to the side. Against Leicester we declared at 327 for 9 and won by 9 wickets. Against Hampshire we made 467 for 4 declared, Dewes and Michael Stevenson making 100 and May making an unbeaten double century. It resulted in a very boring draw. During the Hampshire innings every Cambridge player bowled, with the exception of me. Sheppard bowled two overs and took a wicket. So did Dewes. Against the Free Foresters we made 362 for 9 declared and won by 10 wickets.

It was now time for us to go on our tour, which we started at Hove. At this time Dewes was top of the English batting averages, with May in fifth position. Valentine and Ramadin, who had been so unsuccessful against us, were top of the West Indian bowling averages. Against Sussex, Dewes and Sheppard put on 349 for the first wicket, John making a double century and David 158. We declared at 471 for 5. I nearly had a disaster. When we did go out to field late in the evening, I put on rubber-soled boots because they were more comfortable on the feet. I had totally forgotten that at Hove when the tide comes in the ground gets a bit damp, and I found myself for the last half hour of play slipping about on the grass as if on an ice rink. Happily I survived.

We only managed to make 154 against Warwickshire at Edgbaston on a turning wicket. They replied with 145 for 8 and the game ended in a draw. Our next match was against Worcester, where again we only managed 270 and got beaten by 8 wickets. Against Surrey we did poorly, making some 208 in the first innings, but held out for a draw making 246 for 6 in the second. In the confident belief that they would bowl us out, they insisted on claiming the extra half hour, which Rimell and I played out without difficulty. We then set off on our bus to Bristol where we made 335 for 8 against Gloucester, and set off back to London to play the MCC shortly before the university match.

One of the MCC players was Mike Ainsworth, who had been a commander in the Navy when I had played for them. He was a distinguished cricketer and subsequently became a schoolmaster. He had a great propensity for playing forward. The batsman who was out before him had been bowled. The ball had gone down towards the nursery end. Nobody had bothered to pick it up. Rimell ran up to bowl as if to deliver the ball, whereupon Mike Ainsworth put his left foot firmly down the wicket to play a non-existent ball. We all thought it was hilariously funny. Those at headquarters did not: we were severely reprimanded.

We went to Lords full of considerable confidence about our batting, though somewhat less confident about our bowling. There were three Old Carthusians playing in the side: May, Rimell and I. It was not usual then to have three boys from the one school in the same side. I imagine it is unique now. John Wait had had a rotten year and was left out of the side. In the result, it was a fairly boring match, neither side making more than 200 runs. We thought that we had left Oxford enough time and enough runs to promote a challenge in their second innings, but they singularly failed to take the opportunity. It was an astonishing fact that while Sheppard, Dewes and Doggart all did well in the university match, May never made any significant score and like Sheppard was never to play in a winning university side. In this game he was run out for 7 in the first innings and made 39 in the second.

Some idea of the quality of the Cambridge batting can be shown from the averages. Dewes scored 1262 runs for an average of 78.7, Sheppard 1072 with an average of 46.42, Doggart 525 with an average of 52.5 and May 637 with an average of 42.46. Dewes played for Middlesex, as did Warr; Doggart and Sheppard played for Sussex; May played for Surrey. Dewes finished second in the national batting average. That winter the MCC side, captained by Freddie Brown, went to Australia and contained Dewes, Sheppard and Warr.

In 1951 Warr was captain. No-one who has heard John speak publicly is ever left in doubt about his enormous ability to amuse. He was then a fit, enthusiastic and charismatic figure for whom the whole side would have gone to the wall. We were indeed lucky in our captains. Insole started with an unpromising lot and welded us into a well-organised and effective team. He had an acute cricketing mind. He was somewhat laconic, nervous and superstitious in the extreme. It was impermissible when Cambridge were batting to move during the course of an over, lest the wicket should thereby fall. It was impossible to explain to him that there was no relationship between the two events.

This superstition was followed and copied by Margaret and by Mary Maxwell, Sheppard's sister; whenever they wanted to get a wicket off the opposite side, they would walk around the ground in the confident expectation that it would occur. When it happened they were confirmed in their view that this was the way that wickets were obtained. When it didn't they were philosophical and merely said they would do better next time.

Doggart was lively, clubable, chatty and enormously enthusiastic. He had little or no problem with the batting of the side but was naturally anxious about its composition. Morris, who had been a blue from the year before and was doing exams, did not get back in the side; nor did Wait. These were unhappy decisions for him to make, which I know caused him anguish. But throughout the season he led with much panache.

Warr had a marvellous way of relieving the tension with some comic remark when things went wrong. The summer of 1951, which was in fact to end in disaster at Lords, was one of the happiest summers of cricket that I have ever played. Because the result of the university match is the measure by which a side is judged, that year is always remembered by the team as blighted. But in truth we had enormous fun and played some very good cricket, and if we played the university match again, I know we would win by a distance.

In 1951 we had two new players who were to contribute enormously to Cambridge cricket, and indeed to cricket in general. Rahman Subba Row was a determined left-hand bat who bowled leg-breaks with considerable distinction. It always surprised me that I seemed to be the only person who could read his googly, but he took a number of wickets with it which gave him immense satisfaction. Robin Marlar I had met on a Butterfly tour of Germany. He had been an outstanding schoolboy cricketer. He came up to Cambridge with a great reputation, which he amply justified. Had it not been for the presence of a large number of highly competent off-spinners then playing on the English county circuit, I have no doubt he would have walked into the test side. We were without Dewes and Doggart, though still with Sheppard and May. It was a more modest batting side but a more varied bowling line-up.

We bowled Lancashire out for 78 and Essex for 120, though this time there was to be no repeat of a record-breaking second-wicket partnership from Cambridge. We next played the South Africans, who included their fast-bowler Cuan McCarthy. He was to reappear the following year as an undergraduate at Cambridge. He was probably the quickest bowler in England at that time and was under suspicion, rightly or wrongly, of being a 'chucker'.

I managed to get a few runs against the South Africans in a low-scoring match, but the thing I most remember is facing an over from McCarthy. I managed to get my bat down on the ball off the first five deliveries. The sixth came at an angle which was totally unexpected. It was at a vastly increased speed. It took my middle stump out of the ground. I had scarcely blinked an eyelid. I still think it came from the shoulder, but I may be wrong. The *Times* said an occasional apparent wrist action at the last second did occasion comment. You can say that again.

The *Times* was also complimentary enough to say that my wicket-keeping that day 'left little to be desired'. I have to say that keeping wicket at Fenners was a real treat. The ball came through at an even height and bounce. The most memorable game that summer tour was against Sussex, when I got my highest score in first-class cricket of 74 and put on over 100 in partnership with May, who got 100. Rain probably deprived us of victory. Against Warwick we made 320 for 9 declared, May making 100. Against Middlesex we made 359 for 6 declared, May and Sheppard making 100. In our second innings we declared at 205 for 3, Sheppard getting another 100, and set Middlesex 321 to win; they ended up at 320 for 9 wickets. It could not have been a better match.

The match against the Free Foresters was always amusing because the side included a great number of ex-England captains, including Gubby Allen and Walter Robins. Gubby by this time was full of pulled muscles, embrocation and bandages, but always managed to get a lot of runs though his bowling days were over. There was a good deal of chat and banter from him and, as always, useful and constructive criticism. Walter Robins, who had been a tremendous cricketer and leader of men, was also not averse to telling the young what the game was about. It was therefore with a good deal of amusement that we listened to him telling us that Fenners was much too good for us all and that the sooner we learnt to play on wickets which were not feather bedded, so much more would our game improve. When he was bowled by Wait first ball in the first innings and by Warr first ball in the second innings, there was a good deal of merriment generated.

The game at Worcester also produced similar banter. Tom Wells, our New Zealand player, who had played full-back in the university rugger match, and was a very useful all-round player, batted left-handed and bowled a bit. He had the indignity to get a pair (a duck in each innings). Staying that night at the Digglis Hotel, we ordered duck for him, which he did not find enormously amusing. We got caught on a turning wicket and were set 170-odd to win. We were 16 for 4 at one stage in our second innings. John Cockett, who was a distinguished hockey blue and eventually captained England at hockey, played the innings of his life and he, together with May, enabled us to beat Worcester by four wickets. The state of the pitch can be gauged from the fact that Rolly Jenkins, who bowled leg-breaks, finished up with seven wickets in all and Dick Howarth, who bowled slow left arm, ended up with six wickets. It was a tremendous victory, more particularly as no-one except May and Cockett scored double figures in our second innings.

Cockett followed that great innings by making 120 against Sussex at Worthing, where we declared at 325 for 9 and bowled Sussex out in their second innings, for 79, thus beating them by 117 runs. Wait took 6 for 18 in 14 overs. We then played Surrey at Guildford and declared at 346 for 7, but the match ended in a draw.

The next game against the MCC was also memorable for me because Warr declared our second innings, when I was 74 not out, leaving the MCC to get 366. In the space of 65 minutes, we bowled them out for 43. I naturally told everyone in sight that I had been deprived of the opportunity of scoring my first 100. We were playing on a pitch that was slightly off the centre, and I remember that once we ran 5 off one ball. Geoffrey Keighley, who captained Yorkshire, was unwise enough to say to Warr that he did not think he was very quick. This simply encouraged Warr to give him a torrid time on a lively wicket before he edged a catch to me at the wicket. I suspect he was very glad to go.

Our next match was against Hampshire at Bournemouth where May played an outstanding 178 not out, but we collapsed in the second innings and lost by 89 runs. We then went and played a two day game against the Army at Sandhurst, which I am afraid we didn't take very seriously. I think we behaved rather badly in the mess, and it ended up in a very boring draw. It was not a particularly good warm-up for the match against Oxford for which we started warm favourites. The *Times* suggested that Cambridge should win their 107th university match, and we looked the better-equipped eleven for all conditions. However, it was not to be.

In what was described by the *Times* as a sober day's play, Oxford batted first. They made 178, to which we replied with 69 for 2. That 69 for 2 became 168 and Oxford went to 159 for 6, thus leading by 180. I had a bad day behind the stumps but it was when Alan Dowding, fielding as twelfth man, ran the length of the field to catch May out, that the really decisive moment came. No-one knew who this young, fair-haired, speedy substitute was, but he turned out to be a great friend. Subsequently he became our boys' housemaster at Radley and we discovered that we were married on the same day.

I got myself run out in a misunderstanding with Rahman Subba Row, about which we have pulled each other's legs over many years. The result at any rate was an unhappy one. I found myself stranded at his end with the wicket being put down at the other.

We had to chase something like 220, but never seriously looked like doing so, thus by 6.15pm we were beaten by 21 runs, and we had the great misfortune to have to go to the Hawk's Club Dinner, which was the Cambridge Sporting Club. To be elected you needed to have been a sportsman of some merit, though there were some who got elected on the basis of who they knew. They had premises in Cambridge where it was possible to eat and drink and socialise. Once a year they have an annual dinner at the Savoy. We were greeted in total silence as a team who had had a marvellous cricketing summer and lost the only match that mattered. All I can say is that, looking back over the years, it was the happiest summer's cricket, apart from this match, that I have ever had. The team was an extremely happy and friendly one, and we were captained with great distinction and no little skill, by Warr. We played some fine cricket – if only, if only…

When I look back on my three years in the Cambridge side I reflect on how lucky and privileged I was to be part of such distinguished sides and to have had the opportunity to play against all the heroes of the day. As a modest club cricketer myself, I was indeed fortunate to share and be part of some high-class cricket, which gave such pleasure to the public and amusement to the players.

6

Family and Friends

Margaret and I went up to Cambridge together in 1949, but it was not until towards the end of our second year that we got to know each other. She was reading history at Newnham. Her father had been an eminent grammar-school headmaster but had died at a young age when Margaret was only 12. She had two sisters and was brought up by her mother, who was a marvellous person. She had very strong principles and she was determined never to remarry.

She brought up the three girls with a great sense of public duty which Margaret continued throughout her life. She won a state scholarship to Newnham from Malvern, though because there was some sort of means test she did not get the financial benefit of it. She had been head girl at Malvern and a distinguished figure there, involved in all the sporting activities, and came away covered in honour and glory.

She became very much involved with Queens' because she had friends in the college. She was frequently to be seen at college matches. She was therefore someone whom I had identified both on the sporting field and indeed in chapel, but had scarcely spoken to. The first time we actually spoke to each other was after a lacrosse match. Queens' had a sporting club called the Kangaroos, which used to do a number of slightly idiotic things, among which was to play lacrosse against the girls. Margaret was captain of the university women's lacrosse team and very sensibly decided that she would not take part in this contest, but would referee. Not many of the men had played lacrosse before, but we found that by holding up our lacrosse sticks above our heads it made it almost impossible for the girls to get the ball. I suspect we won quite easily. After the match we were invited to have a cup of tea, where I met Margaret. Thus the first immortal words between us were, 'Would you like a cup of tea, Mr Popplewell?' It was not exactly the start of a great romance and at that stage it proceeded no further. However, in the summer of 1950 Margaret was 21, and her mother laid on a party at the Dorothy Café. I was not among those who initially got an invitation, but apparently some people fell out – thus, together with three other Queens' men, we were invited. We clubbed together and bought her a Parker Knoll chair, which was quite a present in those days and now sits in my study.

It was an immensely entertaining party, and I met her mother and sisters for the first time. Margaret declined to dance with me, not then knowing just how awful a dancer I was. Prudently I danced with her mother, which apparently made a good impression when I subsequently wanted to ask her if I could marry her daughter.

I next fell in with Margaret on the first day of the Christmas term 1950, as I was walking back from a lecture to go back to Queens' for lunch. She had been in Austria at a summer school and had obviously had an enormously good time with a lot of amusing foreign students. When I asked her how she had enjoyed the summer she took this as an opportunity to explain in full detail how each day had been spent. Finally, at about 2.15pm I suggested that we each went off and had lunch and that she should come and have tea with me on another occasion to continue the story. This she did, and during the winter term while I was reading for my bar finals, although notionally doing an LLB, she was frequently to visit me and encourage me in my studies. There was, however, no sensible prospect at that stage of our relationship proceeding further. She was much attached to another Queen's man called David, who had in fact gone down.

However, we met up at the university football match at White Hart Lane where I managed to purloin her toffees – this generated a certain amount of correspondence. She wrote to me at 'Guildford, Kent': in Yorkshire, where she had written from, her perception of the home counties was somewhat vague. However, I received the letter and wrote back. At the beginning of the lent term I managed to get two tickets for Cyril Fletcher in 'Mother Goose' and asked her to come with me, which she did. It was hilarious. Thereafter, matters moved, as they say,

9. Cardinal's Ball, 1951. 'We get engaged.'

with some despatch. I proposed to her on seven successive nights and she turned me down six times. I began to doubt her judgment. She felt a responsibility in breaking off what had been an informal engagement to David, and it involved much determination and soul searching. Being the person she was, she felt an obligation to see David and explain, which she did. Finally she agreed to my proposal. Years later, when we went to a family wedding at Cambridge, we were walking along the backs with the four boys and we came across an indentation in the ground. I went all solemn. I summoned the boys around me. I pointed out the hole in the ground. I said to the boys, 'That hole was made by your father proposing to your mother'.

I was going to be called to the bar in the April, and on our visit to London we went off and bought an engagement ring. My parents had heard about Margaret and sent my sister up to see whether she approved. My sister and Margaret got on like a house on fire and so the word went back that all was well. At the beginning of the Easter holidays I took her to see my parents, who thoroughly approved.

We still needed the approval of Margaret's mother, and so at the beginning of the summer term she came down to Cambridge together with Margaret's younger sisters. Margaret took them punting, leaving me with her mother. We had an exceedingly good tea, during the course of which her mother did her best to put me off marrying Margaret, and then suggested that if I wanted her approval than I had better ask for it. Anyway, all was well and so we announced our engagement in May Week. There was of course the caveat that there was little or no prospect of getting married in the immediate future. I had to make my way at the bar and Margaret had not completed her degree and was then going to go to Hughes Hall to do a Post Graduate Certificate in Education. Goodness knows when we would have an income.

The summer term was enormous fun. I was playing cricket and doing some work for my LLB, but was pretty relaxed because I had already been called to the bar and had got a degree, whereas poor Margaret had to work for hers. Happily she defeated the examiners and we ended the term with a number of parties. She had been alarmed when my mother told her that Popplewells never fail exams.

She then went off to Hughes Hall to learn to teach and I started off at the bar. She spent a term teaching at St Paul's Girls' School, which I am sure was a very good grounding. She stayed in a house in Hammersmith with a family called Oved who ran Cameo Corner. Mr Oved was a marvellous man and used to bring pieces of jewellery of great value and beauty to show Margaret, and when we eventually got married he gave her a beautiful pair of earrings. At the end of her year she got a job teaching at the girls' grammar school at Chislehurst, while I was still struggling at the bar and staying with my sister at Earl's Court. She earned, with London allowance and with the benefit of a university degree, something in the order of £750. I was, at the end of my pupillage, still earning nothing. It was quite impossible, according to our parents for us to get married on that sort of salary, even though we could see no reason why not.

Our parents were united in their opposition, in the belief that we were bound to have children as soon as we married. Thus, we endured an engagement of some three-and-a-half years. This would be quite an anathema to the modern generation. I think our parents took a very grave risk. It was all quite unnecessary because when we did get married we were earning no more and we did not have any children for some three years thereafter. However, we respected our parents and endured a somewhat nomadic existence. Margaret commuted to London from time to time, and we would meet in the holidays up in Yorkshire where Margaret's mother still lived.

Going to Yorkshire at that time really was a day's march. You got a train from King's Cross to one of the stations in Leeds, then went across from one station to another station in Leeds and caught a further train to Harrogate and Ripon. I generated a good deal of amusement among the Yorkshire folk with one of my journeys up there. Having got to the second Leeds station, I enquired which was the train for Ripon, and I was told it was, 'Back a't Pullman'. There standing at the platform was the Pullman train, so I climbed in to the back of it. It started off. People began to undress and get into bunks. I thought this was rather a strange way to travel on what was essentially a suburban journey to Ripon. When the guard came and looked at my ticket he was very cross. He told me I was on the wrong train but he knew people like me who were trying to avoid paying the full fare and explained that it was a Pullman train from Leeds to Scotland, first stop Harrogate and second stop Glasgow. I only just had time to pacify him when the train stopped and I leapt out, thankful not to be carried on to Scotland. It turned out that the phrase 'Back a't Pullman' didn't mean the back of the Pullman, but the train behind the Pullman. I was regarded by the north-country folk as being a slightly soft southerner.

Christmas in Ripon was a splendid affair. It invariably snowed. When it snowed it did so for a while, and it was therefore impossible to get out of Ripon, and I was contained for an appreciable period of time. However, there was plenty of social life. Though Margaret's mother's house was Victorian in its building and in its heating, she always made me most welcome and seemed to think I was a good thing.

Eventually, after three-and-a-half years, in August 1954 we got married in Ripon Cathedral, which was Margaret's parish church. My mother was heard to say that she had never heard of anyone getting married in Yorkshire. She couldn't imagine life outside London, and she had a wonderful way of saying tactless things. John Vaizey was my best man. Unknown to me, he was suffering a serious illness. He took to his bed through the Saturday morning while I tried to get him back on course. Happily he did, and we had a marvellous wedding in the cathedral and a reception at the Spa Hotel. In those days married couples

10. Wedding day, 7 August 1954, Ripon Cathedral.

were not encouraged to stay, so by five o'clock we were leaving the reception and driving off to Doncaster, where we had dinner before spending the night at the Bell at Barnby Moor. As we drove away the heavens went black. It poured with rain and up in the hills it fell as snow, sufficient for some children to make a snowman, although this was August. It seemed an unhappy augury for our married life, but if it had any message it turned out to be a false one.

At the Bell at Barnby Moor we were woken early in the morning by a bang on the door and a message that Margaret's mother had phoned. These were not the days of telephones in bedrooms and so I had to walk the length of the hotel to speak to her. All sorts of images passed through our minds. We knew that there had been a family party after the wedding for the bridesmaids, ushers and friends, and we thought that perhaps there had been some serious accident. Happily it was merely for Margaret's mother to say thank you for a present that we had left for her. However, Margaret left her mother in no doubt that this was an inappropriate time to ring, and she never repeated it with the other sisters.

We then went to Bourton-on-the-Water and to Southampton and crossed to St Malo for a honeymoon at Benodet in Brittany. Margaret's mother had been kind enough to lend us her pre-war Wolsley car and we had a very agreeable time at Benodet, which was then a small sailing village with only a few hotels. How we had come to choose it I cannot now remember. We managed to get ourselves thoroughly sunburnt one day, which was unwise, but except for the undue attention paid by the owner of the hotel to Margaret, we had a very good time.

During the course of the summer we had bought a tiny house at Elmstead Woods, in Kent, for £2900 and a local-authority mortgage of two-and-a-quarter per cent. Elmstead Woods was, as the name implies, an area covered in trees. Some of the trees had been cut down and 20 jerry-built houses had been built in a close. I started to lay a concrete path to the garage. Unfortunately I did this wearing old gym shoes, with the result that my feet got somewhat blistered and I had to walk up the aisle with a very delicate tread. However, it was our home. It had three bedrooms, a bathroom, a sitting room, a dining room and a kitchen, plus a tiny garden. Behind us was the rest of the wood, which was an attractive feature. We asked the builders what plans there were for the woods and we were assured that there were none. We hadn't, however, been in the house for more than a week when the bulldozers went through the wood and some 400 houses identical to ours went up. It was the beginning of the post-war building boom.

Chislehurst, which was our nearest village, was then a very old-fashioned village of the Tunbridge Wells or Beaconsfield variety. It possessed a very good cricket club, the West Kent Cricket Club, which I joined and which used to have a splendid week. Sadly, I hear that it has gone into serious decline. It had a golf club which was also very smart, and altogether it might be described as a nice neighbourhood. One of the social events of the year was the West Kent cricket dance, held at the end of their cricket week at the golf club. I was deputed to approach a number of worthies to persuade them to donate prizes for the raffle or tombola. I had a list of names carefully prepared from previous years, and I sent off about 50 letters indicating that I hoped they would be generous again and that in due course I would call on them. I duly signed and addressed the letters and gave them to my clerk to stamp and post.

I was therefore singularly ill-prepared for the reception I received at the first home at which I called. He was, if I remember right, an ex-Army officer who was a pillar of the local society. He opened the letter and when I explained who I was and what my mission was he exploded

'You damned pup – what cheek you have'. He thrust the unstamped letter in my face and slammed the door. It turned out that my clerk had failed to stamp any of the letters.

The walk to the station was nothing too much and the journey into London was easy. The Corgi which I had bought at Cambridge came in very handy for Margaret to go to school, if I had to have the car to go out to some distant court. And there we lived for some five years. We had quite an agreeable social life. David Kemp, later to become a second master at Tonbridge School, became a great friend and introduced us to a number of people. There were two splendid sisters called May, one of whom married Desmond Perrett QC, who became my pupil. We were not particularly friendly with other people in the close save for two unmarried ladies who were teachers. We also came across Brian and Boo Cubbon and their son John. Brian was to have an outstanding career in the Civil Service. He had the misfortune to be blown up in Northern Ireland with the minister, but recovered to become the permanent secretary at the Home Office.

In August 1957 Nigel was born. He was due at the end of July. It so happened that the American bar was visiting England and we had been invited as part of a young barristers' organisation to go to Buckingham Palace with the Americans. There was great discussion firstly, as to whether Margaret could go in her pregnant state, and secondly, as to what would happen if she gave birth while she was there. Happily he was late. We went to Buckingham Palace and did not have to make the announcement in the paper, 'Suddenly at Buckingham Palace to Oliver and Margaret Popplewell ... '

We engaged a Norland nanny, who I think did not entirely approve of us. Nigel was not an easy child. He had the habit of staying awake for three-and-a-half hours after being fed, and, having just gone off to sleep, then needed replenishing. As the walls of our house were breeze blocks we got little or no sleep, though things did improve slowly. Andrew was born in January 1959. We had decided that, having a nurse in the house, we would take ourselves off for a good dinner, which we did – at Cominetti's in the Old Kent Road. Though an Italian restaurant, not all the staff were Italian. When we asked for the *hors d'oeuvre* we were told that 'it had taken a most terrible bashing that night'. We set off back to Chislehurst at about 11pm or so to find that there was a thick fog and that something was starting to happen. When we got back we notified the district nurse and the doctor. The doctor arrived first without the gas and air; the district nurse got lost and arrived later. At one time it looked as though I might have to deliver the baby myself. Happily for everyone, this did not happen. Next morning when I went to drive to work I found my car had run out of petrol, and we had no telephone, so that if I had had to go and find a doctor or district nurse it would not have been possible.

Margaret had by this time given up teaching. I was practising more and more on the Oxford circuit and found travelling from Chislehurst to Gloucester somewhat inconvenient. Since we had no telephone, if I were suddenly given a brief in Gloucester I could do no more than send Margaret a telegram delivered by the post office with the message 'Gone to Gloucester – length of stay indefinite'. It was not an easy life for Margaret, but she managed wonderfully.

There was one occasion when we had invited two couples to dinner on a Saturday night. They had also recently got married but had not met Margaret. On the Tuesday I went off to Abingdon quarter sessions presided over by a lovely Pickwickian figure, Stephen Benson. My client was alleged to have stolen lead from a roof and Brian Neill, later Lord Justice Neill, was prosecuting.

Our case was not reached on the Tuesday – and the same thing happened on the Wednesday, Thursday and Friday. Because each day we thought the case would start, I stayed locally. On the Saturday we started at 10am, the jury went out at 6pm and returned at 8pm. I arrived back at Elmstead Woods at about 10.30pm to find our guests leaving, having been marvellously well entertained by Margaret in my absence. Life as a fat cat it was not.

After five years we decided to move. The sensible direction was out north and west of London. We got the details of a house at Chartridge in Buckinghamshire from the estate agents. We had some musician friends called Geraint and Winifred Jones, who lived at Little Missenden. We had met shortly before we got married when we went to a friend's wedding, who told us that there was a musician friend of his who had a Rolls Royce and would give us a lift. We speculated that he must be a dance-band leader. In fact, Geraint was a distinguished organist and harpsichordist, and Winnie played the violin. We became instant friends and two marvellous holidays in their Rolls were taken round Europe, in particular Italy and south Germany, where Geraint was recording organ music for the BBC. Geraint was a superb guide, taking us to lovely picnic spots and finding marvellous things to see and do; every day ended with a bucolic evening. They were kind enough to go and have a look at it to see if it was worth our travelling down to Buckinghamshire. The Jones's were very enthusiastic. It was a Georgian house with a Jacobean cottage at the back and it had, according to Winnie, a gin cupboard just inside the front door. This seemed an enormous attraction, though we misread it for gun cupboard. We went down to see it, fell in love with it immediately and made an offer which was accepted. The owners did not wish to leave immediately and we had to make arrangements to raise the money.

At that time house prices did not significantly change in value but we managed to sell our little house at Elmstead Woods for some £3900 which was a good profit. and we bought Lime Tree Farm for £6000. It needed a good deal of work doing on it because the state of the wiring was somewhat elderly, there needed to be a soakaway and various other works had to be done. We got the builders in to dig the soakaway and they were still not quite finished when we got possession. The threat of imminent flushing of water lent some despatch to their activities. For some reason the owners were reluctant to go, and we had to threaten them with court proceedings before they eventually left. There was a most lovely barn as part of the farm buildings which sadly had fallen into disrepair. When we bought the house it became clear that the cost of repairing the barn was out of all proportion to the value of the house. We now very much regret that we didn't do it, but we simply did not have the money then.

The house needed to have the roof totally rebattened, refelted and retiled, and to this end we engaged a builder who came with scaffolding for an entire month. He took off each tile, rebattened, refelted and put the tiles back. The whole exercise cost £200. When we needed one of the chimneys done 20 years later we were told that simply to hire the scaffolding for a period of time would cost 10 times that amount. Lime Tree Farm was a Georgian house built in 1727 and it formed the front of a Jacobean cottage which was built about 1660. The inside was built on several levels, which made it somewhat inconvenient for carrying objects from room to room; however, it contained a dry cellar, which was a good selling point. It had fine panelling and an inglenook fireplace, and we fell in love with it straight away.

We brought up our children here. In 1961 Matthew was born, in 1964 Alexander and in 1966 Eddie Jim. Matthew was two-and-a-half years old when he died from a cot death. How or why it happened we shall never know. He was a happy, lively, healthy child and his death was and continues to be a very great sadness.

In 1963, when my sister died, her daughter Nicola came to live with us. It was quite a culture shock for her to be surrounded by boys and for us to cope with a teenage girl in the 1960s. She had gone to Queen Anne's, which was her mother's old school. It was, I think, too academic for her, and the staff did not seem to be able to manage pupils who were unenthusiastic about work. Eventually she went to America, where she married Barry and lives happily; they now have four children and live in upper New York state.

We engaged a whole series of au pair girls from different countries, most of whom were an enormous success. They found the house extremely chilly, there being no central heating. One girl had spent her life in Algeria and had come back to metropolitan France after the trouble. She failed her Baccalaureate and was sent to Lime Tree Farm as some form of punishment. She had never seen snow in her life and she arrived in one of the bitterest winters this country has ever seen. She was enormously stoic and seemed to enjoy life with the Popplewells. Our first au pair girl was called Doris. She came from Germany and was a slip of a girl. Years later she brought her husband to see us. She was now a grandmother and she produced the menu of the Bell at Aston Clinton, to which we had taken her on her last night. In 1961 it made interesting reading: avocado 1s 3d, steak 4s, a bottle of wine 7s 6d. She had also got pictures of Nigel and Andrew and was delighted to show her husband all round the house and recount how much she enjoyed life with us.

In 1972, during the Lords test match made memorable by Massie's fine bowling, when he took 15 wickets, I got to know Ross Edwards, who was in the Australian side; he came from Western Australia. He was older and more mature than some of the others in Ian Chappell's rather unloveable side. He was a fine fielder and a stylish batsman, and a distinguished hockey player. He once had the misfortune to be out for 99 in a test match. We became firm friends, and on the Sunday before the Trent Bridge test match in July 1972 we invited him to our house. He came down with Greg Chappell and young David Colley, who was on the verge of breaking in to the test side as a fast-bowler. In the sunshine Ross and I played eight sets of tennis against the young men, and beat them. They were quite exhausted, but I packed them off to London and thought no more about it. However, unknown to me I had nearly struck a blow to England, because on the Wednesday Jack Fingleton wrote in the *Times*: 'It would be strange if a tennis mishap had bearings on Trent Bridge. There was no play on Saturday in this match [Australia vs Middlesex]. On Sunday Colley played eight sets of tennis and on Monday could not raise his right arm above his head.' It was all to no avail. In the test match Colley made 54 and took two wickets in England's first innings; the match ended in a draw, though not before Ross made 170 not out in Australia's second innings.

On another tour Ross and Ashley Mallett – the Australian off-spinner – were quietly having supper at our house when some men from the village came to enquire if we knew of anyone who could turn out for the local cricket side next day. They were astonished to find that there were two test players in the village, but were unsuccessful in persuading them to play.

We were lucky in making immediate friends. Margaret fell in at the butcher's shop with Marianne Fry, with whom she had been at Malvern. Marianne was married to Alan, who was an inventor and designed in those days washing machines for Bloom and Colston. They lived in a Victorian house in Chesham and had three children, Roger, Stephen and Joanna. Stephen Fry was even then a somewhat wild child and had the habit of taking off the heads of flowers in people's gardens. But he was plainly highly intelligent. He used to come to our children's parties. I ran them like a detention centre. After the children passed the age of four or five it was an all-boys party in which they played games before tea, had tea lasting five or ten minutes and then back to more party games, all done at the rush followed by some silent films. I don't think the Frys had parties like this. One day on his way home Stephen said to his mother, 'Mummy when you grow up can you choose who you marry?' There was a pause and Marianne said, 'Yes of course, darling'. After another pause Stephen said, 'You mean, Mummy, you could have married Mr Popplewell?'

The Fry family became close friends and shortly after Joanna was born they moved to Norfolk where they bought another enormous Victorian house, which was very gloomy. However, it had a lot of outbuildings where Alan could carry on his business as an inventor, having left the Bloom and Colston organisation and set up on his own. Here he flourished.

We had taken the children to various places for holidays. Once we set out to go to Brittany. This proved something of an adventure, because we took the two older boys together with Nicola and a friend of hers. We went in two cars with an au pair girl. We were intending to go from Southampton to St Malo. In those days the cars had to be lifted onto the ferry by crane. There was a strike by the crane drivers, so that when we arrived in Southampton we were told that our boat would not sail and accordingly we had to find accommodation for seven people. It so happened that the British Association was holding its annual conference at Southampton, and rooms were at a premium. However, we managed to find a friendly pub which took us in. Margaret was dressed for travelling and wearing trousers. She enquired whether it was permissible to go into the dining room without changing (it only shows how manners have changed) and the waiter said he would go and find out. There was then broadcast over the hotel tannoy, 'The lady with the large party can keep her trousers on for dinner'. Happily we found food; we caught the boat the next day and had a long drive to get to our destination.

On two or three occasions we had taken a cottage at Swanage, which had been a great success, but when the Frys moved to Norfolk they suggested that we might come up for the summer and enjoy the East Anglian air. To that end I went up to stay with the Frys in February. Their house was not warm. There were six inches of snow – and that was inside the house! However, nothing ventured nothing gained, so I drove from their house to Sheringham to see whether it would be suitable for a summer holiday. There was something like a gale blowing and the spray was coming up over the promenade. It seemed a most unlikely place to take small children for a holiday. However, I persevered, and about a quarter past one on a Tuesday in February I found Gasche's Swiss restaurant which was open. There were about 40 people having lunch; I got the last place and I thought it couldn't all be bad. Thereafter we took a house in Sheringham for three years, which was a great success.

While we were there, Margaret's sister Rosemary and her husband Robin came up and brought with them a boat to sail at Blakeney. As a result, during the winter I went to the boat show and bought a Mirror dinghy. None of us had ever sailed before but we took it to Sheringham on the top of a car and launched it from the beach. It seemed perfectly simple. The wind happened to be in the right place to sail out from the beach and to sail back again. It seemed to us to present no difficulty. We were to learn a different lesson later.

After three years at Sheringham it became clear that the house we had rented would no longer be available. It occurred to us that it might be sensible to buy something for ourselves, as we had fallen in love with Norfolk and by now had got to know a number of friends. Accordingly Margaret went and approached a number of house agents and found a small cottage in Little Walsingham in the Friday market. After some negotiation we purchased it from the next-door neighbour who was an artist called Chapman. There was a certain amount of work to be done but it provided us with a holiday house for a great number of years. Because it was in the Friday market we decided to call it Friday Cottage. We deliberately chose not to install television so that the children could read books and play games. From time to time they would wander round Fakenham or Norwich looking wistfully into the windows of electrical shops like children deprived of food. However, it was undoubtedly a good idea. We persuaded them that it was in fact not possible to receive television because of the position of the cottage. This cover was somewhat blown when we let the house and tenants brought their own television sets and aerials.

The Frys continued to be part of our lives because Stephen's career at Uppingham came to a somewhat abrupt end when he was expelled. Then he went on a tour of the country armed with other people's credit cards, which resulted in his being arrested and prosecuted. He gives a graphic description of all this in his book *Moab is my Washpot*. There came a time when he was up before the magistrates for them to decide whether he should have bail, whether he should be sent to the crown court and how he should be dealt with. I was then at the bar and went down with the Fry parents as a friend of the family to see if I could assist. Alan very sensibly said that he couldn't guarantee that Stephen would remain at home, and so the magistrates sent him to Pucklechurch Remand Centre.

When he next appeared before the magistrates I spoke up for him as a friend of the family. Stephen in *Moab* is very appreciative of my efforts. I don't think I did anything particularly remarkable, but in the result, the magistrates sensibly put him on probation. Thereafter he picked himself up, went to Norwich City College where he did 'A' levels and did very well. He was then awarded a scholarship for Queens' College and thereafter took Cambridge by storm, both intellectually and artistically and was part of a great Footlights group. His transition from Cambridge actor to writer and actor seemed easy and assured. He rewrote the lyrics of 'Me and my Girl' and had a great number of acting successes, both on the stage and in films and television.

He was invited to act in the play written by his friend Simon Gray about the spy Blake. We booked to see it because Stephen was in it, but by the time we went to see it he had opted out. It was, I have to say, an exceedingly boring play. On that ground alone one could understand why he didn't want to be part of it, but in fact he obviously had some sort of problem and vanished to the continent. He was sighted from time to time, but it was not clear where he had gone. Marianne rang Margaret up in some distress because their house in Norfolk was under siege by press photographers. Alan had gone to the continent and made contact with Stephen and they wanted to bring him back to England without any fuss so that he could quietly settle down with the family and sort himself out.

Margaret immediately offered the use of our cottage, warning Marianne that the neighbours might be a bit nosey and therefore to use her maiden name. She was to tell the neighbours of their wish to be quiet and hoped that the neighbours would not think they were being stuffy. Alan and Stephen therefore flew from Holland to a landing ground in Norfolk. He was collected by car and driven to Walsingham, where he spent something like a fortnight incognito in our cottage while the press continued to surround the Frys' house at Booton. The neighbours still don't know what was going on next door.

Margaret had introduced Stephen to his first Wodehouse book at the age of 12, for which Stephen said he had always been enormously grateful. We manage to see a certain amount of him in Norfolk. He is not only one of the nicest young men but also one of the cleverest, without any pretensions, and his encyclopedic knowledge is astonishing. He claims no great credit for it because he says he can look at something he reads and then has total recall. Nevertheless, it is a very remarkable facility. We much admired his performance in 'University

Challenge' when the oldies defeated the young undergraduates easily and Stephen was the star of the occasion. He was kind enough to invite us to the first night of 'Wilde', which we much enjoyed as indeed we did all his other acting performances. Above all he is not only witty and intelligent but exceedingly kind. Like a comedian who wants to play Hamlet, he would like nothing more than to be an outstanding cricketer, which he has to confess is well beyond his actual abilities.

There were two others whom we were lucky enough to know who burst like stars across the firmament. The first was John Vaizey, who I first met at Cambridge. Because of illness described most graphically in his book *Scenes from Institutional Life,* he had not been in the services and was therefore younger than us. But he was enormously engaging, full of dry wit and a great companion. He and I joined the University Labour Party and indulged in the usual undergraduate criticism of government policy. He was already clearly a distinguished economist, and was rewarded with fellowships at both Oxford and Cambridge. He wrote a number of articles and books about the economics of education, on which he became an expert, and ended up at Brunel University. Having been best man at our wedding, we continued to see a lot of him and his American wife Marina. We became godparents to each other's children and enjoyed an intermittent correspondence. He and Tony Crosland were much involved in education, and John's allegiance to the Labour Party resulted in his being appointed to be Lord Vaizey in Harold Wilson's somewhat controversial honours list, which included Lord Keagan. John was astute enough to be critical of all this – and gradually (though I suspect I had no part in it) he moved to the right. I suspect the education of his children played some part. In the result, he ended up as an advisor to Margaret Thatcher. Sadly, illness overtook him and he died at a young age. But his intellectual brilliance and his acute wit remain with me to this day.

The other star came from Norfolk. Judith Chaplin had a meteoric career. After success at Cambridge she first of all taught, then after her first marriage went to Norfolk Education Committee, where she met Margaret. Then by way of the Institute of Directors and the CBI she became one of John Major's advisors. She was very keen to be an MP, but being intelligent and attractive, selection committees (particularly the women) rejected her time and time again. Eventually she was selected for Newbury and won her seat, only to go for a routine operation which she didn't survive. Her loss was a tragedy for her friends and indeed for the Conservatives, who lost an enormous talent.

I once suggested to her, when she was with John Major, that judges needed an increase in pay, and with that directness accompanied by charm which was her hallmark, she rather witheringly told me that they had no difficulty in finding people to be judges, and she thought no increase was necessary. She was a real star and politics is the worse for her death.

Margaret and I considered ourselves immensely lucky to have met, known and admired the talent of Stephen Fry, John Vaizey and Judith Chaplin. They greatly enhanced the fabric of our lives.

Norfolk has been a great blessing. I now have so many friends there that it is difficult to fit them all in when I pay fleeting visits. Next door to Friday Cottage across a loke was a house occupied by Taffy Humphries, who was a farm labourer. He use to keep an eye on Friday Cottage and also housed our dinghies in his barn. We had by this time not only got a Mirror dinghy but also an Enterprise. We started sailing from Blakeney. It was quite a different experience from sailing off the beach at Sheringham. Blakeney has a very narrow channel without much depth of water. It is possible only to sail for about three hours either side of high tide, and woe betide the boat that does not get back before the tide goes out, because then it is a long walk through mud. The Mirror had a dagger centre-board, which meant that running aground necessarily involved coming to a complete halt.

At very high tides the marshes would be completely covered and it would be possible to take the boat across the top of the marsh. This was very exciting particularly on a run. The difficulty was that the depth of the water was somewhat ill-defined. We once found ourselves running across the marsh and wanted to go about. I therefore got out of the boat in order to turn it round, only to find the marsh contained a good number of gullies, and I went six feet down into water. Gradually we learnt the elements of sailing, and managed to teach Nigel and Andrew. Eventually came the day when we allowed them both out in the Mirror with us hovering around like mother hens, but they both proved competent sailors and eventually bought themselves a Fireball, which is really a plank with an enormous sail. They had very great fun with this, turning it over on regular occasions, but being young and active they thoroughly enjoyed it. Alexander and Eddie Jim in their turn learnt to sail, and in due course they would bring girlfriends up to Norfolk. Putting their girl friends on a trapeze was one way of testing out their ability to survive as Popplewell wives.

One day when I went up to Norfolk to collect the keys of Taffy's barn, he told me that he hadn't got them any more. I told him not to mess about and to give them to me. He replied that the trustee in bankruptcy had got the key and our boats had been impounded. It transpired that he had gone bankrupt and the trustee, perfectly properly thinking the boats were part of his assets, had kept the key. After some negotiation we managed to get the boats released. Further, we decided that it might be a worthwhile exercise to buy his cottage, which we did. We decided it would be prudent to allow Taffy and his wife to continue to live there and not to charge rent, so as to avoid any problems with the Rent Restrictions Act.

After about five or six years Taffy's wife died and he moved out. We therefore got possession of his cottage. It required a very great deal of renovation before it could be made habitable, and we then had the problem of what to call it. There were all sorts of suggestions, such as Taffy's Cottage, and so on but in the end we settled for Thursday Cottage, which caused a good deal of amusement for people who came wandering around looking at houses in the square. We were thus left with two cottages of which we only needed one. In the result, we sold Friday Cottage to an agreeable cleric who discovered an inglenook fireplace in the sitting room. He subsequently sold it to the present owners, who have done a great deal of work on it. They too found all sorts of old treasures of which we were wholly ignorant.

Almost every year since we were married Margaret and I managed to take ourselves abroad after leaving the children at boarding school – most frequently to France. In the summer of 1987 I saw an article in the *Evening Standard* extolling the delights of Normandy. In particular it referred to the fact that property was not expensive, and given that the exchange rate was something like 11 or 12 francs to the pound, it was certainly attractive.

Accordingly we took the car to France and looked around. There were some lovely old timbered houses in the Suisse Normande. Living as we did in the English countryside it didn't seem a particularly good idea to do the same in France. The idea basically was to find a holiday

11. On holiday. Margaret and O. B. P.

house by the sea where we could enjoy ourselves, have friends to stay
and provide a haven for children and grandchildren.

We drove down from Calais and ended up at Carteret, on the
Cotentin peninsula, and stayed at a marvellous hotel called The Marine.
We visited a number of properties, none of which we liked, and then
went to Coutainville, a small seaside resort near Coutances. There we
engaged a Monsieur Barasson, an *immobilier*, who took us to visit a
house which consisted really of two cottages joined together in a small
hamlet. It had a small, enclosed garden and a garage and we liked it
enormously. However, we thought that with four bedrooms it was too
large and too expensive, and so we said goodbye to Monsieur Barasson
and took ourselves off to Mont St Michel for the night.

We managed to arrive at Mont St Michel in time for the last tour of
the mount, which was enormously exciting, and then stayed the night.
We had dinner in a room overlooking the sea and watched the tide
come in. That night after we were asleep, Margaret woke me up at five
o'clock in the morning and said, 'We must go back and buy the house'.
So we got up early, had breakfast, watched the tide come in and raced
back to Coutainville.

By 11 o'clock we had sat down with the owner, a Monsieur Catelan,
who was a French schoolteacher. We agreed a price and it was arranged

that in order to give him time to buy another house we should all exchange properties in December. French law required that we put down a deposit on the house, which we did. We decided to buy the house in the children's name. This necessitated producing their birth certificates, marriage certificates and so on for the French bureaucracy. Andrew and his wife Debs were, I think, in India, and Eddie Jim had gone walkabout in Spain; getting hold of them in order to fill in the documents proved a very difficult exercise. In the result, Eddie Jim was not contactable, so I had to have his share. The French authorities were exceedingly troublesome. They refused to recognise a birth certificate unless it had been produced from Somerset House within the last three months. They required details of the marriage arrangements between the children and the marriage arrangements between Margaret and myself. When we explained that we had got married in Ripon Cathedral, that requirement seemed to go by the board.

But the greatest stumbling block was the big financial crash in October 1987. Thus, what seemed a good financial idea in September turned out in November not to be so good. Likewise, getting all the documents to France at the necessary time proved a nightmare. I became enormously familiar with the abilities of various courier organisations and with French bureaucracy and by the end of December all had been achieved and the documents were duly signed. Subsequently, I had to convey my share to Eddie Jim. This could be done freely in England without expense, but in France it cost quite a substantial amount of money. We quite understood why buying and selling a house in France was such a problem. The only advantage that we could see was that the *immobilier* acted on behalf of both vendor and seller. There seemed to be no property surveys or investigation of title save for an enormous document setting out in very great detail the names of the various parties to the transaction, but in the end it proved a very worthwhile purchase.

In Easter 1988 we set out with a van full of furniture and moved in. The children came for Easter, bringing with them a nameplate for the house. After Friday Cottage and Thursday Cottage in Norfolk we thought that Maison Mercredi would be a more appropriate name for this house rather than No 7 Le Val, and so we christened it. Subsequently, we have had enormous fun there, for ourselves, for the family and for their friends and our friends.

12. Family, 1970s. From left: Nigel, Alexander, Margaret, Ed, Andrew, O. B. P.

Meanwhile, the children grew up. Nigel and Andrew went to a local prep school in Chesham called Winterbourne, which was the pre-prep of a school called the Beacon. The Beacon was a very successful day school run by a formidable headmaster called Masters. When Nigel got to the age of seven and was about to be moved up from Winterbourne to the Beacon, we took the view that it was time for him to go off to boarding school: to Winchester House, where I had been. This caused a good deal of upset, because Masters had made it a rule that he would not take anybody in the Beacon who had not been to Winterbourne and vice versa. We were the first people who had broken this rule. He allowed Andrew to stay on at Winterbourne, but was adamant that Alexander and Eddie Jim would not go either to Winterbourne or the Beacon. Thus, Andrew and Nigel went off to Winchester House. It is customary now for parents who send their children off to boarding school at all, let alone at the age of seven, to be regarded as hard-hearted, uncaring and insufficient parents. It was not universally so at this time. We took the firm view that the relationship between us and the children was enhanced by their being with their contemporaries during the term, without the hassle of parents breathing down their

13. Family party, 1994. From left: Andrew, Nicola, Alexander, Sally, Ingrid, Clare, Margaret, Ed, Nigel, Debs and grandchildren.

neck every night over their prep or other matters, and that to learn to live with other people at an early age was a good discipline in life.

Alexander and Eddie Jim went to Chesham Prep, a local school, and eventually on to Winchester House. At Winchester House they all prospered, both academically and on the games field. Andrew and Eddie Jim became head boys and Nigel became captain of cricket. Having sons as head boys at Winchester House gave rise to one complication, which was that the mother was required at sports day not only to give away the prizes but also to make a speech. The speech always had to include an appeal to the headmaster to give the boys a half holiday, which was enormously popular with the school. Luckily for Margaret both Andrew and Eddie Jim had left school at the Easter term, so she was not faced with this awkward prospect.

At one stage Nigel and Andrew were in the same form, with Andrew getting better marks; this gave us cause for some concern. Nigel seemed wholly unconcerned about it and kept talking about his very clever little brother. Also, when he got Andrew to help him he got quite good marks. When the question of the public school arose we thought it might be better for them to be parted. However, the school and the

14. Family, 1990s. From left: Margaret, Clare, Ed, Andrew, Nigel, Alexander and grandchildren.

boys were firm in their view that it would be better for them to go to the same school. The question then arose as to where they should go.

It was customary in those days for boys to go to the schools of their father, and so we had chosen Charterhouse for Nigel and Andrew. Leonard Halcrow, who was housemaster at one of the houses, was an old friend, and we therefore put the children down for his house. We discovered, however, that Charterhouse in the 1960s seemed to have a problem with drugs, about which the school seemed somewhat indifferent. Apprehensions about the school were confirmed when we learnt that the cricket master had taken the first eleven up to Lords to protest about the South African team appearing. Whatever one's views about apartheid, it was singularly inappropriate that boys should be indoctrinated in this way.

Finally, about two months before Nigel was due to do his common entrance exam Halcrow, who was a bachelor, found the burden of running a house too much and decided to retire. With all this in mind I came home one evening and said to Margaret that I thought that we would not pursue Nigel's entry to Charterhouse but find another school which was more suitable. We therefore approached Radley, where Dennis

Silk was the warden and where Simon Langdale, an old cricket friend, was one of the housemasters. On one of his 'Going out Sundays' we took a very recalcitrant Nigel over to Radley to introduce him to Simon and Dennis to try and persuade them that he would be a suitable boy to enter their school. They were good enough to say that they would take him provided he passed his common entrance, which he did easily, and accordingly he went off to Radley.

There then ensued a most terrible row at Charterhouse. The incoming housemaster thought that Nigel had been removed because of him. I had not in fact met him and had to write an apologetic letter so saying, and it was of course quite impossible to go public on our criticisms of the school. And so the matter had to rest there, with a good deal of ill-feeling on the school's part. Subsequently Andrew got a scholarship to Radley. In those days the award did not increase as the terms went by. Although he started with a scholarship worth a third of the fees, by the time he left it was enough to pay for about a fortnight.

Both Nigel and Andrew flourished at Radley, did particularly well at games and were very great friends. Alexander and Eddie Jim did not then have quite the same close relationship. Alexander was not a great games player though highly intelligent, and the question then arose as to where he was to go. Naturally he was put in for Radley, where he got an award which was worth £100. We had at that time all four boys at fee-paying schools. My practice at the bar was not such that we could continue this without some financial assistance. Margaret's mother helpfully contributed, but of itself it was not enough. Accordingly, we asked Dennis Silk if we could possibly put Alexander in for scholarships elsewhere. Dennis was kind enough to say that if he did not succeed elsewhere he would keep Alexander's place at Radley, which was a very generous offer.

Accordingly, the luckless Alexander was put in for Tonbridge, where he got an award of some £750, and thought not unnaturally that he had done rather well, which he had. However, this was not sufficient, and so for the third time he was put in for a scholarship – this time for Charterhouse. He went to Bodeites, where John Mash, who was Halcrow's successor, was now housemaster. This seemed to repair some of the damage done to our taking Nigel away. In the result, Alexander got the third scholarship, which was worth four figures, and that was the end of his having to take scholarships.

Whether we did the right thing or not I am not sure. Certainly Alexander flourished at Charterhouse, where the academic standard was generally of a higher level than at Radley. He was taught by two PhDs. One of the difficulties about Charterhouse, however, was that it was very much Surrey-orientated. At weekends the place more or less closed down, so that unless you lived in Surrey you were left with one or two other people in the house with very little to do. Radley, on the other hand, while its academic record was not as good, had a multitude of activities going at the weekends, with the result that the boys there were not particularly enthusiastic about coming home for the day.

In due course Eddie Jim got a scholarship to Radley, and he too flourished both academically and on the sports field. Thereafter there was a constant succession of children taking 'O' and 'A' levels. Our holidays in Norfolk were interrupted with cries of ecstasy and groans of agony, and it was with great apprehension that we awaited the dreaded envelopes. Nigel did not have a great respect for authority at Radley, and Dennis wrote a rather scathing report about him wasting the opportunities available to him. His masters obviously had low expectations of his performance in 'A' levels and so recorded in their reports.

When his 'A' level results came out he discovered to his excitement that he had got an A in one subject. This entirely changed his life. He came rushing down from the bedroom saying that he was going to stay on an extra year and take Cambridge entrance, and thereafter his whole way of life improved out of all recognition. He played a vigorous game of rugger in the fifteen and captained the cricket eleven with very great success. And at the end of it all he improved his 'A' levels and sat an entrance to Cambridge and got in. The reports he received at the end of his career at Radley could not have been more different from those he had received throughout most of his time.

Andrew, meanwhile, pursued the classics. He had a major part in the Greek play at Radley where something went wrong and 200 lines were missed out. Nobody seemed to notice except the Ellingworths. Richard Ellingworth and I had been at Winchester House together. He had been a distinguished classical scholar and had ended up in the Foreign Office and was following the text in the original Greek. His son Henry had also been at Winchester House with Andrew and was in the play at Radley. He was one of the brightest children of his generation, and because his parents were often abroad he came to stay with us quite often. He was a very engaging young man, and after some interesting adventures is now busy exercising his mind in computer problems in the US. It was intended that Andrew should go to Cambridge and either read classics or law, and to that end, having got good 'A' levels, he sat a scholarship for Trinity Hall. When he went for his interview he was told by the admissions tutor that he was a right little public-school boy. Having been to a public school, he could scarcely help that, and in the result, he neither got a scholarship nor was offered a place at Trinity Hall. He had come from Radley with an extremely good CV, a distinguished academic record and a great sense of responsibility. He had many qualities to offer and it was incomprehensible that Trinity Hall should turn him down. It was a supreme example of political correctness.

Dennis Silk, to his eternal credit, was so incensed that he took the papers to Downing where John Hopkins, the law tutor, admitted him to the college. During his time at Downing he was given an award and he ended up with a first. An admissions tutor who is so incompetent as not to be able to identify someone who might get a first reflects somewhat sadly on the quality of the tutors. At that time they had security of tenure. This one was probably a product of the revolutionary and bolshie attitude of the universities in the 1960s. Trinity Hall's loss was Downing's gain – more particularly as at the very young age of 38 Andrew became a QC. We often wonder what happened to the admissions tutor, and whether his failure to spot a first-class candidate had the slightest effect on his subsequent career. Sadly, I doubt it.

Alexander cruised through Charterhouse without any apparent effort and followed Andrew to Downing College where, being enormously numerate, he read economics. We confidently expected that Eddie Jim would easily pass into Downing and follow what had now become a family tradition. He had a good academic record at Radley, and played hockey, cricket and racquets for the school. He was quite a talented musician and was a thoroughly responsible boy. The school made the mistake of putting him in for classics and foreign languages. For some reason he and the admissions tutor did not see eye to eye. In the result, to everyone's intense disappointment he did not get in. It was a most shattering blow and one for which we have never really forgiven the college. In the result, he went to Bristol, where he met his future wife on day one. They never looked at anyone else, they married, have three children and lived happily ever after. If it was possible for good to come out of this disaster, that was it.

At university all led lives of typical undergraduates. They seemed curiously enough not to be interested in politics. Nigel read sciences, Andrew read law, Alexander read economics and Eddie Jim read modern languages. Apart from Andrew, who ended up with a first, they all got upper seconds. Nigel had three years in the Cambridge University cricket side and ended up being vice-captain. Andrew played some hockey and cricket and became a member of the Hawk's Club. Alexander took to rowing and ended up with an oar having made four bumps in either the Lent or the May races, though not, it is fair to say, against very distinguished opponents. Eddie Jim played racquets, cricket and hockey at Bristol. Then there was the question of what they were to do when they came down.

In his last year at Cambridge the university had played against Somerset, and Nigel had made some runs and taken some wickets. Peter Roebuck, who had been in the Cambridge side the year before and was now a full-time member of the Somerset side, suggested that he might like to play a bit of professional cricket during the summer, which he did. At the end of the summer, after a comparatively successful number of appearances, he was offered a contract. He had as a schoolboy gone to South Africa with a team called The Crocodiles which included people like David Gower, Christopher Cowdrey, Paul Downton and so on. He had also been on an MCC tour to Bangladesh, so that he had some cricketing background. Having been born in Kent he had gone to Kent Nets, but had not impressed them and subsequently he joined Hampshire's second eleven, where he and Mark Nicholas met up. Hampshire did not offer him a permanent contract and so he decided he would take up Somerset's offer.

Meanwhile he had been taken on by Cheltenham College to teach sciences by Richard Morgan, who had previously been a master at Radley. Also on the staff was Eddie Butler, who was then captain of Wales at rugger, and no doubt parents were very impressed by the fact that the staff included Nigel Popplewell, Somerset cricketer to look after the cricket, and Eddie Butler, Welsh rugger player, to look after the rugger. In the result, it didn't work out like that, because Eddie Butler was away a lot of the time in the winter term looking after Wales so that Nigel played a part in running the rugger, and in the summer term Nigel had the whole term off to play for Somerset.

Somerset at this time was just starting on a run of success. The side was captained by Rose and contained Ian Botham, Joel Garner and Vivien Richards, as well as Peter Roebuck and a number of other considerable players. Nigel was lucky to join at this time, but he certainly contributed to their success, including three one-day cup finals, all of which they won. Initially he opened the bowling and in his first summer took some 50 or 60 wickets, but as the years went by he bowled less and less frequently with less and less success. It always seemed to me a criticism of the coaching that with an easy action as a medium-paced bowler he never improved. Why he did not I have no idea, but clearly there was talent there. It was customary then for the coach to be an old member of the eleven who was given something of a sinecure. The other members of the side of course were not particularly competent to identify weaknesses or skills, and really it was left to the individual player to work out his own salvation.

However, his batting did improve and he ended up by opening the innings. He was unlucky one year in that until the last afternoon of the season his had been the fastest century of the year. On the last afternoon he was pipped at the post by O'Shaughnessay in a game in which the batting side were given runs in order to encourage them to declare, and so lost the opportunity of winning the Lawrence Trophy for the fastest century of the season. After a few years at Cheltenham he decided to move to a school at Taunton. He was by this time married and living there.

After some seven or eight years he became disenchanted with the cricketing world, with the Somerset side, cricket in general and travelling in particular. He suddenly announced he was leaving cricket and to our immense pleasure decided to become a solicitor.

Nigel became quite a well-known figure in the Somerset team, being frequently on television. I was quietly walking around Lords one day during a test match when a small boy aged about nine rushed up to me with his autograph book and said, 'Oh Sir, can I have your autograph?' I patted him on the head in a rather patronising way. Nobody had ever asked me for my autograph since I had been at Cambridge, when 50 'Popplewells' changed hands for one 'May', and I said to him, 'Sonny, you don't want my autograph'. His little face fell and he turned to me and he said, 'Oh but sir, aren't you Nigel Popplewell's father?'

Meanwhile, the troubles that had been brewing in the Somerset side blew up into a major squabble. The catalyst was the decision to replace Garner and Richards with Martin Crowe. Crowe, from New Zealand, had first played for Somerset in 1984 when Garner and Richards had tour commitments. He had a splendid season making nearly 1900 runs with six centuries and taking some 44 wickets. But it was his enthusiasm and ability to inspire the younger players which marked him out as a person of real character.

In 1987, Essex sought leave to have the use of Crowe's services. Somerset were faced with a problem. They could not keep Crowe and also Richards and Garner. In the result, they chose to keep Crowe and to dispense with the services of Richards and Garner. The matter was not handled with a great deal of sensitivity. Botham vowed to leave if Richards and Garner went. A major row ensued for several months.

There was thus a frenzied meeting which Nigel, now retired from the scene, attended. I suggested to him that as a dispassionate observer who was no longer involved but who had been present throughout the period, his views were likely to carry a good deal of weight, and that he ought to speak. In the result, he did, not at great length but with great courage. He persuaded the meeting that it was in the best interests of the club that Viv Richards and Joel Garner would have to go and expressed his dismay at the lack of commitment of some of their players. There is no doubt that his intervention was the decisive one. It was all fully reported in the press. Margaret suffered a good deal of upset, because Nigel was never a very smart dresser and a number of papers highlighted the fact that he was wearing an old jersey with a lot of holes in it.

Although by now he was married to Ingrid and living in Taunton, he decided that he would do the solicitor's exam. It necessitated his coming to London to do the common professional exam because he had got a degree in science. At the end of that year he had to do the solicitor's final. We have always underestimated his capacity. It was immensely hard work coming to London every week and returning home at weekends. When we looked through the list of results of the final we started somewhat pessimistically with those with conditional passes and worked gradually up the list to find to our immense surprise and delight that he had in fact got a first. Clark Willmot & Clark, a very well known firm in Taunton, were kind enough to take him on.

Nigel was articled to Alan Pendlebury, who had been a partner in Walterson Moore many years before and who had often instructed me at the bar. He was now one of the senior partners with Clark Willmot & Clark. Thereafter Nigel became a partner, and subsequently moved to Bristol with Burgess Salmon, where he runs their tax affairs, a subject in which he has specialised. There was an occasion some years ago when he gave a presentation at the Castle Hotel to businessmen after the budget, attended not only by businessmen but by local worthies including Dennis Silk, who was astonished to see his erstwhile, tiresome pupil now a pillar of respectability giving advice to distinguished people. He and Ingrid, his wife, are great outdoor people. They walk the hills and go camping with their three splendid children, Alice, Harry and Thomas. Ingrid was a highly competent doctor, who sadly left medicine because consultants above her were plainly jealous of her abilities – she has now become a gardening expert.

Andrew left Cambridge after a slight tiff with his tutor, to whom he had apparently failed to say goodbye. He retaliated by leaving a Belisha beacon which he had somehow illegally acquired outside the tutor's room, Margaret having said that on no account was she going to take it home. Andrew passed the bar exam and was called to the bar while I was still in practice. On one occasion I led him in front of James Comyn, who nearly fell off his bench when I announced that 'I appear for the plaintiff with my learned friend Mr Andrew Popplewell'. He was lucky enough to get pupillage in Bob Alexander's chambers with Richard Aikens, now Mr Justice Aikens. Aikens thought that he was rather a mouse-like creature who didn't seem to have very much spirit. But when he wrote to John Hopkins to enquire about Andrew, Hopkins reported that he was one of the wildest undergraduates they had had in the college. Among the pupils that year were some eight firsts, and it was by extraordinary good luck that they took him on as a tenant. His progress was swift and at the age of 38 he took silk. He married Debs, a doctor, who is a distinguished dermatologist at Great Ormond Street Hospital. They too have three children, two girls and a boy, who have got involved in the filming world. Anna played the vampire's sister in 'The Little Vampire'. Laura played Lyra in the dramatisation of 'Dark Materials' on Radio 4. Both she and Anna had parts in 'Love in a Cold Climate'. Fred, aged seven, is playing Michael Darling in a film of 'Peter Pan', presently being shot in Australia.

During his vacations Alexander had sensibly gone off to work for Mercury Asset Management (now part of Merrill Lynch), and when he came down from Cambridge they offered him a job, he being enormously interested not only in dealing with money, particularly other people's, but in making money – an activity for which he was ideally suited. He has remained ever since, flourishing in the city environment. He married Sally and now has three girls. They have become great Norfolk enthusiasts and Thursday Cottage is very much part of their life – the girls have taken to sailing like ducks to water. Sally, meanwhile, loves doing up houses, for which she has a real genius.

When Eddie Jim went to Bristol, almost the first person he met was Clare Finzi. Her grandfather was a distinguished composer, her aunt was Jacqueline du Pré and her parents were the authors of the recent book which was turned into a film about Jacqueline. Ed and Clare were ideally suited to each other. They got married and went to live in the wing of her parents' house at Ashmonsworth. After the furore over the book about Jacqueline, to which Clare took grave exception and to the behaviour of her father, they moved to near Swindon. Ed read modern languages at Bristol and in his gap year went to Spain and also to France and became proficient in both those languages. When he came down from Bristol he was undecided as to what he would do and went into the Civil Service – in the Home Office, which he quite enjoyed but where his salary was really of a very modest sort. He therefore decided, somewhat to our surprise, to become an accountant. As he had never been enormously numerate, it was a very brave thing to do. He was determined to make his own way in life and in the result, he went to Coopers & Lybrand in Reading who treated him exceedingly well, and he got through the accountancy exam and stayed on with Coopers. After two or three years he was headhunted by Thames Water and joined them. He was put in charge of various operations in which Thames Water were involved, which included going to America, Turkey and Indonesia to supervise operations which Thames Water were conducting jointly with the host country. Indonesia was in a state of some turmoil, and he had to go around with an armed escort. Subsequently he was promoted to be a controller, which meant that he no longer had the heavy round of travelling abroad. His French has been immensely helpful in dealings with Maison Mercredi, where both he and Clare, being keen garden lovers, have had plenty to do. They too now have three children.

After giving up teaching at Chislehurst when we moved, Margaret did some part time teaching locally but her involvement in education took on a new lease of life when in 1974 she was elected to the County Council. Chesham had always sent three members to the County Council. The Conservatives had masqueraded under the title of either independents or ratepayers. One day when we were seeing the children off to school Ann Brooke, a friend who lived close by us, suggested to Margaret that as she herself was intending to stand for the County Council, Margaret might like to do the same. Neither of them had any previous experience of politics, nor had they seriously been involved in the affairs of the town. However, we did a lot of canvassing. The political climate was such that the Conservatives were on a high and in consequence both she and Ann were returned as members of the council.

Margaret made an immediate impact on the council because on the first day that she spoke the officers and the chairman were talking to each other while she was addressing them and she suddenly said, 'Mr Chairman do I have your full attention?' This brought her to the notice of the powers that be and she was put on the Education Committee and was subsequently chairman of the Schools Sub-Committee and of the main County Education Committee. It was a time of reduction in pupils, and as a result she was required to chair a large number of public meetings where the numbers of pupils had fallen to such an extent that a particular school was no longer viable. The idea that a school might close aroused a great deal of fury in parents and the suggestion that they might actually drive their child an extra two miles to another school fell upon somewhat deaf ears. The fact that they did that every Saturday when they went shopping was not the point. The public meetings were hostile and angry. Little or no effort was made to appreciate that some schools were no longer either commercially or educationally viable and there needed to be rationalisation. It was a very wearying process and one that she did not enjoy. However, in the end the rationalisation policy was pursued, to the general benefit of the community. But her major contribution to education in the county was to fight off Shirley Williams's proposal to abolish grammar schools in Buckinghamshire. She fought a long and hard battle with her and Margaret Becket and managed to keep the schools open until finally the Labour government fell. It is somewhat ironic that the present government has made a U-turn and now is all in favour of selective education. The academic success of the Buckinghamshire schools is a testimony to Margaret's courage and determination.

For about 25 years, until Margaret became High Sheriff of Buckinghamshire, she sat as a magistrate, which she did with great skill and enjoyment. She was chairman for some years and she also was also much involved in the Buckinghamshire Probation Committee, of which she was also chairman. It was a good example of public service without expectation of honour or reward.

After her second term on the Education Committee she decided that she would not stay, because of the difficulties of being a political wife married to a judge. Her interests were primarily in education and not at all in politics, but she felt strongly about it and therefore retired. She would have been chairman of the council had she stayed on, but it was not a position she actively sought and would have involved a political career. She was fortunate enough thereafter to be invited to be a member of the Independent Broadcasting Authority (IBA) under the chairmanship of George Thompson and thereafter went on to the Independent Television Commission (ITC) under the chairmanship of George Russell. For some seven years she was at the heart of independent television. She was much involved in the allocation of franchises in 1994 and was plainly regarded as a valuable member of the commission. Margaret Thatcher had been persuaded that granting the franchises to the highest bidder was not very sensible. An elaborate scheme was therefore devised whereby there was a quality threshold after which the highest bidder, provided they could show a proper financial backing, was awarded the franchise. Normally the television companies and the ITC had a friendly relationship including a certain amount of socialising and entertainment, but all this ceased during the year when the franchises were being considered. One or two applicants found themselves as the only applicants and obtained the franchise paying almost the barest minimum. Others had strong competition and in the result, a number of very well-known television companies failed to get their franchise. This resulted in two companies taking the ITC for judicial review. Sensibly, the courts observed that this was a matter of discretion for the ITC, that they had applied the right test and that the courts simply would not interfere.

Margaret's membership of the IBA seemed likely at one time during the Aitken trial to give rise to some problems (of which more later), but in the event nothing happened. Among her many public activities were running the Oxfordshire Association for the Deaf for some years, being a governor of a number of state and private schools, being a member of the Council of Buckinghamshire University, and more particularly starting up the Thames Valley Partnership, which she did when she was High Sheriff. This partnership, as the name implies, was a combination of disciplines dedicated to preventing crime. Private business was involved, and after a slow start it became an important organisation for fighting crime, for which Margaret must take a good deal of credit. She was on the staff of the Open University, which conferred a doctorate on her.

In 1992 she became High Sheriff of Buckinghamshire. It was customary for the High Sheriff of Buckinghamshire to be sworn in in the crown court. Accordingly I arranged to go and sit so that I could perform this ceremony. Andrew also came down to welcome the new High Sheriff on behalf of the bar, so it was very much a family occasion. I observed to the new High Sheriff that for the first time in 37 years of our married life she would have no right of reply.

Historically, the High Sheriff was responsible for the safety of the High Court judge in the county. In the days when High Court judges went on assize, they moved from county to county with their retinue and baggage and were greeted at the county border by the High Sheriff and conveyed to the county town. The assize system involved judges going to all parts of the country to dispense justice. Because of the dangers then obtaining, it was the High Sheriff's responsibility to ensure that the judges arrived and left safely. Subsequently the role of the High Sheriff was a social one in relation to judges. When the assize system still operated it was frequently the position that judges would stay the weekends with the High Sheriff and be royally entertained. Thereafter the High Sheriff took upon him or herself the responsibility of entertaining judges, of arranging visits to interesting parts of the county and generally being responsible for their welfare.

However, apart from the social side of the High Sheriff's responsibilities the High Sheriff was very much involved in the affairs of the county. There was scarcely a day in the year when Margaret was not attending some function of a civic nature, either large or small but essentially related to county activities. Unfortunately I had to work on a great many of the occasions. It was an absorbing year in which she got

15. Margaret, High Sheriff of Buckinghamshire, 1991.

to know a great number of people in the county and met with all sorts of organisations and bodies of which hitherto she knew little. She herself made no little contribution to the welfare of Buckinghamshire.

On 20 April 2001 Margaret had a heart attack and died. She had had arthritis since she was 30 and had been in constant pain since. She had had numerous operations on her shoulder, hands, legs and knees, and had a pacemaker for a number of years. She never complained. She was the bravest of the brave. Her whole life reflected her deep religious conviction and her sense of public duty, and she set high standards for us all. Her love and laughter enriched the fabric of all our lives. As someone wrote after she died, 'When she left a room the light somehow seemed to fade'.

7

First Steps at the Bar

In September 1951 I became a pupil of Douglas Lowe at 12 King's Bench Walk. If I have to analyse why I had decided to go to the bar in the first place, I think that it arose from reading an autobiography of Patrick Hastings called, I believe, *Cases in Court.* It was the excitement generated by his descriptions of cases he conducted which persuaded me to want to be part of it. I had not been a public speaker at all at school, nor indeed very much at university. I did take part in some moots, though not very successfully. The union had not been part of my life at Cambridge. I had never stood on a public platform, and such after-dinner speeches as I had made at university had been, on reflection, pitiful in the extreme.

Nowadays pupils are prepared for what life at the bar is like. They visit chambers as part of their training. They have practical demonstrations. They see themselves on video. They have ample opportunity to learn some of the trade. Not in my time. John Wrottersley was a senior barrister. His uncle had been in the Court of Appeal. His wife was a friend of my mother's. I was introduced to him so that he could give me some advice. I suspect that his practice had then fallen off. He was destined to be in the legal department of British Rail. He was a railway buff: it turned out to be an ideal place for him. When I went to see him he was obviously disenchanted with life in chambers. He told me that the clerks were unhelpful and that there really was no work and that it was a long struggle and an unrewarding profession. He concluded by saying that I would do very much better to seek my fortune elsewhere.

He was the first practising member of the bar to whom I spoke. I confess that I found his words chilling and very depressing. However, having passed my exams, I was determined to have a go at practising. Through a Charterhouse connection I had an introduction to Anthony Hawke QC, who was then the Common Sergeant, one of the judges at the Old Bailey. He met me, encouraged me to practice and arranged for me to go and be a pupil to Douglas Lowe.

Douglas Lowe was a god. He was tall, handsome, charming and urbane. He had run in the Olympics in 1924 and 1928 in either the 440 yards or the 880 yards, as they were then called, and won gold medals. His chambers were at the bottom end of King's Bench Walk, near the river. It was a splendid sight to see him emerge from his chambers, leaving for court. He maintained his ability to move fast. Thus his pupils were required to run to keep up with him, and it was a very breathless little group that arrived finally at court.

Emerging from his room was a musical comedy. Douglas was enormously well mannered. He would stand aside to enable the pupils to go first. The pupils, in deference to the great man, would stand aside to let him go first. This went on for some time. Each person moved round the other in an undignified *pas de deux*. Finally everyone would try unsuccessfully to go through the door together. Douglas was a man of immense kindness. He and his charming wife Karen took enormous interest in Margaret and myself. We were once royally entertained at the Ecu de France, which was beyond our wildest dreams as well as our pocket. When we got married he sent us a splendid wedding present.

He was totally honest. On reflection he was not, I think, a very great lawyer. It was customary for pupils to copy down the drafts of their masters' opinions and pleadings. Douglas always started his opinions with the magic phrase 'I have carefully considered these papers'. I remember the terrible scene that was caused when the papers were returned by some solicitors suggesting to Douglas that he had really not done his homework properly. This caused Douglas immense chagrin. On enquiry, it transpired that he had omitted the magic words at the beginning of his opinion, thus leading the solicitors to the conclusion that the work had been less than well researched.

His pleadings were involved and were not, as I subsequently discovered, masterpieces of draftsmanship, nor were they a good example for pupils to follow. Douglas had what might be described as a general practice. He did a good deal of common-law work and a very small amount of crime. But he had almost no work either in the magistrates court or in the county court. While it was of immense interest to see work at a higher level, it was not perhaps the best training for a pupil like me, who was to spend his first five years at the bar in the magistrates court.

Douglas had the most elegant room which was beautifully furnished. In it sat Percy Harris, who had recently been Douglas's pupil and had now become a member of chambers. He subsequently took silk and became a circuit judge. One of my fellow pupils was John Owen, subsequently to become Mr Justice Owen. I was enormously envious of him because at the end of his year's pupillage he was going to chambers in Birmingham, where it was said he had an uncle who was a solicitor. He would thereby start to earn money immediately, which seemed a far-off prospect for me. In the result, he flourished on his own ability and had a very large practice on the Midland circuit.

My first case with Douglas involved a libel action brought by a man who claimed to have found a cure for cancer. He gave the cure a number, which turned out to be his telephone number. One of the Sunday papers said that he was a fraud. He then brought proceedings for libel. Douglas was led by Sir Godfrey Russell Vick QC. He had recently been chairman of the bar. He was to sit with Mr Justice Lynskey on the Lynskey tribunal. He was a very distinguished figure. I had met him previously at Cambridge, because he was a great sportsman, and he was kind enough to take an interest in my progress at the bar.

We went round to Sir Godfrey's chambers to have a consultation with him the night before the hearing. Sir Godfrey, while a formidable figure, was not a very great lawyer. When his clerk came in to announce that we were in Court 5, Sir Godfrey enquired from the clerk which judge we had got to hear the case. The clerk replied 'Mr Justice Devlin'. Sir Godfrey turned to me and said 'Mr Justice Devlin has recently been appointed and we shall have to be very careful not to bounce this young judge'. I did not realise then how inapposite that comment was. Nobody was ever likely to bounce Mr Justice Devlin, least of all Sir Godfrey. Mr Justice Devlin's rise from Puisne judge to the Court of Appeal and the House of Lords was meteoric. He had a razor sharp mind and a habit of not suffering fools gladly.

The case was tried by a jury. The Sunday newspaper was represented by Gilbert Paul QC, later Mr Justice Paul. He was indeed a terrifying figure. He had a deformed leg and therefore he stumped when walking. I shall never forget the way he stalked our client in cross-examination, pacing up and down the front row of the court. He totally destroyed him with rapier questions. It was a fine theatrical performance. It encouraged me in the belief that I had indeed joined the right profession. Little did I realise that that ability was not given to many, and in any event it was the result of many, many years of forensic experience.

The next case that Douglas had was a defended divorce. In those days it was not unusual for the parties to be represented by silks when their marriage broke up. The court then decided who had been responsible. The purpose of these bitter contests was to secure the benefit of the financial consequences which in those days depended wholly on the allocation of responsibility for the break-up of the marriage. In this particular case the husband had been having an affair with the au pair girl, and the wife petitioned on the grounds of his adultery. The husband cross-petitioned on the grounds of the wife's cruelty. Part of the allegation was that she played the gramophone record 'So Long' throughout the day over a period of years. Mr Justice Karminski tried the case. Douglas was led by Fearnley Whittingstall QC and Colin Duncan appeared on the other side. It was a fascinating battle of tactics and advocacy. In the result, I think both parties were granted a decree.

The third case which I recollect was before an official referee. Official referees try detailed and complicated building disputes. I forget the details of the case but one thing sticks in my mind – as I subsequently discovered, Douglas's opponent was not regarded as the most trustworthy. I had no idea then that there were some at the bar who could not be trusted or had a reputation for sharp behaviour. Thus when during some adjournment Douglas asked me to stay and look after his papers, it never crossed my mind that the object of that was to prevent our opponent from sneaking over and having a quick look at the proofs of our witnesses. Such is the naivety of young men.

There came the wonderful day when the clerk came into Douglas's room with a set of papers and said 'Mr Popplewell, there are some papers for you'. My excitement knew no bounds. It was a set of papers to draft a divorce petition. The solicitors were Levett and Son. John Levett and I had read law at Cambridge together. He thought it safe to entrust this case, which turned out to be an undefended divorce, to me. I read the papers from beginning to end no fewer than a dozen times, as if my life depended on it. Indeed it did. I drafted the petition. Douglas vetted it and off it went. I thereby earned my first money at the bar, the princely sum of £2 4s 6d.

Then came the great day when I went across to court and put on my wig and gown, to conduct my first case in court. I met the wife petitioner outside court. She confided in me that she had never been in court. I forbore to say 'snap'. We went into court and 20 minutes later I emerged, having persuaded the judge it was an appropriate case to grant a decree. My client was now successfully divorced from her husband. It could not be described as the forensic triumph of all time. At least I had not lost my voice. I had called the judge my Lord. I had managed to ask the right questions without leading. The result had pleased the client. A small celebration that night completed an exciting day.

I was Douglas's pupil for a year. I read his papers and started to write opinions of my own in his cases. He was kindness itself in correcting them. He once had to point out that phrases like 'instructing solicitors really must do more investigation in this case' were unlikely to assist the lay client. More particularly, the solicitors were unlikely to continue to send further instructions. Gradually I found fewer corrections on my opinions. There was one magic day when I discovered that, apart from the phrase 'I have carefully considered these papers', my opinion had gone out as Douglas's draft unamended.

Chambers comprised a somewhat diverse group. The head of chambers was Gerald Gardiner QC, later to become the Lord Chancellor. He was a most distinguished figure and advocate. He had a very large practice of the highest quality, little of which was funnelled down to rest of chambers. He was a somewhat austere figure, of whom pupils stood in awe. It was the customary etiquette at the bar to address fellow members by their surname, but to say 'Good morning Gardiner' always seemed to me to be less than courteous and somewhat impertinent. I therefore used simply to say 'Good morning'.

Another member of chambers was an elderly member of the bar called B. B. Stenham, who then had a pupil, John Archer, subsequently to take silk in my old chambers. He had a curious mix of practice: commercial clients and some criminal work. Additionally, there was

Michael Underhill, later to take silk and become a judge at the Old Bailey. We were to meet frequently on opposite sides on the Oxford circuit. He had also recently been Douglas's pupil. He appeared to me to have little or no work at that time. In another room was John Lawrence, whose practice seemed of the most modest. Percy Harris, who sat in Douglas's room, only occasionally seemed to have any work.

There was no interchange of views between the various members of chambers. On one particularly dreadful occasion one of Douglas's chairs was borrowed by another member of chambers without permission being sought. It was as though the crown jewels had been stolen. Adam was the clerk; he was an old-fashioned clerk who, I am sure, organised the chambers well. Unfortunately, he appeared to have an aversion to income tax. When he died his drawers were found full of income-tax demands for members of chambers. They had never been put on their bill. The sad consequence was that very large sums were required from them because of Adam's default.

Douglas had the somewhat strange practice of not allowing his pupils to take part in conferences in his room. Quite why, I never understood. It is in fact one of the more important aspects of a pupillage to be present at conferences, partly to see how they should be conducted and partly also because if a conference were thought necessary it formed part of the pupil's education and understanding of the case.

I thus had an agreeable year under Douglas's pupillage. From time to time I would go down to the Old Bailey and London Sessions, where I would put on my wig and gown and sit in the row for barristers in the hope of getting a brief. In those days before legal aid had taken off, and indeed for many years after, any prisoner who had the sum of £2 4s 6d (£2.22) could ask for what was called a dock brief. This enabled a prisoner armed with that sum to choose any member of the bar who was robed and happened to be in court to appear for them. It was considered bad form, when it was announced that a prisoner was to be put up who wanted a dock brief, for counsel to leave the court. This sometimes resulted in eminent members of the bar, who were engaged in some other case before the court, finding themselves having to appear in a case for what was then the minimum fee, much to their own and their clerk's annoyance.

However, for the young it was a source of income. Indeed also for some of the old, because one of the saddest features of that period was to see elderly barristers who had no work clutching some old brief which they had once had in their youth, sitting in court and pretending that they were fully engaged. In fact, all they were waiting for was the crumbs from these dock briefs. That they were most of them no good did not make it any less sad.

Occasionally there was also a legal-aid defence which was handed out by the clerk of the court. The clerk was a very important figure. A prisoner would be put up in the dock and would be asked if he or she pleaded guilty or not guilty. Sometimes the prisoner would plead not guilty and ask to be represented. The clerk would then ask whether the prisoner had any money, to which the answer would be 'no'. The clerk would there and then award legal aid, and would pass a message to the judge that a certain barrister should have the brief. The judge would look into the middle distance and, announcing the barrister's name, say 'Would you be good enough to appear on behalf of the prisoner?' The judge had no idea who the barrister was, but it was a kindly way of enabling young barristers to do a little work and it resulted in a fee of £4 7s 6d (now £4.37).

It was also part of the continuing education of a young barrister to see criminal practitioners at work. It was an entirely different way of life from the way that Douglas conducted his practice. While the judges in the civil courts seemed to me august, distant and rather academic characters, those conducting criminal trials at that time seemed to be something out of the nineteenth century. They were very frightening, particularly to young people. Unlike the present day, juries were not encouraged to retire to consider their verdicts. Indeed, the usual admonition to the jury after a summing-up, sometimes of less than half an hour, went something like this: 'Members of the jury, that's all I have to say. Would you now like to turn among yourselves and tell me whether you find the prisoner guilty or not guilty.' It was an infrequent occurrence for jurors to say that they wanted to retire to consider.

The quality of advocacy in the criminal court seemed to me to be at a fairly low level. The theory which had been dinned into me that the accused was innocent until found guilty and that the burden of proof was on the prosecution seemed to be a concept wholly unknown at that time, either at the Old Bailey or to London Sessions. Sentences too seemed to be draconian. For a probation report to be asked for was such an uncommon event as to warrant comment. Those who conducted prosccutions either at the Bailey or at the London Sessions at that time seemed to me then, and indeed now, to have proceeded on the basis that anyone charged could only be there because they were guilty and that the court's time was being wholly wasted by pathetic attempts by defence counsel to challenge the evidence. I confess that at that time and subsequently for a number of years, I thought that to describe London Sessions and the Old Bailey in those days as courts of justice was doing damage to the English language. In due course a quite different breed of prosecutors and thence judges took over the reins. The ordinary notions of justice then started to permeate the conduct of criminal trials both at the Bailey and at London Sessions and the judges there now properly enjoy a high reputation.

I was fortunate enough to obtain a brief at London Sessions by way of legal aid. It was for a man who had stolen some goods. He was hotly pursued by the police in Sicilian Way off Kingsway, caught, arrested and charged. It was my first criminal trial – indeed, the first case in which I had to cross-examine any witnesses. I was armed with Archbold's *Criminal Pleadings and Practice*. I bore in mind all the rules of evidence that I had learnt in my bar exams. I avoided as best I could leading questions of my client. I attempted to put into effect the art of cross-examination, which Sir Patrick Hastings described so vividly in his book.

Alas, what seemed easy on paper proved difficult in practice. My attempts to persuade the police officer that my client had not admitted his guilt were fruitless. No doubt today simply to suggest that a police officer had made it up would have ensured his acquittal. In those days it did nothing more than to ensure that a conviction was inevitable. So it turned out. I emerged from that case considerably chastened about my ability as an advocate. Nor was I much consoled to be told by Douglas that there really was no defence. Every young member of the bar believes that his or her client is either guiltless in a criminal case or faultless in a civil case. The ability to assess a case was one of the lessons it was necessary to learn in order to become a successful practitioner.

In the same way, every pupil believes that his or her master is the fount of all wisdom and that the master's views on law are unarguable, and that a case is lost only because of the stupidity of the judge, who has failed to appreciate the quality of the master's argument. It was only later that I came to realise that while Douglas possessed a fund of common sense and charm, his views on law were somewhat suspect. It was also borne in on me that not every case that we lost was due to the judge's failure to understand the brilliant argument of my master.

One of the more amusing cases that Douglas had was when he was against a litigant in person. I remember nothing about the facts of the case save that the litigant had once appeared in the House of Lords as a litigant in person. He had succeeded on that application before their lordships, who had congratulated him on the quality of his advocacy. This, I believe, had occurred some 40 years before. It was a compliment the full effect of which their Lordships could scarcely have contemplated, because he then became a vexatious litigant, bringing action after action, to the great distress of a number of perfectly ordinary law-abiding citizens. In this particular case, while we were in the Court of Appeal, Douglas was called a criminal abortionist by this litigant. This was too much even for the urbane Douglas Lowe. It was I think the only time that I knew him completely to lose his temper. A scene of what to me was unparalleled amusement then occurred before their Lordships.

I was due to finish my pupillage in July 1952. It was clear to me that there was no prospect of staying on as a tenant in those chambers. It was equally clear that even if there had been a prospect of staying on, there was no work for a young man. What I wanted was a chambers where there was a lot of small work available which could be handed to a young man to cut his teeth on. Neither Percy Harris nor Michael Underhill at that time were generating enough work to pass on. Thus the question arose as to where I was to go to look for chambers.

Getting a tenancy then, as now, is the single most important step which young barristers take. It may well be that they can stay on in the chambers where they have been a pupil. If they have been a pupil in a good set of chambers, by and large that is the very best step that they can take. They will know a number of the members of the chambers and will have met some of the firms of solicitors who bring work to chambers. The clerk will have had an opportunity of assessing their merit. Other members of chambers will have got to know their abilities and therefore would be happy to entrust some devilling work or returns of theirs to them. That was not the situation that faced me. I had no contacts other than Anthony Hawke, nor indeed any strings to pull. Douglas was kind enough to enquire of other sets of chambers whether they would take me on, but in the result, I managed to find chambers through a totally different channel.

In the summer before I started with Douglas I had been on a cricket tour with the Butterflies to Germany. Among those taking part, unknown to me before, was a solicitor called Ken Gardiner. He was in the firm of Gardiner and Co., which was a well-known firm of solicitors in London, dealing with insurance work. Although I did not know it at the time, the senior partner was Geoffrey Gardiner, Ken's older brother. As I understand it the father had left the practice to Geoffrey as partner and Ken simply as a solicitor.

When we were in Germany playing cricket, I talked to Ken about what I was going to do at the bar and that I was going to be a pupil of Douglas Lowe's. He said to me that if I ever needed any help I was to get in touch with him. And during the summer of 1952 I did. He was kind enough to suggest that I might like to go and see the chambers of Ronnie Armstrong-Jones at 5 Essex Court. Ronnie Armstrong-Jones was Tony's father. In those chambers was Hugh Griffiths, whom I had last seen playing cricket when he had come to play for the Free Foresters at Cambridge. I remembered him from being the school fast-bowler at Charterhouse.

Acting on Ken's advice I went to see Hugh and talked to him. He was kind enough to suggest that he would have a word with Ronnie and so also did Ken. Ken's firm provided Armstrong-Jones' set of chambers with a substantial amount of work. All I knew about them was that they were a 'running-down set', that is to say they dealt exclusively with motor-accident cases. I knew nothing about motor-accident work, nor about insurance. I understood that there was a lot of small work about and that there was an opportunity there to earn some money. Accordingly on a day appointed, I went to 5 Essex Court to be interviewed by Ronnie.

Douglas's room at 12 Kings Bench Walk was full of the most lovely furniture, and although the chambers were at the top of some stone stairs the rooms were all well furnished and comfortably well decorated. When I first went round to Essex Court I thought I had gone to the wrong place. The tiled walls on the staircase made it look like a public lavatory. Hugh Griffiths was then sharing a room with two – if not three – others, in what can only be properly described as a cupboard. I was shown into Ronnie's room which, while nicely furnished, was very small. Ronnie himself was a very shy man and this manifested itself in a very marked stutter. He always talked as if he had a plum in his mouth, and was a very nervous advocate. But he overcame this handicap and succeeded in building up a large and successful practice almost entirely confined to motor accidents. He disliked appearing in the Court of Appeal or doing Factory Act cases. Above all he was very good at public relations and he went out of his way to be exceptionally charming to solicitors and claims managers who were the life blood of chambers' practice. He was particularly good at encouraging the young men in chambers and persuading work their way. He also had a quiet flair for cross-examination. I remember in one case he persuaded a court that a witness who had taken a solitary drink before lunch must have been paralytic by the evening.

He was obviously fairly unenthusiastic about this young man who was being thrust upon him by Ken. Nor was he wholly receptive to the suggestion that I could come in and be a tenant. He observed that there really was no room in chambers. I looked wildly round his room and suggested that I might sit in a corner. This fell on somewhat stony ground but eventually, no doubt with the assistance behind the scenes of Hugh Griffiths and Ken Gardiner, I was invited to become a tenant.

At that stage the chambers did not have the fixed rule of only having tenants who had been pupils in chambers. The purpose of that rule was so that other members of chambers could see and judge the quality of the pupil and more importantly could judge whether the pupil would be likely to fit in as a person with the rest of chambers. Life in chambers is lived at a very close personal level. You need to get on with those with whom you are going to work for 30 years. This rule did not apply at that time, but immediately after I became a tenant it did. I was too pleased at becoming a tenant to appreciate the significance of it.

Unknown to me, my arrival in chambers caused some distress to Raymond Kidwell. He at that time was pupil to Patrick O'Connor, subsequently to become Lord Justice O'Connor. Raymond had won almost every prize at Oxford and was about to become a tenant. He suddenly heard that this fellow Popplewell from outside chambers was being wished on chambers by Ken Gardiner, and imagined that his prospects of becoming a tenant would thereby be damaged. Happily this anxiety turned out to be unfounded. Within a few weeks of my arrival he too became a tenant and harmony was restored.

It was a remarkably friendly collection of barristers. In one room, which was known as the colonels' room, because they had all been colonels during the war, were Frank Cassels, later to become chairman of London Sessions, Toby Springer, later to become a stipendiary magistrate, and Ken Barraclough, later to become Chief Metropolitan Magistrate. In another room was Ted Eveleigh, later to be Lord Justice Eveleigh, and Niall McDermott, later to be a minister in Harold Wilson's government and in charge of some international lawyers in Geneva.

In yet another room was Ted Branson, father of Richard Branson, and Maurice Holmes. Maurice Holmes's family had run a transport business. When the transport industry had been nationalised he had decided to come to the bar and practice. Most of his work at that time was in relation to the transport world. He subsequently left chambers to become chairman of London Transport. Other members of chambers were Hugh Griffiths, later to become Lord Griffiths, Michael Ogden, later to become Sir Michael Ogden QC, Raymond Kidwell and Patrick Bennett, both of whom later became QCs, and Robin Carey Evans, who left the bar at an early age.

In a room on his own was Mark Van Oss. Mark Van Oss was an elderly bachelor who had a practice almost wholly unconnected with that of the rest of the chambers. He was regarded as a great fount of wisdom on the subject of pleadings. But he was terrifying to young men because if ever you went to see him to ask him for assistance he would require full details of the investigation that you had concluded so far. If it did not seem to have involved any great deal of work, off you would be sent packing to complete your investigations before seeking to pick his brains.

Ronnie Armstrong-Jones had his own room, which I have described, and in yet another room was Patrick O'Connor. Patrick's room one can only describe as the size of a broom cupboard. It had, if my recollection is right, a broken-down sofa, two chairs and a table. Patrick had one of the largest practices in chambers. To me, coming from the rather smart King's Bench Walk, it appeared as though I had left the Savoy and come to a doss-house. My room, which I shared with Michael Ogden and Martin McClaren (later to become an MP and PPS to Alex Douglas-Home), was in the wig shop. At the entrance to the passageway from Middle Temple up to Fleet Street there was a little wooden building which had originally been a shop, from which wigs had been sold before the war. The shop had either gone out of business or been taken over, and it was now part of chambers annexe. The shop retained its glass windows, and in this little wig shop the three of us sat.

It had a number of disadvantages. It had no telephone, so that if the clerks wanted to get hold of us somebody had to come down. If a solicitor wanted to speak to one of us we had to go into the main building to speak to them. There was little or no heating. Ronnie's idea of economy was to allow, even in the coldest time, the use only of a one bar fire. The walls were wooden and the cold was extreme. On the other hand in the summer the glass windows acted like a greenhouse. If the door was open the heat could be reduced, but that encouraged visitors to the Middle Temple to treat the building as if it was an information centre.

Presiding over this set of chambers was the head clerk, Harold Standring. He was splendidly Victorian. He had old-fashioned ideas about behaviour, about discipline and about how solicitors should be treated. It was indeed no bad thing to be brought up in that world. There were still solicitors who were known as ambulance-chasers. They would go to the scene of an accident, leave their calling card with the victim and then seek to appear for them. There were some who conducted cases on a contingency basis. It was of course forbidden by the Law Society in those days, but now is all the rage. It did not prevent some solicitors from acting on the basis that if they won they would get something back from the client. There were solicitors then, and indeed for a considerable part of my time at the bar, who either would not pay counsel's fees or were very slow to pay them. Harold did his best to sort out the sheep from the goats and to protect the members of his chambers from being exploited by disreputable solicitors.

I remember one occasion when I had a brief returned by Harold on the basis that the solicitors were not the sort of solicitors with whom chambers wanted to do business, as a result of previous incidents. There had been a time in the past when a cheque was enclosed with the brief but that had gone. The minimum fee had recently gone up from one guinea to two guineas. In real terms, a two-guinea brief resulted in the receipt by the member of the bar of £2 4s 6d. Of that £2 4s 6d the barrister got two pounds. The shillings in the pound which made the two guineas went to the clerk and the other 2s 6d was the clerk's fee. Under Harold was William Roberts, subsequently to become our head clerk and a distinguished chairman of the Barristers Clerks

Association. Although Harold had general responsibility for the work of chambers it was William who really looked after the young men, talked to the solicitors and the managing clerks about their prowess and obtained work for us.

Chambers in those days had about four or five solicitor clients. They were all doing general insurance work and in particular motor-insurance work – Hewitt Woolacott and Chown, Gardiner and Co, Berrymans, L. Bingham & Co. and Ponsford and Devenish. There were other firms which sent us some work, but these were the principal solicitors and were carefully nurtured. One very large and distinguished firm of solicitors who did insurance work had a policy not to send chambers any of its work. It apparently went back to some frisson before the war when papers had been sent down to Ronnie. In the papers was a note from the senior partner to insurers, suggesting that they should not instruct Mr Armstrong-Jones because it was their experience that he frequently returned briefs at the last moment. Ronnie was a person who was not prepared to take any criticism lightly. He looked up his records. He found that what the senior partner said was not accurate. He insisted on the senior partner writing to the claims manager telling him that what he had been told was quite untrue. Not unnaturally, this did not endear Ronnie to the senior partner. The result was that thereafter, and certainly right up to the time that I left chambers, that firm of solicitors scarcely ever instructed us. The fact that, by 1983 at any rate, all the parties involved were either dead or retired did not in any way affect the continued frisson.

In chambers, because of the diversity of the work, we used to keep a list of witnesses ranging from medical witnesses, both pro-plaintiff and pro-defendant, to road-traffic experts, to factory experts, to trampoline experts, fire experts and so on. The idea was that any member of chambers who came across an expert witness would record his or her name and details on the list with suitable comments. This gave rise to one or two humorous entries, although it was in fact a serious document. One member of chambers had entered the name of Mr A, and another had written under 'comments', 'Surely he is dead'. Yet another member added his views: 'This is not so, it's merely the appearance he gives in the witness box'.

In 1951 'running down' had a rather pejorative connotation. It was not highly regarded by other members of the bar as being either very intellectual or very smart. The chambers practice broadened, firstly into general insurance work, then into building work and then into commercial work. But for the young people in chambers the first few years were spent travelling around the country appearing in magistrates courts on behalf of defendants. We were instructed by insurers to represent dangerous and careless drivers. We went to inquests to seek to avoid damaging admissions being made by a driver, so that when the Fatal Accident Act claim came to be dealt with in the High Court, insurers' liability for damages would be minimised.

As almost all the drivers whom we represented in the magistrates court had indeed been guilty of some traffic offence, victories were few and far between. It was, however, a marvellous nursery in which to learn the art of advocacy. The prosecutors in the London area were instructed by the solicitors for the Metropolitan Police. They were young rising solicitors mainly, who were anxious to pursue their career through successful prosecutions. There was therefore not much love lost between them and us. They saw us as tiresome young members of the bar who were always trying to take technical points and show how clever we were.

At that time litigation in solicitors' offices, particularly those doing insurance work, was mainly conducted by managing clerks. They had no or little legal training except what they had learnt by years of practice. They were battle-wise and knew every trick of the trade. Their assessment of young members of the bar was probably a very shrewd one. Below them were youths 17 or 18 years old who came out to court with the young barrister. They usually demanded to be taken by car. They almost certainly required to have their lunch paid for them. Their main topic of conversation was either football or pop music, and their assessment of the young barristers' performance was in direct proportion to the quality of comfort in the car, the standard of meal provided and the interest shown by the young barrister in the turgid discussions of football and music.

The stipendiary magistrates in the London area were for most part tolerant of the young men doing this work. They recognised that broadly the motions had to be gone through and honour satisfied. They generally listened with an astonishing amount of patience to what must have been enormously inept cross-examination. There were, of course, some fierce and unattractive stipendiaries who made life a misery for the bar. It was not surprising sometimes that their patience wore thin. However, there was a splendid stipendiary at Greenwich before whom I frequently appeared. After my third unsuccessful defence of a careless driver in one morning, he turned to me and said 'Mr Popplewell, I do hope some time you will get a case where you can have a victory'.

About the various magistrates courts where we appeared, there were of course many stories told. The chairman of the Bromley Bench once said 'There is a doubt in this case but we are not going to give you the benefit of it'. Minnie Ling, who sat at Dartford Magistrates Court for years, was a terror. Her only words in court were 'We convict'. Sometimes this was pronounced before the defendant had a chance to give evidence, in which case there would be a joyful trip to the divisional court to set the conviction aside, but those occasions were rare. There was one celebrated occasion when she suddenly announced 'We acquit'. The look of surprise and horror on the face of all those in court could only properly be described in a Bateman cartoon.

Outside the immediate London area, magistrates in the country regarded the appearance of counsel with very great suspicion. They were thought likely to lead the magistrates into confusion and error, and were only there because the litigant was plainly guilty. At Beaconsfield Magistrates Court the chairman at one time had been a Commissioner of the Metropolitan Police. He had now retired. He had a hearing aid. When the police officer was giving evidence against the defendant the hearing aid was switched on fully, so that the chairman could hear. When counsel for the defendant rose to cross-examine, that was a signal for the hearing aid to be switched off – ostentatiously. When the defendant came to give his evidence, the hearing aid remained off. But when the prosecutor or policeman got up to cross-examine again, the hearing aid would be switched on. Thus the chairman could savour the difficulties which the defendant had in explaining himself. The clerks too were a law unto themselves. They directed magistrates on points of law and sometimes on questions of fact, until they were discouraged by higher courts. They were generally rude to young counsel and interfered in a number of cases often to show that they were running the court. But all in all it was a tremendous training ground, and in addition to teaching us the geography of the London area it enabled us to make our own terrible mistakes without doing our clients any real damage.

I remember two particular examples of over-questioning. I was defending some careless driver in a magistrates court and getting nowhere in my cross-examination of a particular witness. He had described my client's car as going very fast, and I tried to pin him down to the precise speed at which he said my client was going. Although I asked him a number of times, he said he couldn't really say and I rather pooh-poohed this, saying that anyone can give an estimate and why didn't he try, or was he trying to deceive the court and so on and so forth. He turned to me, and looking me straight in the eye said, 'Well if you really want to know, I have never seen a car go as fast as that in all my life!'

The other incident involved a friend of mine who was defending a man called Danny charged with driving under the influence of drink. This was in the days before the breathalyser, and counsel for Danny called in support of his client's evidence a man who was a distinguished local worthy who explained that he had known Danny for a long time. He said that Danny was not the sort of person to behave like that and that he, the local worthy, could vouch for the fact that he was a thoroughly sensible young man who would never have behaved in the way alleged. And he went on to say that on the particular day when the incident was alleged to have occurred he had seen Danny and could vouch for his condition. The local worthy was cross-examined 'up hill and down dale' as to how he could possibly remember the particular day, but he stood his ground. At the end of the cross-examination, counsel for Danny was about to release the local worthy, who had made a very good impression. Unhappily, his instructing solicitor tugged his gown and in a hoarse whisper said, 'He's got a diary so he can prove the date'. Counsel stood up and said, 'Just a moment. Do you have a diary?' To which the local worthy replied that he had. 'Do you happen to have the diary with you?' He replied that he did have it with him. 'Would you mind looking at it and seeing if that helps you?' So the local worthy fished in his pocket and got out the diary. He opened it at the particular date. There was then a pause and the local worthy went white; the judge intervened and said, 'Well come on, tell us what it says'. In a faltering voice the local worthy read it out as follows: 'Danny dead drunk again'.

Life at the bar in 1951 could not be more different from today. Firstly, it was a very small community consisting of no more than

2000–3000 barristers, whereas now there are some 10,000 barristers practising in London and on circuit. While there was nothing like the same difficulty about getting into chambers as there is now, there was little or no work for the young barristers when they did get into chambers. Almost all the aspiring barristers tried to make a living by giving lectures, talks and other forms of activity. The most talented, of course, were able to go back to their university and tutor potential lawyers.

I managed to get some lecturing at Ealing College sponsored by the local council, for which I received the handsome remuneration of two pounds per week. I started the lectures in October and went through to Christmas when there was a holiday break, and then there were another eight weeks in the New Year. I began with 24 in the audience but of course as the weather got bad and Christmas approached, the numbers started to dwindle. This was potentially disastrous because unless there was an audience of 16 the local authority would no longer support the course. I therefore had to devise ways and means of interesting the audience so as to ensure that they turned up the following week.

I rapidly realised that the more intricate details of the law of tort were of singularly little interest to most of them, whereas stories about Crippen were likely to excite the interest of even the most unenthusiastic students. Thus, at the end of each week I would announce that the following week I would be discussing, in all the gory details, how X came to be murdered, how Y came to be charged, what the result of the case was and what lessons were to be learnt. Although my numbers got as low as 18, I managed to keep them going until Christmas. I then announced that there would be an entirely new programme in the Easter term which would be of immense interest to them now that they had had some familiarity with the law. Thus for two years I managed to earn what seemed a fortune giving these lectures. Whether the students ever profited by it I never knew. I also sat on and chaired a number of wages councils, which helped to resolve pay disputes in those industries where there was no national agreement. This was very interesting and rewarding, though not financially. It provided an insight into industrial relations and helped to hone my mediation skills.

It was absolutely essential to have some form of income, because life at the bar was not exactly all silk and money. In my first year I earned £202. The clerks took the clerk's fee and the shillings in the guineas. The fact that I earned that amount did not mean I actually received it in the year. Solicitors were very slow in paying; additionally in those days any legal aid civil work resulted in a payment of only 85 per cent of the fee marked. The reason for this was apparently based on the theory that as there were always bad debts of about 15 per cent for the bar, the government thought it would not enrich the bar and deducted 15 per cent. Thus, for a great number of years the bar subsidised the legal-aid scheme to the tune of 15 per cent. Although legal-aid work was guaranteed payment, because it took so long to be paid (and still is), it always seemed something of a government racket.

In my second year I made £592, including two briefs which were marked in double figures. This was truly exciting. The normal brief fee for appearing in a magistrates court or at an inquest, certainly in the London area, was £2 4s 6d, two pounds for the barrister, 2s 6d for the clerk's fee and the two shillings in the guineas were for the clerk. One day it was decided by the clerks that no-one in chambers should appear in the magistrates court or at inquests for less then three guineas. This decision was made in order either to increase the reputation of the chambers or to increase the earning power. However, its practical effect was considerably less enchanting.

The next brief to come down to chambers was for me and was marked two guineas. The clerk rang up the solicitors and said that 'Mr Popplewell does not do cases in the magistrates courts for less than £3 3s'. The solicitors, no doubt much miffed, said, 'Very well, please send the brief back and we will go to another set of chambers who will do it for two guineas'. It has to be said that while this was only a temporary hiccup it was a matter of considerable importance to me at the time.

In those days it was *de rigueur* to wear a black jacket, pin-striped trousers, to carry a rolled umbrella and have a bowler hat. The number of bowler hats that I left on the train were legion, and constituted a very considerable outlay. The purpose of having a bowler hat, I believe, was to enable the bar to take off their hats to the judges when they recognised them. This was fine in theory, but to me as a young man at the bar, High Court judges were virtually unknown. There was a very learned judge called Mr Justice Slade who had been a skilled advocate and had appeared for William Joyce in his trial for treason. He was distinguished-looking, and for about eight years I took my hat off to him whenever I met him. One day when I did this a friend of mine with whom I was walking said, 'Why did you take your hat off?' I replied, 'That was Mr Justice Slade'. He pointed out that it was not Mr Justice Slade, and that although he bore considerable similarity to him he was but an ordinary junior member of the bar like me. He must have been somewhat astonished that, week in and week out, this young barrister took his hat off to him.

There was a very strong code of conduct. When barristers were called to the bar, certainly by the Inner Temple, they were provided with a book called *Conduct at the Bar*, with all sorts of strictures as to how young barristers ought to behave and warning them against doing anything which might bring them or their reputation into disrepute. Barristers were not allowed to indulge in business, and most particularly they were not allowed to tout. The idea of a barrister going to the office of a firm of solicitors for a conference or consultation or having a party to which solicitors were to be invited was total anathema.

There was an Inner Temple ball in aid of charity, the Gainsford Ball, to which we decided to go. Margaret cheerfully rang up a number of our friends to invite them to come. She knew nothing of the etiquette of the bar. Among those she invited was a solicitor friend of ours, who at no time ever provided me with any work. We were godparents to each other's children. I had to explain to Margaret that this was wholly unacceptable, and that these nice solicitor friends would have to be told that they could not come to this dance.

These rules sometimes reached absurd proportions. I once went to Gloucester to do a case instructed by Geoffrey Gardiner, the senior partner of Gardiner & Co. We travelled down in the train together, which we were allowed to do, and we stayed at the same hotel in Gloucester. However, I was required to dine separately from him so that there was no appearance of my touting for business. The whole thing was quite absurd and led to a good deal of ill-feeling between the solicitors and barristers. The solicitors felt, not unnaturally, that they were being treated as second-class citizens. To be seen drinking with a solicitor – or even worse, with a solicitor's managing clerk – was regarded almost as a capital offence.

The bar was divided into circuits. Unless one wanted to practise entirely in London it was necessary to join a circuit. The southeastern was very popular circuit because it was within range of London, and there were a number of members of my chambers who were members of the southeastern circuit. Ted Eveleigh was a member of the Oxford circuit, as was Martin McClaren. It was thought sensible that I should also join the Oxford circuit, so that if there was any work that they could not do on circuit, it might come my way. At the time, if a solicitor wanted to brief a member of the bar who was not a member of that particular circuit, that solicitor had to pay what was called a special fee, and a junior from the circuit had to be instructed. It was a restrictive practice which was designed to ensure that each circuit could provide enough work for the barristers on it.

Accordingly I joined the Oxford circuit, which was one of the smaller circuits. The assize system still operated, and thus at the beginning of each term a High Court judge would set out, starting at Reading then onto Oxford, Gloucester, Worcester, Hereford, Newport, Shrewsbury, Stafford and Birmingham. At Birmingham the Oxford circuit and the Midland circuit had equal rights of audience. It did, however, give rise to a good deal of dispute. If a case started on the Oxford circuit, say at Stafford, and had to be moved to Birmingham, only an Oxford circuiteer could do it. Likewise, if a case came from the Midland circuit (such as Warwick) to Birmingham, only a Midland circuiteer could do it. Even more arcane were the rules governing appearance at Birmingham quarter sessions, where I believe sometime in the early part of the century an agreement had been struck between various sets of chambers as to who or who was not allowed to appear at Birmingham quarter sessions. Luckily I was never involved in this dispute, as I did no criminal work at Birmingham.

One advantage of a small circuit was that everybody knew everybody and it was possible for discipline to be regulated. If anyone stepped out of line the word soon went round the circuit. The leader of the circuit would send for the luckless barrister, who would be admonished as to his or her future conduct. These old-fashioned rules may now seem outdated, but it ensured that there was trust between the bar and the bench and trust between opposing barristers. The general public may not appreciate how important it is that such a trust should exist, and only when the rules are bent by some unscrupulous advocate does the system start to break down. Because it was a small circuit it was possible to know one's opponents well, to know their weaknesses and their strengths, and to appreciate the camaraderie of the bar. Nowhere was it better to be found than on circuit. To be constantly against another barrister, to be in court against that barrister over a period of days or weeks, to stay in the same hotel and suffer the same trials and tribulations from the judges, cemented a great deal of friendship.

At the beginning of each assize the clerk of assize would read the commission directed to the judge or judges. The High Sheriff would present the judge with the several writs and precepts and then the judge would start trying the serious criminal cases. The reading of the commission was a formidable undertaking and was a matter of great solemnity. We had two great clerks of assize in my time: Tumin, father of Sir Stephen Tumin, and Bill Lewis, whose reading of the commission was a work of great oratory. Sometimes the clerk of assize would have a legal-aid defence which he could hand out to young counsel. Sometimes there was a dock brief. Once selected, the barrister would go and see the prisoner down in the cell. It was vitally important to obtain the £2 4s 6d before acting for the prisoner, because most of the cases were so hopeless that there was no possibility of getting anything from the prisoner once convicted. It was some years before the dock brief was abolished. It was as well, as it was an unattractive feature of the system. But for those of us who were without work it was often worth visiting a criminal court, either at quarter sessions or on assize, firstly, to be seen by solicitors (this did not count as touting), and secondly, there was always a possibility of a dock brief or a legal-aid brief.

Thus one Monday morning I was sitting at Gloucester quarter sessions when a prisoner asked for a dock brief. He selected me. His crime was stealing lead off the roof of a church. I went to see him. I was wise enough to get the money off him. He told me his tale, which was essentially that he was on the roof but he was only there as a lark. I was required to put forward this unlikely story, which I did on Monday, Tuesday and up to Wednesday lunchtime – at which time the jury for some reason disagreed.

The Clerk of the Peace very kindly allowed me now to have legal aid, which in those days was £4 7s 6d however long the case lasted. I went into the adjoining court and fought the case on Wednesday afternoon, Thursday and Friday, when the jury returned a verdict of guilty. I returned home to Margaret, who enquired what I had been doing. I was able to tell her that I had been in court every day of the week. She was naturally excited about this and said, 'Well how much money have we made?' I explained to her that I had made £6 12s, of which 12 shillings had to go to the clerk. Thus I had earned the princely sum of six pounds. She was very pleased. I then explained to her that what with the cost of travelling down to Gloucester and back and of staying in a hotel, my expenses totalled some £25, whereupon she said that she hoped that I would not be in court the following week.

On circuit there were hotels where the bar were required to stay, known as the bar hotels. If you were in an assize town during the assize and did not stay at the bar hotel, questions would be asked. It was customary to entertain the judge at one or more of the circuit towns. At Gloucester this was done at the Bell Hotel, where the bar stayed. In those days it was possible for the hotel to provide not merely bedrooms for the bar, who might vary in number from 2 or 3 to 30, but also to provide private rooms where we could all meet and discuss circuit affairs. They were immensely valuable occasions for the young members of the bar. All the senior members of the circuit would be present, discussing the affairs of the circuit, questions of advocacy, questions of etiquette and generally indulging in legal gossip. The dinners were of a high quality. The circuit had its own wine, which was paid for out of circuit funds and kept in a cellar at the hotel.

When the judge was invited to dinner the judge would sit at the top table with the senior members of the circuit. After a dinner where there were no speeches, younger members of the circuit would be brought up to sit next to and try and entertain the judge. It was for the young person a somewhat frightening business, but it enabled the judge to get to know one or two younger members of the bar, which made appearing before that judge subsequently much less daunting. A great deal of drink was consumed, which is what the public perceive to be commonplace among barristers. Thereafter there was quite often bridge played and cases settled before the next day's work started.

Having finished at one assize town, the judge would move on to the next assize town to be greeted by the High Sheriff of the adjoining county, and legal work would all start again. There were local bars at the time, though mostly confined to the big cities. On the Oxford circuit there was a flourishing bar at Birmingham. They tended to do a lot of work at Shrewsbury and in Stafford as well as at Birmingham, but less at the periphery of the circuit such as Gloucester, Newport and

Oxford, which is where I tended to have my practice. Ted Eveleigh had a big circuit practice and found increasingly that so far as the smaller work was concerned he was not able or willing to do it. Accordingly some of it came into my hands.

Solicitors on circuit tended to view a barrister as a jack of all trades, with the result that if a solicitor thought you were worth instructing he or she would send you not only personal injury work and criminal work but divorce work too. Quite often difficult points of landlord and tenant law were sent, and indeed on more than one occasion I was asked to advise on abstruse chancery matters and tax problems. It was often difficult to persuade a solicitor out in the country that one's knowledge of the law was not total and that they it would be far better off to employ some specialist counsel in the more recondite matters with which they were concerned. But of course, in my anxiety not to turn away work I have no doubt that on occasions I took on cases for which I was not properly qualified.

Solicitor advocates were comparatively uncommon. They were then allowed to appear in the county courts and in magistrates courts but not at quarter sessions or in the High Court. Even though they were allowed to appear in the county court it was quite often that in the more serious cases they instructed counsel. The local judges encouraged this practice by often being as beastly as they could to solicitor advocates.

The first day of the assize in any particular town was always marked by the High Sheriff having a luncheon party to which the bar were invited, whether or not the High Sheriff knew them and whether or not they in fact had any particular work at the assize. Thus out-of-work barristers could find themselves being fed very well on the first day. At some quarter sessions, particularly at Oxford city sessions, it was then customary for the city to provide lunch for the bar throughout the session. This again attracted the attention of young barristers. Quite properly, for reasons of economy the city decided that enough was enough and discontinued their generous provision.

Oxford city court was the scene of one of my more amusing cases, which involved Bob Hawke, subsequently the Prime Minister of Australia, who was then a Rhodes scholar at Oxford and aged 25 or so. He had had a distinguished sporting career and was close to getting into the university cricket side.

On this occasion he and another undergraduate called Jimmy Allan, who was the university slow left-arm bowler, were members of the University Air Squadron. They had gone to their annual dinner. Sometime after midnight, one of the company was not feeling very well, and so Hawke and Allan set out in their van to take this friend back to his college. It was now well after midnight. The rain was pouring down. Having safely delivered this young man they decided to return to the University Air Squadron grounds. They came down The High and were minded to turn into Longwall.

A police car saw them and gave chase, thinking that it was a stolen van. They got alongside the van and started indicating that the van should stop. Hawke took little or no notice and there was then a pursuit down Longwall and into the University Air Squadron grounds. When Hawke and Allan got out in the pouring rain they were seized by the police who arrested them on the grounds that they had stolen a van. Hawke was not much given to lying down under this sort of suggestion: he told them in no uncertain terms what they could do with themselves. The matter was only resolved when an official from the University Air Squadron pointed out to the police that the van was indeed Hawke's.

The police then announced that they were going to arrest and charge Hawke with dangerous driving. This they proceeded to do. The next thing that happened was he was up before the magistrates court defending himself. All his friends from Vincent's, the Oxford sporting club, sat in the gallery, cheering and making something of a nuisance of themselves. None of this much appealed to the magistrates, who found him guilty and fined him.

I was therefore instructed by the AA solicitors to go and appear for Hawke at the quarter sessions in front of a retired judge who was sitting in Oxford. One of my problems was that although Hawke had a very good driving record, he had had the misfortune to borrow either a policeman's helmet or a Belisha beacon on 5 November, had been charged with an offence and had pleaded guilty. His parents knew nothing about this and he was very anxious that they shouldn't. I was anxious that the recorder should be told what a good driving record he had. To lead that evidence, however, would have allowed my opponent who was prosecuting to ask him questions about this previous conviction. My opponent was a senior member of the circuit. I expected him to say that he would not ask about this conviction. However, he didn't, and told me I must take my own course. I still think he behaved badly. I was then left in the dilemma, which I resolved by not making any mention of his driving record.

Our troubles started at the very beginning. Allan was our star witness. However, he was at Worcester College, who were engaged that day in a rugger cup final. It was likely that we would need Allan early in the afternoon. The captain of Worcester Rugby Club came to see me and I pointed out the problem of Allan playing rugger in the afternoon. It was therefore arranged that the match should be brought forward and be played in the morning so that hopefully we could have Jimmy as our witness in the afternoon. All went quite well in the morning. The police officers did not do very well in the box and we made considerable headway. Hawke was a good witness and stood up to cross-examination by my opponent.

Then came the moment when we needed to call Allan. So I told the recorder that my next witness would be a Mr Allan and the usher went down the corridor crying out, 'Mr Allan, Mr Allan, Mr Allan'. He came back after a while and told the recorder that there was no answer. The recorder then asked where he was. I said that he was on university activities but was expected at any moment. Very shortly Jimmy arrived, out of breath and somewhat dishevelled. The apocryphal story was that he was given a 'Hawks' tie to wear. We brushed him down and tidied him up. He was 19 years old and undaunted by the grandeur of the court.

The recorder said, 'Where have you been young man?' Jimmy, without batting an eyelid, replied, 'Playing rugger, sir!' The recorder, 'You think that is important?' 'Yes sir, very important.' 'Why?' 'Cuppers final!' said Jimmy. 'Oh, did you win?' 'No.' 'Serves you right!' exclaimed the recorder; and then, 'Which College were you at?' Jimmy replied, 'Worcester College'. There was a long pause and the recorder said, 'Ah, my father's old College!' From that moment we never looked back. Hawke was triumphantly acquitted and we spent a very good evening at Vincent's celebrating. I was paid the princely sum of 15 guineas for this trial.

As it was to be my only, or at any rate my only substantial, triumph for a good number of years, I bored everybody in sight with this story. Time passed. Bob Hawke returned to Australia. He became a famous trade-union leader and then became Prime Minister of Australia. One day I received a letter from a Ms d'Alpuget, telling me that she was to write the definitive biography of Bob Hawke. She understood that I had appeared for him many years before and asked me to repeat the story on the tape which she had sent me. I thought it proper that I should consult Hawke before I recounted this tale. This I did. He replied that he had no objection and thus the story appeared in the biography written by Ms d'Alpuget. She is now Mrs Hawke. Many years later I met Hawke in Australia House when I was involved in the cricket world and reminded him of our encounter so many years before. I saw him again at the World Cup more recently, together with his wife, and we enjoyed a good laugh about the whole incident.

Although there was a strict code of discipline at the bar it has to be said that there a good number of ploys and doubtful tactics that nowadays would be frowned upon. 'Level playing fields' and 'cards on the table' are now current words in legal language. They did not exist in the early 1950s. Certainly some of the solicitors' managing clerks were as sharp as anyone. I remember once during a case in the High Court waiting in the corridor outside the court for the case to come on. The very experienced and crafty managing clerk from my solicitor's firm suddenly vanished. When he reappeared a few minutes later I said to him, 'Where have you been?' and he said, 'I've just been having a word with the witnesses so that the truth may more clearly emerge'.

There was another managing clerk who once instructed me in a case at Shrewsbury in front of Mr Justice Byrne. It was a damages only in that liability had been admitted. It was therefore a question for the judge to assess how much the case was worth. It is open to a defendant to make an offer to a plaintiff of a certain sum, the effect of which is that if the plaintiff does not recover more than the defendant's offer the plaintiff has to pay the defendant's costs after the offer. The offer is made by money being paid into court. For obvious reasons the judge is not aware of the amount which is paid into court and therefore gives his judgment wholly ignorant of it.

The managing clerk and the judge's clerk had been old friends. A judge's clerk's responsibility is to arrange his judge's affairs, to make sure the judge's papers are in proper order, that his time is efficiently spent and that his cases run smoothly. The judge's clerk and the managing clerk went out for a drink in the evening after all the evidence had been heard but before the judge had given judgment. The judge's clerk said to the managing clerk, 'I expect you have got some money in court, haven't you?' To which the clerk replied, 'Oh I couldn't possibly tell you that!' The judge's clerk said, 'Oh go on, I won't tell the judge'. My clerk said, 'No, no it would be quite wrong to tell you that'. However, after a number of drinks the judge's clerk persuaded the managing clerk to tell him that not only was there indeed money in court but exactly how much, namely £1500. This conversation was all unknown to me.

The next day the judge gave his judgment and finished up by saying, 'And taking everything into account, in my judgment the proper sum for damages is £1750'. The plaintiff's counsel asked for judgment in that sum whereupon I got up and said, 'I ought to tell your Lordship that there is £2000 in court'. This meant that the plaintiff had to pay our costs from the date of payment in. The managing clerk had knowingly misled the judge's clerk, and no doubt the judge's clerk had told the judge what sum was in court. None of this should have happened, but it gives some indication of how litigation was conducted in those days.

When I went on the bench I had Ken Wright as my first clerk. He was very experienced but a bit of a lower-deck lawyer. When he died I was extremely lucky to be looked after by Paula White and Rita Spence, who were marvellously efficient, charming and delightful to work with. They made my time on the bench, particularly on circuit, a real pleasure.

Very gradually my practice broadened and increased. Thus, on circuit, apart from civil work, I started to do some prosecuting at Gloucester, Oxford and Reading. In London I began to get some work in the road-haulage world. Maurice Holmes in our chambers had originally been involved in a transport undertaking which had been nationalised at the end of the war. He decided to come to the bar and he practised substantially in road-haulage litigation. In those days anyone who wanted to run road-haulage businesses needed to have various licences. This applied both to passenger and to freight. It was a world of its own as far as litigation was concerned. So far as passenger licenses were concerned, the objectors were bus companies running passenger services and most particularly British Rail. So far as freight was concerned, the objectors were almost always competitors.

These hearings were before inspectors in various parts of the country. They were enormously experienced and very able, as indeed were the practitioners who specialised in this field. There were a number of members at the bar who did this particular work, but more especially in East Anglia there were immensely able solicitors who had something of a monopoly in the work. Not only did they appear for these transport undertakings in applications for licenses but they were busy buying and selling vehicles and haulage businesses on behalf of clients, and for them it was lucrative. Because of their experience in this type of litigation, which they conducted themselves, they scarcely had need for counsel. However, occasionally they found themselves in some other place and accordingly they used to instruct me from time to time. Likewise, I was instructed by British Rail to oppose coach companies wanting to run a service in competition with them. This had two aspects. Although the brief fees were not very good the rail fare was provided and it was first class. This was a degree of luxury to which I was unaccustomed. The difficulty in the litigation was that often the alternative journey provided by British Rail was almost always wholly unacceptable. Thus, a coach company would want to run a coach, say, from Cambridge to Great Yarmouth for the day. It would go direct to Great Yarmouth, deposit passengers at a point where they could spend many hours enjoying whatever it was they wanted to see there, and return at a fixed time back to Cambridge.

The alternative which I was instructed to put forward was for the passenger to get a British Rail train from Cambridge to another station where, if the passenger were lucky, there would be another train waiting to take him or her to yet another station. If the passenger was unlucky and the train had gone there would be a delay of an hour. There might or might not be another train which was then ready to go to Great Yarmouth. The cost was invariably higher than going by bus and it involved a number of changes. It was dependent upon other trains running to time and it allowed the unfortunate passenger considerably less time in Great Yarmouth than that which could be enjoyed going by bus. It was a somewhat unrewarding argument which no amount of skilled advocacy could improve. Not surprisingly, the number of successes were somewhat limited. But it gave me a broader outlook on other types of litigation, for which I was always grateful.

Defended divorces were a feature of life when I started at the bar. The result of a trial affected the whole future of both husband and wife. A wife who was found guilty of a matrimonial offence might well find that she was deprived of any maintenance. It might also be that access to the children might be limited. Thus, defended divorces were fought as bitterly as any other piece of litigation. There were enormous difficulties in divorce litigation. There could be no divorce by consent. If it were thought that the parties had colluded then the Queen's Proctor, who was an official appointed by the court, could interfere and set aside the divorce. If one party forgave the other by having intercourse for one night, that was said to condone and that would prevent in most circumstances a decree nisi being pronounced. Connivance, another magic word meaning encouragement of an offence, might disentitle a party to be divorced. Equally, although the parties might have been at loggerheads over the years, if they had continued to live together and their behaviour did not amount to what the courts said was cruelty, they would remain united.

Thus, many and devious were the devices adopted by the litigants to try and ensure either in a defended case that they could win the action or in an undefended case that were not prevented from being separated from their husband or wife. Allegations of cruelty were often the most difficult to prove or disprove. Thus, what seemed a trivial event often got magnified out of all proportion and the throwing of a custard pie could become paragraph 24 of a petition containing some 70 similar paragraphs

So far as undefended divorces were concerned, they went through, if not actually on the nod, usually quickly and simply unless the judge happened to be somebody who did not believe in divorce. In those circumstances life was exceedingly difficult, because a lot of the evidence consisted of some enquiry agent who had obtained a confession from the husband or of some maid who had been in an hotel and seen the husband in bed with some third party. Everyone knew that this was simply a device to find some ground to enable parties who wanted to be divorced to get divorced. For the bar it was a very lucrative trade. It required no very great advocacy. Three or four undefended divorces in a morning were soon got through, and they were a considerable money-spinner.

In the event the powers that be decided that undefended divorces could be done equally well by solicitors and thereafter there should be divorce effectively by consent. The bar, I think very unwisely, fought against this as a matter of principle, saying that the breaking up of a marriage was a very solemn business and could not possibly be left to solicitors. It was a wholly untenable position and did not reflect well on the practitioners in the divorce division. Nowadays, guilt or innocence is comparatively unimportant, while money and children are the essential elements in this type of litigation. But I have to say that conducting defended divorces made me realise that other people's lives were not entirely straightforward, and as a young married man I learnt things which have never ceased to astonish me about how other people conduct their lives.

Gradually over the years my practice grew. My first appearance in the Court of Appeal arose out of a right-of-way dispute in Cheltenham. They are an immense source of litigation and very rewarding for the lawyers. This case, Sabatella vs Newman, arose out of an argument between two neighbouring shopkeepers somewhere in a backstreet of Cheltenham. My client owned the path between the two properties which led up to the back of both properties. The next-door neighbour had a right of way 'at all times and for all purposes to pass and repass on foot'. The thorny question that confronted the county court judge was whether that allowed the next-door neighbour and his employees to wheel their bicycles up the path, to park them at the back and whether there could be coal and other goods delivered up the path to the next-door neighbour.

This interesting point of law was further complicated by the claim by the neighbour that there had been a right to use the path in this way over many years, and that right had been exercised 'nec clam nec vi nec precario' – neither secretly nor by force, nor by permission. If the right had been exercised unchallenged for 12 or 20 years there was an unlimited right to use it. This involved calling some of the more elderly inhabitants of the area to describe how they had pushed prams up the path, how they had been there as children and how the path had been used over very many years. Additionally, we argued that a bicycle could not be used as it was a vehicle, and the path was to be used on foot. There was a marvellous Irish case which seemed to indicate that a foot passenger was only allowed to carry what a normal foot passenger carried – this did not entitle someone to carry sacks of provisions or coal.

All these weighty arguments were fully canvassed before the county court judge. The judge took a dislike to my client, whom he thought was being difficult and obstructive, and resolved most of the points of law in favour of my opponent. However, it seemed to me that there was a good argument that the judge had got it wrong, so we decided to appeal. I spent a great deal of time in preparing the case and reading up a lot of law. My opponent, Douglas Draycott, who subsequently took silk and became Leader of the circuit, was a fine advocate but not a particularly industrious one. I arrived at the doors of the court with some 30 authorities. He appeared at 10.25am clutching an out-of-date *Halsbury Laws of England* and asked me what on earth I had got all that law for. The laugh was on me, because although I argued the case for three days he was not called upon by the court and won easily.

I gradually acquired clients from insurance companies and had retainers from them. These were the days when there were steel mills and iron foundries. At Newport there was a whole group of steel manufacturers. A visit to them was an exciting experience because they took no notice of visitors. Some of the equipment was woefully out of date and great sheets of white-hot metal were constantly being moved around the floor of the mill in what seemed to the outsider a most haphazard manner. Additionally, molten metal was frequently conveyed above the mill floor in buckets in the most alarming way.

The standards of safety in factories in those days, both there and more particularly in Birmingham and Coventry, were very low, and accidents were frequent. The unions were very much at the forefront of this litigation, and provided a first-class service to their members. Curiously enough, there was a reluctance among insurers to instruct counsel who appeared for the unions and vice versa. It was borne of some sort of prejudice and profited no-one. Any member of the bar who did plaintiffs work was able to bring a breadth of knowledge of their systems when appearing on behalf of insurance companies and vice versa. Gradually the prejudice evaporated, and consequently firms like W H Thompson and Shaen Roscoe became regular clients.

It was customary in the early 1950s for plaintiffs who were badly injured to seek to have a jury. The general rule then obtaining was that if there were a serious injury a jury was best equipped to deal with it. As juries were never allowed to be told how much they could award, it always seemed to me to be a somewhat bizarre way of proceeding. It was also thought that juries would be much more sympathetic to a badly injured plaintiff. I was involved in one jury action in which it was certainly not so. Mr Pericinotti was an Italian who had dived off the West Pier at Brighton when the tide was out, into about three foot of water. There were notices telling him not to do so and the area from which he dived had indeed been cordoned off. However, the result of the accident was that he was now in a wheelchair. He brought his action against the pier company, which was insured and for which I appeared. It was quite clear at the end of the plaintiff's case from the jury's comments that they were wholly unwilling to find in his favour. In the result, the plaintiff's counsel agreed that the jury should be dispensed with and the matter go on before the judge, who found in our favour.

The question of whether there should be a jury or not was decided by a master, a minor judge who dealt with a good number of the interlocutory applications. From the master there was an appeal to a judge and from a judge to the Court of Appeal. Patrick O'Connor QC was leading me in a case for a badly injured plaintiff and we had obtained from the judge a jury. Our opponents decided to appeal. We went over to the Court of Appeal at 10.30 for the hearing. Patrick told the solicitor on the other side that by 11 o'clock he would have to buy Patrick and me a cup of coffee because they would lose easily. In those days the Court of Appeal was reluctant to interfere with what was regarded as a judge's discretion.

It was however part of Lord Denning's crusading mission to get rid of juries in civil actions if it were possible. He chose this case among others at the same time to lay down that juries in personal injury cases were in effect no longer to be granted. Thus, at 11 o'clock we retired and bought our opponents coffee. Sensibly, when we sought leave to appeal to the House of Lords, because this was quite contrary to previous practice, the defendants bought off the action by settling it. Further cases in which juries were sought totally failed. Thus, for all practical purposes jury trials in civil actions save for libel, slander and false imprisonment, went. Years later I was to be involved in the question of whether there should be a jury trial when I came to deal with Jonathan Aitken's libel action – but more of that anon.

It was customary for members of the bar to sit as recorders in various places throughout the country acting as part time judges at quarter sessions, as the name implies, four times a year. The recorders were chosen to sit on their own particular circuit. On the Oxford circuit they ranged in importance from places like Oxford and Gloucester down to Abingdon and Burton. In 1970 I was invited to become recorder of Burton-on-Trent, which was a great honour. A number of distinguished members of the bar had previously held the post and moved on to more senior positions. One recorder had occupied the post for some 25 years. I duly went up to Burton with Margaret and my clerk William, and was sworn in with much ceremony. Thereafter I used to sit on average four weeks in a year.

Because it meant being away from fee-earning work, the cases were dealt with with very great despatch. The organisation of the court at Burton would put to shame the rather leisurely way in which cases are currently conducted. To begin with I would get all the papers some time before the sessions started. Thus I was usually able to detect what the real point in the case was and therefore how long it was likely to take place, and indeed whether a plea of guilty was likely; it was customary for two or three contested actions to be completed in a day because counsel, particularly from Birmingham, also wasted no time. The borough was exceedingly kind and generous and I was invited to lunch with the Mayor every day. It was extremely hospitable of him and I enjoyed it. However, the conversation had some limitations because I sat between the Mayor and his wife and she was never allowed to express any views of her own. Whenever her views were canvassed the Mayor would say, 'Oh my wife thinks this or my wife thinks that'. It did tend to make conversations somewhat stilted.

Burton jurors had a mind all of their own. There was a case of a black man who was alleged to have attacked a policeman with a knife. The jury went out and acquitted him in the face of very strong evidence. When this result was announced there was a jury waiting in the court to try the next case. That jury was duly sworn. It was a case of shoplifting. A lady had gone into a supermarket, had taken 233 tins of kitty food off the shelf, secreted them around the numerous pockets of her coat and emerged without paying.

When she was stopped by the store detective her defence was that she did not realise that she had got the tins on her. Not unnaturally, this case aroused a good deal of mirth. When the jurors went out everyone assumed that they would be back in a few minutes with a verdict of guilty. Not a bit of it. They were out for an hour and a half and came back and acquitted her. Sometime later that week, the Clerk of the Peace happened to fall in with one of the jurors. It is a criminal offence, of course, to disclose what happens in the jury room, but the Clerk of the Peace could not contain himself and asked this juror how they had arrived at the result.

The juror's explanation was very simple. He said that they had retired, had a cigarette, elected a foreman and very quickly decided that the lady was plainly guilty. Then one of the jurors spoke up and said, 'If that black man who carved up the policeman is going to be acquitted why should we convict this poor old biddie?' The others all agreed, and that is how they returned their verdict. As comparative justice it could not be faulted, and the young man who had been defending no doubt went home thinking he had had a tremendous victory.

Tales of what happened in the jury room are always apocryphal. I remember a case on circuit where a QC was defending in a perfectly hopeless case. He made an impassioned plea to the jury but was nevertheless surprised that the jurors were out for four hours before returning a verdict of guilty. When he went into the pub, after the case, to have a drink he fell in with one of the jurors, who congratulated him on the way that he had conducted the defence. The QC was much pleased. He enquired why the jury had taken so long to reach its verdict. The explanation was a simple one. They had all retired, they had elected a foreman, they had had the customary cigarette or two and they decided clearly that the accused was guilty.

However, as they were leaving the retiring room to return to court one of them asked whether they shouldn't tip the jury bailiff. There was no immediate agreement, so they retired back to their jury room where they discussed that very important matter. Having had a long argument, they eventually agreed that indeed they should. So they then again left the retiring room to return to court. But somebody then observed that they hadn't agreed how much. So back they went into the retiring room again to debate this most important point. There was no immediate agreement, and thus a total of some four hours went by from the time they went out before they fixed upon a sum which was appropriate.

Colonel Randall was the youngest colonel in the Royal Corps of Signals. The British Government had succeeded in selling a vast quantity of tanks (I believe they were Centurions) to the Shah of Iran. This had brought a great benefit to the British arms industry. It was now necessary to secure for the British wireless industry a contract for the wireless equipment in those tanks. There was intense competition from the Americans and there was also competition amongst the various wireless manufacturers in the UK. It was Colonel Randall's task on behalf of the government to evaluate the respective qualities of the wireless equipment produced by British manufacturers and then seek to secure a contract from the Iranian Government for their installation. In those days, as may well be the case now, it was impossible to secure contracts of this sort without a good deal of palm-greasing. In order to get a sample piece of wireless equipment into Iran, it was necessary to tip customs officials. In order to see anybody who mattered in relation to the contract, further handouts had to be given, and this went right to the top. The British Government had a slush fund under the auspices of Millbank Technical Services, which paid the Shah £1 million through his charitable foundation, The Pahlavi Foundation, and a further £1 million to Sir Shapoor Reporter, the Shah's right-hand man, in order to seek to obtain these contracts. Sir Shapoor Reporter had been awarded an OBE in 1969 and a KBE in 1973 for 'services to British Industry'. Thus, the whole of this contract involved bribery and corruption on a fairly substantial scale.

The colonel saw no reason why he should not get his share. Accordingly, he accepted from Racal, one of the wireless manufacturers, a sum of money as a result of which he and two members of the organisation were charged with corruption. It was said that the management of Racal itself knew nothing of this, although this proved to be the subject of much debate in the defence of the two officials from Racal.

Colonel Randall's defence was really twofold: firstly, that he had not accepted any bribes, and secondly, that if he had, everybody else was doing so and there was nothing wrong with it. It was not very easy to run those two defences in harness but the question of the Shah and his right-hand man being paid by the British Government caused me some disquiet. We had material which would have enabled us to run this as part of our case if necessary. However, it was perfectly obvious that if that became public, any further contracts between the British Government and the Shah would be put in jeopardy. Accordingly, it seemed to me that, while I could not prevent Colonel Randall being tried, it would not be in anybody's interest that he should be tried publicly and that the best way for him to be dealt with was by a court-martial. To that end I went to see the Attorney General who was then Sam Silkin. I explained to him that I was instructed to run the defence, that Colonel Randall was doing no more than the British Government had been doing, that we had material and documents to support that and that I was instructed if necessary to make this public during the course of the trial. I therefore suggested that it was in nobody's interests, least of all the British Government's, for Colonel Randall to be tried at the Old Bailey with all the publicity there attending, but that a court-martial which could be conducted much more privately was the appropriate forum for the trial. There were sufficient powers in a court-martial to deal with Colonel Randall if he were found guilty, to deprive him of his pension if that were thought necessary and thereby to avoid the possibility of severe damage to the British industry.

Sam Silkin simply could not understand the point that I was seeking to make. He seemed wholly indifferent to the damage it would cause to the government or to industry and simply refused to contemplate any alternative mode of trial. Thus the trial took place. The involvement of the British Government in paying bribes to the Shah and his right-hand man became public knowledge and the colonel and one of the Racal employees were convicted. As it happened no damage – or no great damage – was done to relations between the government and the Shah, because within a short period of the trial there was the revolution in Iran, the Shah was deposed and the question of future arms contracts with the British Government became academic.

One of my more amusing clients was a successful conman. Like all successful conmen he had great charm, ability and a powerful personality. His particular scheme was to buy an option on a flat in Nice for which he paid very little and then to advertise to retired licensed victuallers that there was a flat for sale in Nice at quite a modest price. To that end he flew out at his own expense some 70 or 80 licensed victuallers and showed them the premises. They were duly impressed and handed over very substantial sums of money in order to buy the flat. They were given some worthless bit of paper showing their entitlement. In due course they each set out at their own expense to Nice to secure the bargain of a lifetime. It turned out no to be so, because when they arrived they found they had no right to buy the flat, the option to buy no longer existed and simultaneous rights had been given to some 70 or 80 other licensed victuallers. It was of course a wicked scheme, but its sheer audacity nevertheless admitted of some admiration, though the judge who gave him (I think) three years didn't think so.

We had on the Oxford circuit some formidable advocates: Teddy Ryder Richardson QC was an advocate of the old school. He scarcely missed a trick and won a number of cases that I don't believe many others would have done. George Baker QC, subsequently to become president of the Family Division, was an engaging Scot who always presented an air of utter sincerity and rectitude to his case, from which the client undoubtedly benefited. Stephen Brown QC, likewise to become president of the Family Division, was a powerful advocate both in civil and in crime. Robert Hutton's family had been in Gloucester for many years. His father had been chairman of Gloucester quarter sessions, as indeed had he. His son Gabriel subsequently became, and still is, a circuit judge in Gloucester. Robert Hutton was a prosecutor of the old school who believed that most defendants were villains and it was his job to bring them to justice. He maintained this role both as an advocate and as chairman of quarter sessions. He was kind to the young bar but a formidable opponent and one who did not suffer sloppy work.

One of the more eccentric members of the circuit was Edward Terrell QC. During the war he had been an inventor of great skill. He had devised a plastic armour which had been of immense value to shipping and had been given an award at the end of the war for his achievements. He subsequently devised the no-spill ink bottle. He wrote a book about his experiences called *Admiralty Brief*, and no-one would could gainsay his remarkable achievements. However, his judgment did not always match his abilities.

There was a dreadful occasion in which he appeared in a murder trial, on behalf of the defence. In those days the sentence for murder was hanging. The evidence against his client was primarily the imprint left by a shoe belonging to the accused. The officer giving evidence about this indicated to the jury that the mark at the scene of which he had taken a cast was consistent with being made by the defendant's shoe. It was of course an important piece of evidence, but by no means conclusive. A more skilful advocate would have been able to establish that there were many other shoes in existence with a similar pattern.

Not so Edward Terrell. With a great flourish he brought out his magnifying glass. He looked at the cast. He looked at the shoe. He handed the magnifying glass to the officer and said, 'Now officer, if you look at the cast with the magnifying glass you can see that they are not the same'. The officer took the magnifying glass. He slowly looked through it at the mark on the cast. He then looked at the shoe, he quietly put down both the magnifying glass and the cast. Then he looked up and said, 'Thank you Mr Terrell. Now that you have given me your magnifying glass I can say without hesitation that the mark on the shoe and the mark on the cast are identical. There can be no doubt about that.' Within a short space of time the jury convicted. The judge put on the black cap and started pronouncing sentence of death saying 'You Edward Terrell', and then suddenly remembered that that was not the name of the defendant.

He had more success in a civil action in which he appeared for a blind man who had fallen down a hole left by some post office engineers. In front of Mr Justice Marshal he lost, and he lost again in front of the Court of Appeal. He got leave to go the House of Lords

16. Oxford circuit dinner, 1972. O.B.P. in middle table.

and opened the case to them by saying 'My Lords, the eyes of the blind are on your Lordships today'. Sitting in the House of Lords was Lord Evershed, who had found against a plaintiff in similar circumstances in a previous case in the Court of Appeal. However, he changed his mind and said, 'The matter does not appear to me today as it appears to have appeared to me previously'. Terrell won his case. Thus, the matter was sent back to the trial judge for an assessment of damages. The trial judge gave the plaintiff a modest sum about which Terrell appealed to the Court of Appeal, which increased it substantially. It was thus a substantial triumph for him.

In 1972 Lord Beeching, who had been responsible for closing a good number of the railways, was invited to look at the assize system, which had remained unchanged since the fourteenth century. The effect of his recommendations was to reduce the number of the courts to which the judges were to go, and more particularly to abolish the Oxford circuit. It was not said so expressly. Simply the Oxford circuit did not appear any longer as one of the circuits. It effectively became joined with the Oxford and Midland circuit. This arrangement was happily well organised so that the leaders were chosen alternately from the Oxford and Midland until such time as it no longer became important as to which circuit the leader belonged.

Because the assize system no longer exists as such, some of the camaraderie which had previously existed has vanished. No longer does the circuit meet as a body. Discipline is more difficult to exercise. It is customary now for important cases on circuit to be dealt with by the circuit judges and not the High Court judges. The effect of this is that often those who wish to apply for silk do not always get the opportunity to appear before a High Court judge.

It was a singularly agreeable idea that the Oxford circuit, on the twenty-fifth anniversary of its abolition, should hold a dinner in London attended by over a hundred old members presided over by Judge Allan King-Hamilton QC, now well over 90, the last leader of the circuit. He spoke as an ex-president of the union with great flair. The evening was full of nostalgia and reminded us all of the happy days that we had had together.

One effect of the abolition of the circuit system was that there were no longer recorders of a particular town save in the big cities. People were now appointed as recorders or assistant recorders in whatever

17. The last photograph of the Oxford circuit, 1972. O. B. P. front row, sixth from left.

town they were required to sit. I had been a deputy chairman of Oxfordshire quarter sessions and under the new system was able to sit at Oxford as a recorder. One immediate effect was that the Clerk of the Peace at quarter sessions, who was an experienced lawyer and who fully understood what the cases were about, was now replaced by a civil servant. It was done in order to provide enough clerks to deal with the new system. A number of those imported had considerably less knowledge than that of their predecessors. In the result, when I did a fortnight's sitting at Oxford after Beeching I was only able to deal with about half of the work that I had got through in one week at Burton. Thus what was thought by the late Lord Beeching as a money-saving and more efficient system turned out, as these schemes often do, to have a totally contrary effect. It resulted in a terrible waste of money, resources and time. Sadly, now the Oxford circuit has vanished, with Oxford becoming part of the southeastern circuit. Cui bono?

8

Bradford

On Monday 13 May 1985 I was hearing a case in the High Court concerning a fireman's pension rights. At about eleven o'clock a note was passed up to me by the usher saying would I ring Tom Legg as soon as possible. (Tom Legg was the Lord Chancellor's right-hand man.) I said to counsel that I had to rise for a few minutes, which I then did and went to my room. My clerk Ken asked me what it was all about and somewhat jokingly I said that I supposed that the Lord Chancellor was going to move me straight to the House of Lords without my first going to the Court of Appeal.

I rang Tom and the conversation went something like this.

Me: 'Tom, Oliver here.'

Tom: 'Oh, Oliver, thank you for ringing; you've probably heard about the fire at Bradford Football Ground on Saturday.'

Me: 'Yes I saw something of it on the television.'

Tom: 'Well, there is to be a public inquiry.'

Me: 'Oh yes.'

Tom: 'It is to be conducted by a Judge and the Home Secretary will be announcing the terms of reference this afternoon in the House.'

Me: 'Yes.'

Tom: 'The Lord Chancellor has specifically asked that you should do this.'

Me: 'Yes.'

Tom: 'And the Lord Chief Justice has given his blessing.'

Me: 'Yes.'

Tom: 'And the Prime Minister has added her recommendation.'

I let a long pause go by while I digested this information. I then said – 'Tom, tell me, how many other people before me have been asked?'

I was naturally much honoured and flattered to be nominated for this inquiry. It was necessary that the matter be kept under wraps until the Secretary of State announced the matter to parliament. It was also necessary to complete the case about the fireman's pension because it was clear that my inquiry would occupy me full time and that it would be impossible to deal with other work once I started the inquiry.

I therefore went back into court and saw both counsel in my room and explained to them that for reasons which I could not divulge we had to finish the case on that day. Therefore they had better get their skates on. Both sensible counsel did indeed do that, with the result that I was able to clear the decks and concentrate on the inquiry.

The next move was to go to the Home Office to see the officials and to be briefed on what was required of me generally. More importantly the first decision was how were we to proceed immediately. Bob Morris was the under-secretary at the Home Office who had charge of me. He could not have been more delightful or more efficient. We met Sir Brian Cubbon, who was the permanent secretary at the Home Office and together we discussed how best to proceed. It was agreed that I should visit Bradford at the very earliest moment, which was in fact on the Tuesday morning. Meanwhile there would be gathered together a team to assist me, and then we should consider how to set up the inquiry itself.

On the same afternoon as the fire at Bradford there had been a substantial riot at Birmingham City football ground where Leeds supporters had broken into the ground, necessitating the use of police horses. The fire at Bradford had claimed the lives of 56 people, with many others seriously injured. At Birmingham a young boy of 15 had died and there had been many others injured. Quite how it was going to be possible to conduct both inquiries simultaneously, one effectively concerning crowd safety and the other effectively concerning crowd control, was not very clear to me. But these were all matters for the future.

The announcement of my appointment in the media received considerable attention and was accorded a note of general welcoming approval. William Rees-Mogg, who had been at Charterhouse with me, said that although I hadn't been in the top class intellectually I was quite a sensible person and no doubt would conduct this inquiry in that manner. Peter May was kind enough to say that if I had not gone to the bar I would have had a future in first-class cricket. That was somewhat generous.

On Tuesday morning I got up early in order to get to London airport to fly to Leeds and thence to Bradford. At about 7am I was in my pyjamas having breakfast when there was a knock at the front door, to which I unthinkingly went. I found a news photographer on the doorstep. He said, 'Lord Popplewell?' I said, 'Well you're close; what can I do for you?' He said, 'I've come to take your photograph'. I had visions of the photograph of the judge conducting the inquiry going round the world in a somewhat *déshabillé* state. I told him to wait while I changed and then discovered that he was taking photographs for the evening paper.

I then went to London airport where I met up with Bob Morris. He was naturally extremely anxious as to how I would cope with the media attention. As we got onto the plane there was a television camera and crew simply filming us going up the steps. No-one said anything nor conducted any sort of interview. I asked Bob what was that all about. He said that in case we never reached Bradford there would at least be a record of our having set off on the inquiry.

With this somewhat gloomy preamble to the inquiry, Bob then proceeded to brief me. Essentially our visit was partly public relations, namely to meet the press and those who had been closely involved in the disaster, and partly to get some first-hand impression of what had happened. Bob explained that my immediate function was to express no sort of view but to explain that I was there to listen and learn. I naturally wished to express my sympathy and more particularly to get some idea of the extent of the disaster.

I was wholly unaccustomed to the attention of the media. Though I had appeared on television on a limited number of occasions I was wholly unprepared for the reception which greeted me when I arrived at Leeds airport. There was a room to which we were directed in which there must have been some 50 or 60 photographers and reporters. One of my abiding memories of photographers during my inquiry was the number of pictures they thought it necessary to take of me. Most would take 20 or 30 and even when I thought it was finished there would be another call to look this way or look that way. Naturally the

18. Bradford City Football Club after the fire, 1985.

press wanted to know my reaction, what the purpose of the inquiry was, who I thought was to blame even at that stage, and so on. Having explained that I was there to listen and learn I went on to use the phrase familiar to those conducting inquiries that my inquiry would neither be a 'whitewash nor a witch hunt'.

The sight of the burnt-out stadium was horrendous and more awful than anything I had ever seen. Flowers had already been laid along the embankment above the ground. But they did little to alleviate the distressing picture of a stadium in ruins. I walked round the ground, accompanied by officials, including the chairman Mr Stafford Higginbottom, and television cameras. I was wearing an old mac which unfortunately lacked a button or two. Margaret saw the television pictures and could scarcely contain herself on my return. A number of my friends also commented on what they described as my 'flasher's mac'.

This visit so soon after the disaster had a very sobering effect. It was gradually borne in on me the enormity of the inquiry in which I was engaged. The other matter which I gradually came to appreciate was the effect of being a personality. I appeared then and subsequently with some frequency on television. People would then recognise me in the street and bend my ear about the problems of football. Thus, for a short time Popplewell became a household name. The fact that it was a north-country name and that I had married a Yorkshire girl in Ripon certainly eased my path in relations with the Yorkshire people.

I also had a good deal of correspondence from various people. One letter went something like this: 'Dear Judge, Were you ever at — School? If so, were you there in 1935? If so, did you play for the first eleven? If so, did you keep goal? If so, did you play against —? If so, did you borrow my gloves? If so, may I now have them back?' I wrote a friendly reply denying any involvement with his school or his gloves and there the correspondence ended.

I also received 12 family trees from Popplewells all over the country wanting to know if I were in some way related. I solved the problem by sending copies of all the trees I had received to every family and letting them work out whether Great Uncle Charlie on one tree was the same person as Great Uncle Charlie on another. It was all amusing stuff and no doubt was of interest to a number of families.

On my return to London it was necessary to set up the framework for my inquiry. It was obvious that the fire at Bradford required the inquiry to be held in public. This was necessary in order to establish precisely what had happened, to enable those who were aggrieved or grieving to express their views and to enable us to decide what if any improvements could be made in relation to crowd safety.

The riot at Birmingham however, raised slightly different considerations. Firstly there were the parents of the boy who had died whose feelings naturally needed to be considered. Secondly I had to consider the position of the two football clubs who were involved and of the police. But I quickly came to the conclusion that no very useful purpose would be served by conducting that inquiry in public. The matter was fully recorded on the television and on video. There was naturally some criticism that I was perhaps taking a more serious view of what had happened at Bradford than at Birmingham and that both inquiries should have been in public. That criticism was of a limited nature and I am still convinced that we adopted the right approach.

My committee, which had the rather high-flying name of Committee of Inquiry into Crowd Safety and Control at Sports Grounds, began to take shape. The Home Secretary had appointed two assessors to assist me, Alan Goodson OBE QPM, who was then Chief Constable of Leicester, and Martin Killoran QFSM, who had recently retired from being Chief Fire Officer of Greater Manchester. Alan was a deep-thinking, hard-working and thoroughly sensible police officer. Martin was a highly experienced fire officer. Both were also used to coping with the media and the press, an area with which I was comparatively unfamiliar.

I made it clear at the very beginning that it was to be my report but that their input was of very great importance. I needed their expertise not only in dealing with matters within their particular disciplines but also in handling the whole inquiry generally. Their assistance was of immense value in the course of the inquiry and on many occasions absolutely fundamental. Their common sense, intelligence and experience was critical to the success of the inquiry. Of course there were times when we had disagreements, but there was never a time when we failed to resolve those disagreements by amicable and intelligent discussion. Without them it would scarcely have been possible to have produced a report, certainly not a report of the magnitude which we did.

We set up base at the Home Office. Neil Morgan was appointed as our secretary, and he could not have been more efficient. He had vast experience of the workings of the Civil Service, which hitherto had been a closed book to me. Knowing who to go to or where to go was of immense value. We additionally had two assistants, Mark Depulford and Jill Hales. They were both comparatively young in the fast stream of the Civil Service and were christened by myself and the assessors as the 'young turks'. They epitomised everything that was best about the Civil Service in that they were immensely hard-working, highly intelligent and enormously efficient. They played a significant part in our inquiry – not merely in organising our arrangements, in accurately recording details of meetings and keeping the vast volume of paper under proper control, but also in having an important input into our thinking.

I think that both the Civil Service and I learnt a good deal about the approach of each other. There is a natural tendency for the Civil Service to be governed by a hierarchal approach. Thus, if I needed some information from the Home Secretary it was not possible for me to go up one floor in the Home Office, knock on his door and ask him or his secretary for that information. There was a procedure which had to be properly followed. This was quite understandable, but on occasions caused some difficulty. I remember once that there was a document that we urgently needed which was sitting on an official's desk. I simply told the civil servants that I was proposing to go to the room where it was and seize hold of it. They threw up their hands in horror, but it certainly saved us two or three days of wasted time. I think they found the more relaxed approach of the judiciary a welcome and refreshing experience. Equally, I found their organisational abilities superb. Above all, their ability to record the minutes of a meeting in an intelligent and useful manner was of enormous importance.

Although I was appointed by the Home Secretary, my immediate remit was to the Minister of Sport, Neil Macfarlane. The Minister of Sport was regarded by the Home Office, housed as he was in the Department of the Environment, as someone well below the salt. When I suggested one day that I might drop in and have a cup of tea with him to discuss how we were getting on, it was greeted with some horror by my civil servants. They wanted to know what it was I was going to talk about, what points I wanted to make, how I would deal with any points that he wanted to make and so on.

Nevertheless, from time to time I used to visit Neil Macfarlane at his office. On each occasion I had a brief prepared for me by my civil servants about the points which might arise, how I should deal with them if they did arise and limiting what I should say in answer to questions likely to be posed by Neil or his civil servants. I have no doubt that his civil servants had prepared the same sort of briefing for the minister.

On one occasion, I remember after we came back that my civil servants were in good humour. When I enquired why they were so pleased, they said 'Ah well, we managed to put a point across their civil servants because their civil servants hadn't briefed the minister about a point which you raised'. It seemed to me a somewhat childish approach. I have no doubt that on many occasions it is necessary for a minister to be briefed by his or her civil servants on matters which are likely to arise which might not have occurred to him or her, and to prepare the minister with answers to difficult questions. But the sort of teatime informal conversation which I had in mind simply did not give rise to that necessity and seemed an awful waste of time and effort on the part of the Civil Service.

Having established our working arrangements at the Home Office it was necessary to set up the public inquiry which was to be held at Bradford. Somebody has to do the preliminary work of getting together the material, obtaining statements from witnesses and getting the arrangements in order. The West Yorkshire Police had been fully involved from an early stage. Their enquiries had been thorough, far reaching and highly efficient. They had a great number of photographs of the scene both during and after the fire. There were television films of the fire and there was a mountain of evidence as to what had happened, which they helpfully provided before we started. I appointed Andrew Collins QC, now Mr Justice Collins, as counsel to the inquiry. It was his responsibility to assemble the material collected, to decide to some extent in conjunction with me what evidence was to be called at the public inquiry and so to conduct the cross-examination of witnesses as to elicit the essential facts necessary to enable me properly to report.

To this end, on 23 May I held a preliminary hearing, at which various interested parties sought leave to be represented. I had some precedents upon which to base my decision. Leslie Scarman, now Lord Scarman, had conducted an inquiry into the Brixton riots. Cyril Salmon, subsequently Lord Salmon, had brought out a report about how public inquiries should be conducted after the Savundra interview on television. I took the view that interested parties should be represented and have the opportunity of asking questions of witnesses. I was particularly concerned that the football club itself, which was likely to be first in the firing line, should have every opportunity to answer criticisms, and that the relatives should equally be able fully to canvas their concerns.

There have been a number of inquiries conducted by inspectors or chairmen which did not follow that pattern, in that witnesses were called before the inquiry and cross-examined by the inquiry without benefit of legal representation. The result was that what one witness said in criticising another witness would not immediately be challenged by that witness. There was thus no-one to correct a hostile approach by the inspector or chairman or counsel to the inquiry, or to point out any mistake of fact implicit in the questioning. No doubt it has some advantages in speed and in preventing the inquiry from getting out of hand. It was also thought that giving a witness the opportunity to rebut any criticism shortly before the publication of the report would sufficiently prevent what might otherwise be thought to be an injustice. I always had my doubts. This did not seem to me to be fair. Nor was it the manner in which Lord Salmon proposed that public inquiries should be conducted. Certainly, the Scott inquiry seemed to me to contain all the disadvantages of unrepresented witnesses having no opportunity properly or immediately to challenge adverse evidence. Also, the argument that keeping lawyers out of an inquiry would shorten the proceedings seemed to be invalid. There is, of course, no necessity for everyone to be represented. Some people's involvement is on the margin. But it doesn't seem to me very difficult to determine at the beginning of an inquiry who the people are who are likely to be in the frame. Simple justice requires that they should be both represented and have the opportunity to challenge adverse evidence. I very much respect Richard Scott, but I certainly wouldn't have conducted an inquiry his way.

The value of the assessors was immediately shown. I was very unenthusiastic about allowing the Police Federation to be a party to the inquiry. Nobody was criticising the police. Individual officers had behaved with enormous gallantry. There did not, so far as the papers were concerned, seem to be any valid criticism that could be made of the police. However, my assessors pointed out that there had been a number of problems in the use of police radios during the fire. It was suggested to me that an input from the Police Federation would be of enormous value. I quickly saw the point of this and they were allowed to be joined as parties.

Before the inquiry began we had been supplied with a mass of documents and reports. It was possible even before the inquiry started to come to a preliminary view as to what had happened. In the result, that preliminary view was confirmed by the oral evidence given by the witnesses. After holding my preliminary hearing on 23 May I went to visit some of the survivors in hospital at Bradford. I was astounded at their courage and fortitude, and indeed at the general reaction of the citizens of Bradford to the great disaster which had overwhelmed them. The grief and anxiety and anguish which the disaster caused cannot be overstated. But the citizens seemed to draw on an inner strength and rallied round. A disaster fund was quickly set up and sensibly administered according to need.

Comparing the reaction of those involved in the Bradford disaster with those involved in some other disasters, one can only be astonished at the wonderful way that the citizens of Bradford behaved. They quietly buried their dead, tended their injured and comforted their bereaved. Not for them the noisy and public whingeing and whining which has been the hallmark of so many other disasters. They did not pursue seemingly endless inquiries as a personal vendetta. They did not seek to use their disaster as a weapon of emotional blackmail on the government, not did they seek to perpetuate publicly the memory of the terrible disaster they had suffered. They behaved with great dignity and no little courage. It is sad that the example so bravely set by Bradford was not followed by others.

Saturday 11 May 1985 was to be a day of celebration for the Bradford City Football Club. They had won the third division championship and were to be promoted. This was their last game of the season. Their visitors were Lincoln City. Before the game started the trophy for the championship was presented to the club. The manager was presented with an award for manager of the year. The vice-president of the Football League attended. So did the deputy Lord Mayor of Bradford, together with civic dignitaries from twin towns in Germany and Belgium. It was indeed a day of celebration. A crowd estimated at some 11,000 attended. As ill-luck would have it, the stand where the fire occurred was to be pulled down on the following Monday and rebuilt.

The match kicked off at about 3pm, and the fire started shortly before half time. In another 45 minutes this stand in any event would have ceased to have been used. The stand where the fire occurred was a wooden stand. A cigarette or a lighted match must have been dropped between the wooden floorboards. There was a good deal of material under the floorboards and a fire started. People in the seats became aware of fire under the floorboards. The police were called. It was not immediately apparent to them that there was any serious risk. The wood roof was covered with a tarpaulin and sealed with asphalt and it rapidly took fire. The burning asphalt added its own fuel to the flames and injury to the spectators. The speed with which the fire took hold was graphically described as 'faster than a man could run'. From the time that the fire first appeared until the time that the whole stand was fully ablaze was probably not more than about five minutes.

There was some suggestion that a smoke bomb had been thrown into the block, causing the fire to start. That was fully investigated by a detective superintendent. No-one in the block concerned suggested that that had taken place. One reporter from the *Daily Star*, however, believed he had seen a smoke bomb being thrown. He was then able to write in somewhat graphic terms in his paper that a smoke bomb caused the tragic Bradford football fire. He added, 'I know that the killer who threw it would have escaped'. When he gave evidence the journalist accepted that he hadn't actually seen anything thrown. He had seen a trail of smoke, he believed that a smoke bomb had been thrown. It was clear from all the evidence that this particular description of the cause of the fire was inaccurate. There never was a smoke bomb thrown nor a killer at large. We disregarded his evidence.

The speed of the fire took everyone by surprise. It was one of the lessons to be learnt from the inquiry. The effect of it was that people did not move at all after the first discovery of the fire. When they did move they were overwhelmed by smoke and heat. It was thought that some of the exit doors had been locked. This proved not in fact to be the case, but a number of the turnstiles were. The available exits were insufficient to enable spectators safely to escape. Luckily there were no barriers at the front of the stand, thus enabling a good number of spectators to escape by that means. When we had to consider crowd control, as opposed to crowd safety, the question of barriers at the front of stands preventing spectators running onto the pitch was at the forefront of our minds. There was considerable comment that if there had been these barriers the death toll at Bradford would have been enormous.

There had been difficulty in relaying messages. It was clear that some messages had never been received, and some that were received were not received in full. This failure in fact played no part in the tragedy. However, it gave rise to considerable disquiet about the proper functioning of police radios in a football stadium. The Home Office Directorate of Telecommunications gave an undertaking to see whether a more suitable personal radio could be produced.

The relationship between the police and the stewards of the ground was also a problem which troubled us throughout the whole of our inquiry, and still to some extent troubles me. The police's view was that they were responsible for controlling breaches of the peace, and for the movement of spectators in and from public thoroughfares into the ground, while the club was responsible for the control of spectators once they were on the club's premises. In 1985, club stewards were often former servants of the club who assisted in opening doors and taking tickets and were rewarded either by some small fee or by the fact that they were able to watch the football free. They often had little or no training in safety matters or in matters of crowd disorder. One of the astonishing features that we discovered during the course of the inquiry was the vast burden imposed upon police forces by the necessity of having a police presence in the ground to prevent disorder. We did our best in the inquiry to seek to devise a division of responsibility between the club and the police.

A football club after all is a private organisation run for profit. It is thus in no different position from any other private individual or body arranging a function. Essentially, it should be responsible for arranging to secure the safety of its own premises and for ensuring that whatever entertainment it allows to take place on the premises is conducted in an orderly way. In a perfect world, if it were found as frequently as it was that there was disorder at a private entertainment, the police should simply ban that entertainment. In practice, the idea of a football match being cancelled because of the risk of disorder is not a practical suggestion. It therefore becomes necessary for more and more police to be involved in the organisation inside the ground for the purpose of public safety. For instance, at Norwich in 1985, a match involving a high-profile visiting team often caused half of the the county police force to be deployed.

Prior to this fire there had been some correspondence about the state of the ground. The West Yorkshire Metropolitan County Council had indeed written in July 1984 that it was concerned about the main grandstand in that the timber construction was a fire hazard. In particular it was pointed out there had been a build up of combustible materials in the voids beneath the seats, and that a carelessly discarded cigarette could give rise to fire risk. There was no reply to that letter, and on 30 April the council wrote again suggesting a meeting to discuss what was required and a meeting was scheduled for the Wednesday after this disaster. The Health and Safety Executive had also drawn the club's attention to a number of matters prior to the fire.

It was quite clear however that there really was no co-ordination between the various bodies responsible for supervising the safety of the ground, and we commented upon this lack of co-ordination. One of our recommendations, which was brought into effect, was that there should be a certification process which required all the various disciplines to ensure that the grounds were in fact safe.

The club itself took a thoroughly responsible attitude to the disaster arising from the fire. In 1983 a new club had been formed with Mr Higginbottom as Director and chairman. Like all clubs at this level, it had financial problems. Higginbottom made no attempt to evade his responsibility. At the inquiry he said that he wanted to say something about the responsibility of the club itself. He said that a great deal of effort had been put into improving the club and a great deal had been achieved since the new company was formed. Many improvements had been made in the running of the club, but as the chairman of the club he accepted responsibility for the executive and management he employed. He added that he also accepted responsibility for the manner in which the club was run and that there were obviously things that could have been done on the day or before that day that would have helped the situation with the benefit of hindsight. He finished by saying 'I am prepared to say there are a number of things we all wish had been done or had been thought of prior to this terrible tragedy'. It was a brave and responsible attitude to what was not merely a public but also a private disaster for the club.

It was not our responsibility to attribute blame for the fire. Our remit was to find out what had happened, to point out the lessons to be learnt and to try to provide for the future. Mr Justice Cantley subsequently conducted the litigation in the High Court and apportioned liability between a number of parties.

One of the suggestions which we would like to have made was to prohibit permanent wooden stands. That, however, was not a practical proposition. We did recommend immediately that the building of new permanent stands of combustible material should be prohibited as a general rule. Given the nature and extent of the fire and the speed at which it had occurred, this did not seem to be an unreasonable suggestion. It was clear that there must have been hundreds of stands similar to that at Bradford with a similar fire risk. If another fire had broken out in a similar situation we would have been heavily criticised for not taking some immediate practical steps. However, we did not appreciate the full effect of this recommendation. Those in the timber trade complained loudly and frequently that they were being victimised, that there was simply no evidence that timber stands were as a matter of fact particularly vulnerable to fire, and that our recommendation was likely to have a very serious effect on their trade.

I confess that I found this reaction somewhat surprising, and indeed intemperate. We were sent a film showing an attempt to set fire to some timber which had been specially treated. It appeared to show how difficult it was for stands of this construction to catch fire. For my part I was singularly unimpressed, having seen the horrific film of the fire at Bradford. However, it was necessary in order to conduct our inquiry properly to hear evidence from all sides. We had no wish to pursue a recommendation which might have been ill-considered, or at any rate considered without consultation with the timber industry. To that end we invited the timber trade to visit us at the Home Office.

The procedure we adopted after the holding of the public inquiry was to invite representatives and individuals to come and see us at the Home Office. The three of us together with our civil servants would then meet in a conference room in an informal atmosphere and listen to any observations or representations that anyone whom we invited wished to make. In addition to those to whom we sent invitations, a great number of organisations and individuals themselves wrote in, either asking to come and see us or to accept written submissions from them. It was all conducted on a very informal basis without any formal agenda and with the objective of learning from the witnesses the valuable points and observations which they were able to bring to our attention.

When we had to consider the question of combustibility of timber, I not only had had the advice of Martin Killoran but also of the fire authorities at the Home Office. Their advice was that as a general rule wooden stands should be replaced with non-combustible stands. But they were equally of the view that provided adequate exits were available they would, for the time being at any rate, be not unwilling to sanction the continued use of existing wooden stands.

We thus awaited the arrival of the timber trade with some interest. A large body arrived. They were clearly exceedingly troubled. To say that they had steam coming out of their ears would be an understatement. For the best part of an hour they addressed us on the subject of the non-combustibility of wooden stands, how the timber trade were being discriminated against, how their members were being put out of business and how the dangers of concrete structures were no less than the dangers from wooden stands. I remained silent during most of the discussion until I could finally stand it no longer. I intervened to ask the simple question, 'Are you saying that a concrete stand is more combustible than a wooden one?' Then there was a long silence.

Eventually they did grudgingly acknowledge that wooden stands were indeed more combustible. I thanked them for their attendance, observed that on this matter I was a pure amateur but that I was dependant upon the expertise of my fire officer assessor and the fire service element of the Home Office. I told them that naturally we would be considering the problems in the light of the timber trades representations. I fear that they went away still full of fire and fury and did not regard themselves as having been fairly treated.

The inquiry into what happened at Birmingham City football ground arose from the fixture between Birmingham and Leeds United. It was the final fixture of the 1984/5 season. Birmingham City had already secured promotion to the first division as runners up, and if they defeated Leeds and Oxford United lost in another fixture then Birmingham City would be champions of the second division. So far as Leeds were concerned, if they won at Birmingham they would be promoted to the first division, but only if Manchester City (who were playing a simultaneous fixture elsewhere) lost. A good deal therefore turned on the result of this match.

It was the behaviour of the visiting supporters that gave rise essentially to the riot. A number of the Leeds United supporters found that the pace at which supporters ahead of them moved through the turnstiles was too slow for their liking. They simply scaled the walls, went through fences and over the barbed wire and into the ground. Others, unwilling perhaps to negotiate that obstacle course, decided to storm the main gate and were assisted by those already inside. A battering ram was used against the gates, consisting of a piece of concrete with steel reinforcing rods about seven feet long. They eventually broke down the gate and poured into the ground. Another group of supporters smashed 40 or 50 feet of metal railings and wooden doors, together with a part of a small brick wall.

During the first half the supporters, now armed with missiles including cans, bricks and pound coins, bombarded the police who were around the perimeter. The Leeds United fans then prepared themselves to invade the pitch. The half-time whistle signalled a pitch invasion from both ends of the ground. There is no doubt that the Birmingham City supporters were greater in number than the Leeds

United supporters, but the Leeds United supporters made greater use of missiles.

The luckless police were ready for this invasion. They formed a double cordon across the pitch to keep the factions apart but they too were bombarded by pieces of concrete, bricks, coins, boards and advertising hoardings. The police managed to keep the warring factions apart and the second half began. At the final whistle the pitch was invaded again by both supporters. Although the police managed to keep the fans apart, they were subject to considerable bombardment. It was described by one of the inspectors as a pitched battle and involved the use of mounted police. It took some time for the police to restore order. It was only the timely and courageous intervention of the police between the rival supporters that prevented a disaster similar to that which occurred at the Heysel stadium. A great deal of damage to property was done, and over 100 police were injured as well as nearly 100 civilians.

About half an hour after the game finished a wall which ran between one of the terraces and a car park collapsed. A young boy, Ian Hampbridge, who was close by, was killed. It was not possible to be sure how the brick wall came to fall. The most likely explanation was that it was due to the surge of people. The young lad was on his first visit to a football match. He came from a respectable family. He was not involved in any violence and was unhappily the innocent victim of the collapse of the wall.

There is no doubt that the primary cause of the riot was drink. A substantial number of visiting supporters came to Birmingham deliberately to cause trouble. They sparked off the Birmingham supporters, whose subsequent behaviour was as bad as if not worse than that of the visitors. The problem of crowd control was one that troubled us both initially and throughout our inquiry for a number of reasons. It was very difficult to identify the cause of violence at football matches. We were assisted by a number of reports and publications. There was the Sports Council Social Science Research Council Report of 1978. Professor Cantor, who was a consultant to our inquiry, gave us valuable assistance, and Messrs Dunning, Murphy and Williams from the University of Leicester provided valuable insight into spectator violence at football matches. In all I must have read 30 or 40 reports, studies and books. At the end of my inquiry I was bound to report that that there was no panacea, no one solution to the problem of violence, and that if violence within the football ground were in fact to be contained it did not necessarily follow that it would not re-emerge elsewhere.

The next problem was how best to deal with hooliganism inside the ground. Segregation of fans was clearly of assistance. But there were always problems of the wrong fans getting into the opposition's terraces. Then there was a question of how the police should control the hooligans on the terraces themselves. At Birmingham the police had been subjected to a hail of missiles including pound coins, which had prevented them effectively from identifying the culprits or being able to take any serious steps to prevent it.

One of the most important suggestions which we made and which has been carried out since was the introduction of closed-circuit television from a control room within the ground. The advantages of this control room have become increasingly apparent. From the room it is possible for the officers to have a view of every part of the ground. They are able to monitor the approaches to the ground and to identify possible areas of trouble. In particular, such is the state of technology that it is possible to film a hooligan on the other side of the ground misbehaving, take his photograph and thereby identify him immediately. The effect of this has been quite dramatic. Confronted with the evidence of misdemeanour, the hooligan has put his hands up and been dealt readily by the courts.

The extent to which the terraces should be fenced so as to prevent the hooligan from running out onto the pitch was naturally and still is a very thorny subject. Quite clearly the presence of fences at Bradford would have enormously increased the number of deaths. The fencing at Hillsborough plainly seriously contributed to the death toll. Suggestions were made for moveable fences or indeed a moat like structure such as to be found at some continental grounds. There was also a suggestion that if fans were fenced in they would be likely to behave like hooligans, though I confess I never found that a particularly convincing argument. Generally at grounds, fencing has now gone.

Then there was the controversy between seating and standing. One of the surprising features of the behaviour of soccer spectators is that they like to stand in a crowd with their mates. That it is uncomfortable and exhausting is nothing to the point. Any suggestion that they should be required to be seated was greeted with something akin to outrage. When we conducted our inquiry we were told that 'all-seating' had been attempted at Coventry, but it had been proved to be totally unsuccessful because the fans had simply broken up the seats and used them as missiles. One of the other matters which we had to consider was the question of membership cards. This had aroused the interest of the Prime Minster, who had apparently been horrified that one of her successful political meetings had been much upstaged by a riot which had occurred at Luton. She was therefore fully committed to the idea of spectators only being allowed into the ground on production of a membership card.

There were two objections to this scheme. The first was what might be described as an objection in principle and the second was a practical objection. The objection in principle was that membership cards were nothing more than identity cards. The suggestion of introducing an identity card naturally aroused the fury of those libertarian groups, self-opinionated and self-elected, which seemed to think that such an idea was a diabolical interference with a fundamental liberty. They chose not to consider that it might have the effect of enhancing the liberty of some other spectator who merely wanted to enjoy a football match. They closed their eyes to the fact that everybody who wants to go abroad has to have a passport, which is no different from an identity card, or that a driving licence is required for somebody who wants to drive a car, or that season-ticket holders on railways require a card, or that plastic cards are now part and parcel of everyday life. They were supported in their objections rather sadly, I have to say, by the media, which, by constantly referring to membership cards as identity cards caused a number of even quite sensible people to believe that their liberty was in some way being curtailed.

In our initial report we were very much in favour in principle of introducing some sort of membership scheme, because we thought that it would help to prevent hooliganism, identify those involved and thereby create a happier place for those who wanted to watch the game in some degree of peace. However, when we pursued the matter more deeply it became clear that there were a number of practical problems which would have made their introduction in full, at that time at any rate, wholly impractical.

Almost all football grounds in this country were at this time old fashioned. Getting spectators through the turnstiles is a time-consuming process. Some of the up-to-date clubs have gone a long way to speeding up the process, but in 1985 they were few and far between. A football spectator is a creature of habit. The figures for Liverpool in 1985 showed that only 65 per cent of the total attendance were in the ground 15 minutes before kick-off and 92 per cent at kick-off. Thus, on average some 9000 spectators were still trying to get into the ground 15 minutes before kick-off and 2500 were still outside when play began.

We were told by some of the most prestigious and responsible clubs that if some sort of membership scheme were introduced necessitating the showing of passes, even if electronically controlled, it would be quite impossible to ensure that there were not a large number of spectators outside the ground at the time of kick-off. The suggestion that spectators might leave a little earlier in order to avoid the crowd was greeted with amusement. In the result, we came to the conclusion that although there were a good number of arguments in favour of membership schemes there were a great number of practical difficulties. It may be that now with modern sophisticated equipment the problem can more easily be tackled.

At Birmingham we were provided with a great number of documents and in particular the film of the riot. Thus, we were able to come to a clear view as to what had happened and why it had happened. One of the problems that continually arose during our inquiry was that those who labelled themselves supporters of club A did not necessarily belong to the official supporters club, nor did the club itself have any power to control their activities. Thus club A's supporters would give the club a very bad name even though they were not members of the official supporters' club. Whatever the club did it was impossible for the club itself to prevent those supporters from continuing to behave in that way. Almost all clubs had official supporters clubs which were generally well run, well managed and well supervised; they did their best to identify and to try and control their unofficial supporters, but inevitably there were difficulties.

In addition to discussing the matter with the senior police officers we interviewed a number of the police officers who had been present at the riot. They had undoubtedly behaved with great bravery. There were police officers of both sexes. It was clear that the rioters had made no exception as to who they had chosen to attack, and a number of women were injured. We also were able to talk to the parents of the young boy who died, and expressed our sympathy with them in their sad bereavement. They were, I think, grateful for the interest that we had displayed, for the trouble we had taken to ascertain the cause of their son's death, and were in no way disturbed by the absence of a public inquiry.

After having conducted our inquiry at Bradford and our investigation at Birmingham, we returned to the Home Office to consider how we should go about writing our report. The Bradford and Birmingham incidents had occurred on the last day of the football season. It was therefore impossible for us to go and see any football matches until August at the earliest, in order to see for ourselves the problems of crowd safety and crowd control. This left us effectively with two options. We could either wait until the autumn or indeed the winter to write our report, when we would have had the benefit of some part of a season's football. Or we could write an interim report with our preliminary views and then consider the matter again more fully when we had had the benefit of more detailed information.

In the result, we decided that it would be sensible to write a report as to what had actually happened at Bradford and Birmingham with preliminary views as to how in the future the problems could best be avoided. Then subsequently we would write a final report in which we could expand upon and if necessary amend our preliminary views about the future. The writing of the report on what actually happened at Bradford and Birmingham presented no real problem. It was no different from writing a reserved judgment with finding of facts.

The assessors and I were unanimous in our views as to what had happened both at Bradford and Birmingham, as to the primary causes and as to the immediate precautions that we thought should be taken. We received written evidence from a wide variety of organisations, from MPs and some 200 letters from members of the public. We also had a report from the fire research station at Bournewood which prepared a detailed technical assessment of how the fire started and spread and its likely effect on spectators. This was an immensely valuable contribution of great interest to those of both a technical and a non-technical bent. It enabled us to place our recommendations about future precautions upon some firm groundwork.

The civil servants were very keen (because apparently it has always been the practice) to write the report themselves. I was told that it was customary for the introduction to be written by the chairman of an inquiry with assistance from the civil servants but that the report itself was to be drafted by civil servants, subject of course to the views of the members of the inquiry. This was not at all my style. Ever since I was at the bar I had never delegated any preparation of my work to anybody else. I liked to do my own work myself and set out my opinion in my own style. Otherwise I could never be sure that the matter would be presented in the way that I wanted. This initially caused some anxiety among the young turks, but by this time they had come to appreciate that a judge did not always follow Civil Service habits. They readily undertook the donkey work of preparing the relevant documents in proper order to enable me to put my report into some sort of shape. Naturally I discussed every detail with the assessors. We drafted and redrafted together and having got the material into some sort of shape we then invited the young turks for their views, which they readily gave and which were of immense value.

I took the opportunity when I was at the Home Office to go the library to look at a report of an inquiry into equal pay of which my father had been secretary sometime in 1940s. I could detect his very dry language not only in the introduction but also in the whole of the report, and while I am quite sure that that report reflected the views of the inquiry I have equally no doubt that it was all drafted in my father's hand.

We were able with all this assistance to get a draft out by early July. Given that we had not started to hear evidence until 5 June this was by any standard a remarkable process. The only difficulty that occurred was that although we were provided with an efficient personal secretary, Nathalie Austrie, it was not her responsibility to type our report. Word processors seemed to be unknown in the Home Office.

It was my custom to dictate my opinions, and I did this with our report. My clerk did some of the typing but in the end we were dependent on the pool at the Home Office, which unfortunately did not seem fully equipped (at any rate at that time) to cope with our demands. Such was the pressure of work that at one time I offered to get two girls from Brook Street to come in and do the work because I was so frustrated by the inability of the typing pool to cope with what we required. Certainly, one of the lessons which I learnt from conducting the inquiry was the necessity for a full-time, fully trained audio typist with proper equipment. In the result, we did get the report to the Secretary of State before the end of July, when it was duly published.

What then happened was something of an eye-opener. This sort of report goes to the Cabinet for it to decide whether it should be published. Plainly it was the type of report which was likely to be published. I was told that it would be published on a particular Thursday, that I would have a press conference in the morning and the Secretary of State would announce the conclusions to the House in the afternoon.

On the Sunday and Monday immediately preceding publication I was astonished to find in the main national newspapers an accurate summary of our recommendations and conclusions, including in particular the support that we gave to the membership scheme much favoured by the Prime Minister. On the Monday I inquired of the the very efficient press secretary at the Home Office how this leak had come about. Was it the printers? Had it come from the Home Office in some way, or from somewhere else? She promised to make some inquiries and about an hour later she came back and told me that in fact the leak had come from No 10 Downing Street.

I was naturally naive at this time about these matters. Leaking is now a part of political management. I asked how it could possibly have happened that there could be a leak from No 10, and whether it had been with or without the Prime Minister's approval. Again she said she didn't know but she would make some enquiries. Eventually she came back to me to say that whereas the press office at No 10 could indeed leak matters without the Prime Minister's express approval, on this occasion it had been done by the press office with her express approval.

I confess in my innocence to have been somewhat shocked at this revelation, until it was pointed out to me that the purpose of this leak before publication was to enhance the stand which the Prime Minister had firmly taken that one way of dealing with the hooligan problem was to adopt a membership scheme. Thus, by getting this fully reported in the nationals on Sunday and Monday ahead of the Secretary of State's statement, it would naturally attract the media and therefore the public's attention. It also of course enabled those newspapers which published it to be able to tell their readers after the publication of the whole report that they had anticipated this particular recommendation. My approach to subsequent news items of a similar sort was a good deal more cynical.

The report, when published, attracted a good deal of media interest. I held a press conference which was well and fully attended, and gave a number of television interviews. The press was supportive throughout, apart from their lack of enthusiasm about 'identity cards' and were as anxious as we all were to deal with the very serious problem of football hooliganism. The Secretary of State presented my report on 24 July 1985. The government gave a positive response to most of my recommendations, and generally it was considered to have been a successful exercise. For a number of days the name Popplewell dominated the headlines, and then happily my assessors and I were able to retire to comparative obscurity while we conducted a more detailed inquiry into the structure of football generally.

Our method was to invite representations and evidence from a great number of interested parties. I wrote a personal letter to all 90 football clubs in the English league inviting them to express their views as to what steps could be taken or recommended to prevent the repetition of the events at Birmingham. I further said I would welcome any views they had about other aspects of our enquiry. I invited them either to write or to come and have a discussion with us. A number of the clubs did indeed give us the benefit of their experience, either in writing or by taking the trouble to come and talk to us. Some indeed did both. Together with the assessors we managed to visit a number of clubs. However, out of the 92 clubs, 50 did not even bother to acknowledge receipt of my personal letter, let alone give us their views. It was I thought rather sad and reflected the very insular attitudes which a great number of clubs held.

In addition to the football clubs and indeed the football authorities we sought the views of others including sporting institutions, police officers, fire officers, local authorities, judges, MPs, St John's Ambulance, sports writers and the producer of a Thames Television film called *Hooligan*. We had 300 letters from members of the public and individual commercial undertakings. There was also a project from pupils of the Curzon Church of England Combined School, Penn Street Village, Buckinghamshire, which was much appreciated. I went to visit the school and took with me a football autographed by the England team, which was much welcomed.

We decided that we must go and visit a number of clubs and see some football matches in England, Scotland and Wales. In particular as a result of the disaster at Heysel, which occurred on 29 May, during the course of our inquiry, we visited Brussels. What had happened was that shortly before the European Cup Final between Liverpool and Juventus was due to take place, English fans had charged into a block on the terraces occupied by opposing fans, as a result of which 38 people had died and some 400 people were injured. It was agreed that we should take into account any lessons arising from those events.

Additionally we visited various sports grounds devoted to rugby union, rugby league, cricket, horse racing, greyhound racing, athletics, tennis, motor racing, stock-car racing and speedway racing. We also went to a number of indoor stadia. Our general working plan was to read the documents and representations and to let witnesses come and talk to us in an informal atmosphere in the Home Office. There was no fixed agenda. Often a witness would have written something which was some guide as to what they wanted to say. We would then use them as a sounding board about particular views which we had in mind. We were constantly developing our thoughts and found these discussions a very useful way of crystallising in our minds more clearly the various arguments in favour or otherwise of a particular proposal.

The press officer at the Home Office suggested to us that if we wished to meet the football press it was no good inviting them to come and see us in the afternoon when they would be busy. Additionally, she thought a meeting in the evening when drinks would be available would be more productive. So we arranged for 20 or 30 of the football correspondents to come and meet us one evening. We provided a good deal of refreshment. We sat among them in an informal way, round a large table. I introduced the meeting by telling them that they were the experts who saw the game week in week out and we were mere amateurs. We were anxious to have their views because they were important and wanted their help as to how to solve the various problems affecting football.

They needed no further encouragement. For some three hours they held forth without taking a breath save to replenish their glasses, and supplied us with a vast amount of valuable material from their experiences. The assessors and I remained almost completely silent except to thank them at the end. They were surprised at the informality of our approach and our obvious eagerness to listen. It paid dividends. When our report finally came to be published we got headlines

'Judge accepts my views', 'Inquiry follows my recommendations', 'As I told the judge' and so on. It was a good example of a successful public relations exercise but none the worse for that.

The basis of safety at sports grounds had been the 'Home Office Guide to Safety at Sports Grounds', which was known as the 'Green Guide'. It was a thoroughly sensible pamphlet which needed to be brought up to date. To that end I set up a working party which Martin Killoran chaired. The members were a very distinguished group of 15 or 16 people. They were all experts in their own discipline. They all had very decided views on what should be in the 'Green Guide'. A lot of their discussions related to the thickness of concrete and tensile strength of railings. They met for a full week in September. From time to time I met with Martin to see how they were getting on. During the course of the week he was in total despair because his very distinguished members were putting forward what seemed to him at any rate to be wholly conflicting views. He could not see at the end of it the slightest possibility of arriving at a report with which all members would concur.

It was then that Martin's management ability came fully into its own, much assisted by the skill of Mark Depulford in the drafting of his report. It contained some 63 recommendations. I was told that it was likely that there would be one or two minority reports and that it was unlikely that the same two or three would agree to any particular proposal. To my astonishment, such was Martin's skill in management and Mark Depulford's in drafting that these great experts all concurred in the recommendations. It was a supreme example of how the personality of a chairman and skill of the drafter could work wonders in a result.

Neither I nor my assessors had very much previous acquaintance with football clubs, nor indeed were we familiar with professional football in general or the football scene in particular. To that end we visited 31 clubs, enduring some fairly monumentally boring football. We went on one occasion to an evening match at Fulham. We stood on the terraces, where it cost, if I remember rightly, some four pounds. The seats in the main enclosure cost, I believe, some four pounds fifty and were almost totally deserted. The facilities on the terrace were Victorian in the extreme but such spectators as there were chose the terraces. The quality of play was of a very low calibre. We could readily understand why spectators might be moved to hooliganism in order to provide some sort of entertainment during a boring evening.

I was once asked how we should deal with hooliganism. I somewhat facetiously told the reporter that we should follow the example of Fulham, where the first time a hooligan misbehaved he or she was taken out of the ground, and on the second occasion the hooligan was brought back into the ground and forced to watch the match. When this was more widely reported Fulham were not very pleased.

On another occasion I went to West Ham. For some reason the Home Office had got anxious about my appearing incognito and unguarded at a football ground, and decided that I should have a minder. I went dressed in clothes that Margaret would describe as somewhat scruffy. I arrived at the ground to be greeted by a plain-clothes police officer dressed a good deal more smartly than the judge and plainly a police officer. He took me round the ground. We were greeted by officers in uniform who recognised him and asked what he was doing with the judge. Thus our cover, such as it was, was well and truly blown.

On another occasion I went to Chelsea. This time I was unaccompanied. I stood on the terraces with about 15,000 other Chelsea supporters. It was indeed quite an experience. The language of the spectators, both male and female, was not for the faint-hearted. The singing was of a high quality and astonishingly well orchestrated. The humour was coarse but funny. There was an incident when the rival goal-keeper was sent off for a foul. He accepted the red card with a good deal of reluctance and was encouraged on his way by the 15,000 spectators in the stand shouting in harmony 'Off, off, off'. When he finally reached the touchline, with one accord and as though synchronised, 15,000 spectators lifted their right arms with their palms upraised. They waved gently towards the referee shouting 'Be merciful, be merciful'. Who orchestrated this or how the crowd was so controlled was impossible to say. Clearly there were leaders in the stand, and any conductor would have been proud of such a well-produced response.

Ian Studdart had produced a film for Thames Television called *Hooligan*, in which he had depicted the activities of some West Ham supporters. It seemed to us that unless we had the views of those who were involved as hooligans, we would not have a complete picture. We therefore approached Mr Studdart and discussed with him his views about hooliganism in general. More particularly we wanted to know whether those whom he had met during the course of his film would be willing to give some evidence to us. There were undoubtedly potential disadvantages in approaching these fans. Firstly, they might totally dry up when confronted by a judge and a chief constable; alternatively, they might be so boastful about their activities as not to make their evidence worthwhile. We were also somewhat apprehensive that their appearance at our inquiry might lead them to go public about their involvement and thus appear to attract some sort of seal of approval from our inquiry for their behaviour.

In the event, we were satisfied that the advantages of talking to them outweighed any disadvantages. We would naturally have to evaluate the quality of their evidence but with the assistance of Mr Studdart we hoped they would be forthcoming.

In the result, two of them attended. They gave us a fascinating insight into the behaviour of football supporters. It was clear from their evidence that part of the reason for their hooliganism was to protect what might be called 'their territory'. Thus, when visiting supporters came to their part of London they were not going to be allowed to be 'cock of the roost', rather like little gangs which form in a street or in an apartment block and dominate that particular area. West Ham supporters were determined to dominate the area of their patch. To that end, any visiting supporter was likely to be subject to attack. When we asked what would happen if we, the members of the inquiry, happened to be present at a football match when they were minded to set upon visiting supporters, they replied that they might well attack us but they wouldn't actually mean us any serious harm; we would just be unlucky bystanders. It was not a lot of comfort.

They told us that there had been an occasion when they had been intending to go to Newcastle. The match had been cancelled. They arranged to meet the Newcastle supporters some way out of the town in order to have their battle. They had had in their group some members of the Army who had been at the forefront of the battle on their days off. While during the week they might happily work with a supporter of a rival club and be friends with them, on football match day they would be deadly enemies.

There had been a suggestion that the National Front had played some part in the increase in the hooliganism. They rejected this view, observing that they would be quite happy one weekend to go and help the National Front to attack some Pakistanis and the following week team up with the Pakistanis to attack the National Front. It was simply part of their culture. Involvement in violence was a necessary form of activity for which football provided the forum.

Other supporters to whom we spoke offered much the same view. Some came from what might be described as the middle class: they owned good homes with good jobs, they were happily married. But on a Saturday with their colleagues they found that, for some reason which they were not always able to explain, they were overcome by the excitement of group violence and did terrible damage to people and property.

Naturally we also visited Scotland and saw some matches there including seeing Glasgow Celtic against Glasgow Rangers. Nothing that we saw in England could possibly compare with the intensity of the antagonism between the two sets of supporters, but the problems of hooliganism were no different there.

We went to rugby league matches where we found that the violence on the field greatly exceeded that of violence on the terraces. It was impossible to distinguish between a rugby league crowd and an association football crowd in its social makeup. At rugby-league matches, families attended full of enthusiasm and loyalty to their team. They were in no way less vociferous in support of their side, but were able to sit cheerfully side by side with opposing fans. It never seemed to occur to anyone at a rugby league match that there was any necessity for segregation. We never found an answer to explain the difference in behaviour between these supporters and soccer supporters.

Drink, we recognised, was an important element in the behaviour of the football spectators. How to deal with it was not an easy decision. Drink had been banned in Scotland inside the ground – not so much because of the effect of the drink but because bottles were used as weapons. There was a strong argument in England for allowing drink to be available in the ground on the basis that, given the size of a crowd, it was almost impossible to buy sufficient quantity inside the ground which would have any effect on a spectator's behaviour. If drink were to be banned inside the ground then all that would happen would be that a spectator would simply drink in the pubs in and around the ground. There drink could be more quickly sold and consumed, and the spectator could therefore arrive at the ground in a greater state of inebriation.

However, the government took the view that it would be sensible to ban drink inside the ground, and to that end introduced a Sporting Events Control of Alcohol Act 1985. That allowed magistrates to grant a licence to sell drink, but it did not apply to any part of the premises from which the sport could be directly viewed. The effect of that was that a licensing bench could give a licence to a bar beneath a terrace from which football was not immediately visible but refuse it for a supporters' box from which football was directly visible, even if the box was glassed in. This was the result of a compromise when the Bill went through the House of Commons. The government was keen to get an act on the statute book to prevent people having drink in the ground. The opposition took the view that if they were going to allow the matter to go through speedily, as the government wished, it was politically incorrect and socially unfair that a spectator on the terrace should be prevented from drinking while somebody in a box should be able to drink freely. It was wholly unrelated to any question of danger. As Lord Justice Holt said in 1796, 'An act of parliament can do no wrong but it may do some things that look pretty odd'.

As a matter of social equality this argument could not be criticised. As a matter of practicality for a large number of football clubs it was disastrous. Boxes had become an enormously valuable asset in the financing of a football club. Supporters had boxes, directors had boxes, sponsors had boxes. From none of these, however much drink was taken, could any damage be done. The result in practical terms was that a spectator in a box had to go behind a curtain to have his drink and re-emerge to watch the match. It was an absurdity which happily has now been resolved.

Shortly after its introduction, I was invited to Wembley to an international match. I went to have a drink. I asked for a gin and tonic. I was told unfortunately that owing to some idiot judge the law did not allow it. I felt suitably chastened.

We finally published our report in the autumn and made a number of recommendations. Generally the report had a favourable reception and the government took on board a number of our views. Sadly, it could not prevent further problems at football matches, and I watched the disaster at Hillsborough with sadness. While there is no doubt that closed-circuit television has made a substantial difference to hooliganism inside the ground, no-one can be complacent that the problems have been eliminated, Nor can we be satisfied about safety. I was taken to a ground in the northeast recently where I sat in a wooden stand some 70 or 80 yards long. I was horrified to see that the stewards were smoking throughout the game, as were a number of spectators, even though the club had been warned that television cameras were to be introduced to film a programme about safety at football grounds. Lessons learnt from disasters seldom last long.

9

Jonathan Aitken

On 10 April 1995 the *Guardian* published an article headlined 'Aitken tried to arrange girls for Saudi friends', making serious allegations about Aitken's connection with the Arabs, about a stay which he had spent at the Ritz in Paris, and about his involvement in arms dealing. On the same evening, Granada Television broadcast a 'World in Action' programme entitled 'Jonathan of Arabia', making a number of similar allegations.

Aitken called a press conference that afternoon. He said:

> I believe I have done nothing wrong. I have certainly made my fair share of mistakes in the thirty odd years of life as a writer, business-man, parliamentarian and minister, but I am prepared to stand on my record as a decent and honourable person in Saudi Arabia and elsewhere, and to defend it not only before the jury of the courts but before the wider jury of all fair minded people. If it now falls to me to start a fight to cut out the cancer of bent and twisted journalism in our country, with the simple sword of truth and the trusty shield of traditional British fairplay, so be it, I am ready for that fight.

Thus started one of the bitterest and most enthralling libel actions heard in an English court. At the time Aitken was MP for South Thanet, which seat he lost in the general election of 1997. From 1992 to July 1994 he was Minister of State for Defence and in July 1994 he was Chief Secretary to the Treasury. It was no secret that he was very friendly with a number of Arabs and in particular with members of the royal household and that he had secured for the British Government a number of very worthwhile arms contracts.

A number of newspapers had been highly critical of his behaviour and his conduct over a period of time. He had decided, as he subsequently told the court, to ignore those allegations. However, when these particular publications took place he decided that enough was enough and issued proceedings. On 11 December 1995 Granada published another documentary programme in their 'World in Action' series, entitled 'The Lisi File'. Effectively, it sought to connect Aitken with a firm called B Marc, which had supplied arms for Iran under the 'Lisi' contract. On 12 December 1995 the *Guardian* published an article, alleging that Aitken had offered to help B Marc win orders for Iraq when it was covered by an arms embargo, as well as an allegation similar to that in the Granada broadcast.

After the writs had been issued in April 1955 and January 1996, there ensued a great deal of exchange of pleadings between the parties. Although the pleadings and the documentation covered an immensely wide field, the allegations really came down to a discrete number: one, that he had procured for the Arabs, and for a particular named prince, prostitutes at the Inglewood Health Hydro, which was a health clinic of which he was director; two, that he had an involvement in a Lebanese-owned arms company named Future Management Services (FMS) and that while a minister he maintained relations clandestinely with them and failed to disclose his directorship in the register of members' interests; three, that in September 1993, as a minister of the crown he had visited Paris to attend an expenses-paid business meeting of various associates of Prince Mohammed and the Saudi royal family, and that he told lies about this visit in order to conceal his misconduct; four, that he had a business relationship with the Saudis which he concealed and that he received commissions which he knew to be derived from bribes received from the royal family; five, that he was involved with a company called B Marc, which had provided equipment for Iran and Iraq contrary to Resolutions of the UN and the parliamentary statements; and finally six, that in December 1980, when he was director of a television company called TV-am, he allowed the Saudis to become a major shareholder without revealing that to the IBA, which had rules governing the foreign ownership of independent television companies.

It was, however, in relation to Aitken's visit to the Ritz that the main thrust of the case lay. From 17 to 19 September 1993 he had stayed at the Ritz in Paris. It was his case that he had gone there with his wife and daughter to have a family holiday before they took their daughter to a new school at Aiglon, near Geneva. He claimed his visit was a purely private one, that there was no business deal involved and there was nothing which could give rise to the slightest criticism.

The *Guardian* learnt from Mr Fayed, the owner of the Ritz, not only that Aitken had stayed at the Ritz on the dates alleged, but also that a number of people, including Mr Said Ayas and Mr Wafic Said, Arab businessmen, were also staying in the Ritz on that weekend. There then ensued a correspondence between Mr Preston, who was at that time the editor of the *Guardian*, and Aitken. It started in October 1993 and continued off and on for the best part of a year. It concerned the details of Aitken's visit to the Ritz. During the course of the correspondence, Aitken was interviewed by Sir Robert Butler, the Chief Secretary to the Cabinet, and by the Prime Minister, and he made a statement in the House of Commons. A neutral observer might well regard it as somewhat bizarre that the busy editor of a national newspaper and the equally busy Chief Secretary to the Treasury should spend their valuable time writing to each other on a regular basis over that period concerning details of a visit to a hotel in France.

Before a case like this comes on for trial, there are a number of preliminary procedural matters about which the general public are usually wholly unaware. Firstly, each side sets out its case – in the case of a plaintiff in a statement of claim, in the case of a defendant in a defence. The plaintiff then issues a reply to the defence and the defendant is entitled to issue a rejoinder. These documents are drafted by counsel and they give rise to requests for particulars, some of which may be agreed to; others may require the order of the court. I was given charge of the case early in 1997 and thereafter all the preliminary applications relating to the case were heard by me. The pleadings in the *Guardian* and the Granada actions followed a similar though not precisely identical pattern, because there were slightly different allegations. The parties amended their pleadings from time to time. By the time we got to trial the defence had been amended, re-amended, re-re-amended and yet re-re-re-amended. At the trial itself I had a bundle described as a 'truncated bundle of pleadings', which ran to 255 pages.

There were a great number of preliminary hearings dealing with all sorts of procedural matters which were heard privately in chambers. At an early stage I was provided with a list of potential witnesses on both sides in the various actions. They numbered some 200 in all. It's inevitable in this sort of case that a judge may either know of or personally know one or more of the witnesses, and I pointed out to counsel that there were two or three witnesses whom I knew socially.

There are a number of ways of dealing with this problem. The judge is obviously obliged to draw this to the attention of counsel. I say obviously because every judge is aware of this obligation, which is no more than common sense. How Lord Hoffman failed to disclose his interest in the Pinochet affair remains a mystery – how he could continue to sit after being reproved by the law lords is even more baffling. A judge can if he or she so wishes then disqualify him or herself on the ground that this knowledge of the personalities involved is so great that even if the case could be tried fairly, it would not be seen to have been tried fairly. There are other situations in which the familiarity with the witness is either so tenuous or the importance of the witness is so limited that the judge need not disqualify him or herself unless there is strong objection from the bar. In this case, having drawn the attention of the bar to the two or three witnesses whom I knew, I asked whether there was any objection to my continuing to hear the case. No sort of objection was raised and, indeed, none could have been raised. Then the matter simply dropped out of any argument.

However, one of the allegations raised was that Aitken had allowed the Saudis to become a major shareholder in TV-am without revealing that to the IBA in December 1980. In 1988 the Saudi interest in TV-am became known. As a result, the IBA required the board of TV-am to take steps to disenfranchise the holding and subsequently Aitken resigned his directorship. By 1988, Margaret had become a member of the IBA under the chairmanship of Lord Thompson. She was a very junior member.

The issue in relation to TV-am was not what happened in 1988 but what happened in 1980, long before Margaret became a member. There was no dispute that in 1988 the IBA had taken a strong view about Aitken's behaviour. There was indeed a minute of the board meeting to that effect. There were no witness statements from any of the members of the IBA. Nevertheless, I felt it was necessary long before the trial started to inform the parties that Margaret was a member of the IBA in 1988, and to enquire whether anybody had any objection. I was assured on all sides that there was no possibility of any objection, that there was an agreed board minute and the issue revolved not around what happened in 1988, but in 1980. Thus the matter closed and I thought no more about it.

However, during the course of the trial there appeared to be some dispute as to what had happened between Aitken and the IBA in 1988. Mr Carman QC, on behalf of the plaintiff, sought leave to obtain a witness statement from Lord Thompson, chairman at the material time, and to call him as a witness. The modern practice at trial is that if a party wishes to call a witness, it has to obtain a statement from that witness before the trial. It then has to be exchanged with the other side so that what is sometimes called 'cards on the table and no ambush' obtains. No such statement had been taken from Lord Thompson, although the allegation about TV-am had been pleaded some two years before.

Accordingly, when Mr Carman QC, on behalf of the defendants, sought leave to call Lord Thompson in the middle of the trial, I refused. That night the evening paper had a headline which suggested that Margaret might well be called as a witness; no such suggestion had in fact been made by Mr Carman QC. Without a witness statement having been obtained from her she would not have been allowed to give evidence, nor indeed could she give any material evidence other than that she had been present at the board meeting in 1988, as to which there was no dispute. She was the junior member of the authority and there were, I think, 11 other members. Thus, her evidence would have been of little or no value.

Next morning I therefore called the parties into my room to see what was going on. It was explained to me that the defendants wished to call Lord Thompson as a witness and to take a statement from him. I observed that as far as I could understand there was no question of Margaret being called to give evidence. She would in any event have been called as a witness on behalf of the defence and Mr Gray QC, on behalf of Aitken, raised no sort of objection. It was obviously not a very desirable situation and, the matter having been raised in the media, it had to be dealt with in open court. In open court I raised the question of Lord Thompson again and the question of Margaret being called. It was clear that I would now have to allow Lord Thompson to be called if the defendants wished, in order to avoid suggestion that I was keeping his evidence out to avoid Margaret having to give evidence. In the result, Lord Thompson produced a statement but was not called. Indeed, there was no sensible possibility of his being called because there really was no substantial issue about what happened in 1988. As far as Margaret was concerned, there never was in fact any possibility of her being a witness. Thus, although it provided the media with some copy, it was, in the result, a total non-event.

More contentious, however, and more important, was the decision I had to make as to how the case was to be tried. By the time I came to take over the case it had been agreed between the parties that the case should be tried by a judge and jury. Libel cases are normally heard by a judge and jury. That had been done my Mr Justice French on 18 June 1996. In May 1997 the plaintiff made an application that the case should be tried by judge alone, that is by me. The decision as to the method of trial is not governed by some idiosyncratic view of the judge, as some of the less-informed scribblers seemed to think, but by certain rules. In this case the Supreme Court Act 1981 provided that in a claim in respect of libel, the action should be tried with a jury 'unless the court is of the opinion that the trial requires any prolonged examination of documents which cannot conveniently be made with a jury'. I therefore had to consider firstly, whether the trial did require a long examination of documents and secondly, if it did, whether it could conveniently be made with a jury. If a trial cannot be conveniently made with a jury, the court has a discretion as to how the trial should be conducted. There were a number of previous cases which laid down the general principles. Lord Denning, in one of the earlier cases, said 'When a man's honour or reputation is at stake it may be of special importance to him to have a jury'. However, the wording of the rule was thereafter changed. The current position was stated by Lord Justice Lawton, who said 'Even if it does require prolonged examination of documents there is still a discretion on the court to allow trial with a jury but the emphasis now is against a trial with juries and the court should take this emphasis into account when exercising its discretion'.

The principles which I had to apply were not seriously in doubt at the bar. It was on the facts as they then stood that the parties made their submissions. On behalf of the defendant, Mr Price QC said it was a simple case which depended on the credibility of the plaintiff, that the number of documents were comparatively limited, that they were not complex and it was the oral evidence upon which the jury would have to rely and determine the issues. Mr Gray QC, on behalf of the plaintiff, said there was a vast number of documents and although a lot of them were comparatively simple, it was the sheer volume of documents which were likely to be used which would require prolonged examination. At that stage the plaintiff had witness statements from 80 witnesses and the defendants from 60 or 70. The witness statements alone amounted to some nearly 1800 pages.

It was also the sheer volume of documents that was a problem. The plaintiffs list amounted to some 600 separate documents and the defendants between them to some 850 documents. They did not simply represent that number of pages. It was obvious to me at that stage that the vast quantity of documents made it wholly inconvenient for the case to be tried by a jury. In that event it was clear that my discretion should be exercised according to the rules against a jury rather than in favour.

This decision was greeted by near hysteria among the *Guardian* scribblers and by other sections of an ill-informed press. I gave leave for them to appeal to the Court of Appeal because of the urgency of the matter. The Court of Appeal, presided over by the Lord Chief Justice, heard submissions from both parties. All the relevant authorities were cited to them, and my decision was upheld. Some of the wilder criticisms in the press about the Court of Appeal decision sadly reflected more on the critics than on the court. By the time the case came on for trial it was even more self-evident that the volume of the material was such that it could not have been conveniently tried by a jury.

One of the more fanciful criticisms made was that a jury would be likely to have found in favour of the defendant, whereas a judge would be so overwhelmed by the presence in the witness box of a Cabinet minister, that he or she would be bound to find in favour of the plaintiff. Nothing of course could be further from the truth. Judges try cases alone every day of the year, frequently involving the credibility of witnesses. We often have to make the decision that a witness is a liar or that a plaintiff or defendant is fraudulent or not in any circumstances to be believed. Part of the exercise of our judgment for which we have years of experience is to make those sort of findings.

Nor did the matter rest there. Months after the plaintiff had thrown in his hand and the *Guardian* had had a tremendous victory, one of their scribblers was still whingeing and whining about my decision to dispense with a jury. I'm afraid it only served to make him look something of a laughing stock.

It was obvious from the very start of the trial that what happened in Paris was likely to be the yardstick by which the rest of the evidence was to be governed. But before that issue became crystallised I had to make yet one further ruling: each party had to set out what it said the allegation meant. The defendant who sought to justify, that is to prove the truth of an allegation, had firstly to set out the meaning and then seek to prove its truth. If the allegation meant something worse than that which it was sought to justify, the plea of justification would fail. To give a simple example: if a plaintiff alleges that an article means he is a thief, but the defendant says the article only means he is suspected of theft and seeks to justify the suspicion, the plea of justification will fail if the conclusion is that the allegation means he is a thief. When a jury is sitting, the judge has to rule whether the meaning alleged by one or other of the parties is capable of having that meaning. It is then for the jury to decide whether it does have that meaning. When a judge is sitting alone, as I was, the judge has to decide not merely whether it is capable of having the meaning alleged, but whether it does have that meaning.

In relation to a company called B Marc, the article and television broadcast suggested that the company had provided equipment for Iran and Iraq, contrary to Resolution of the UN and various parliamentary statements. There was no dispute that the article and programme were suggesting this. So far as the plaintiff's involvement was concerned, it was his case that the article and broadcast meant that he knew what was going on. The defendant didn't seek to justify that he actually knew what was going on, but that he ought to have known what was going on.

Although the difference to a layman may seem slight, there was a difference. I had to decide, reading the article and looking at the television broadcast, whether the meaning was that he actually knew or whether it was merely an allegation that he ought to have known. I was addressed on the subject. I re-read the article and looked at the broadcast on a number of occasions. I came to the clearest conclusion that both the article and the broadcast were saying that he knew what was going on. Thus the defence of justification of the allegation that he ought to have known could not be sustained. Accordingly I ruled in the plaintiffs favour. No-one looking at the programme or reading the article could have had any doubt as to their meaning.

This decision too caused affront to the *Guardian*, which seemed to think that if only there had been a jury it would have got a 'better' decision. It wouldn't, because I would have ruled that the article was incapable of bearing the meaning which the defendant suggested.

The events of the visit to Paris read like a detective novel. Its eventual *dénouement* was due to some fine work by a *Guardian* journalist and its investigators. The plaintiff had planned to travel to Paris and Geneva with his wife and their youngest daughter Victoria. They intended to cross by ferry on Friday 17 September to go to Paris and do a day's shopping. Having stayed overnight in Paris, they then intended to go onto to Geneva where they had arranged to stay with the Ayas family, one of whom was godparent to Victoria. The purpose of going to Geneva was to take Victoria to her new school at Aiglon College, Villars Geneva. She was due to arrive as a new girl that weekend.

Prior to going to Paris, the plaintiff was required as Minister of State for Defence to take the place of the Foreign Office Minister and go with the Duke of Edinburgh to Kracow to attend the reburial ceremony of General Sikorski. The plaintiff had intended to fly from Kracow to Paris at about 1pm in order to join up with the family. However, the obsequies to General Sikorski took longer than anticipated, with the result that he missed his commercial flight to Paris. He went back to London via Balmoral on the Queen's Flight with the Duke of Edinburgh. He finally got to Paris at about half past nine in the evening and went to the Ritz Hotel, where he was staying. His room was booked by his Arab friend Said Ayas. His story was as follows.

When he got to the Ritz he was invited by Said Ayas to dinner, and then learnt that his wife and Victoria had gone to Geneva. Thus, he spent the Friday night at the Ritz by himself. On the Saturday he spent the whole day in Paris without his family. He arranged to go and see his daughter on the Sunday, in the late afternoon. According to him he spent the Saturday jogging, reading and writing. His wife, who had originally intended to come back on the Saturday night to join him, rang to say that she would come back to the Ritz on the Sunday morning.

19. Trial of Jonathan Aitken. From left: George Carman QC, Jonathan Aitken, O.B.P.

According to Aitken, she arrived late in the morning. She had a bath. They talked. Somewhere about 1.30pm he left the Ritz and went to Geneva, where he saw his daughter for about half an hour. The reason that his wife remained in Paris on the Sunday was, according to Aitken, to see a doctor about some ailment on Monday morning. To that end, during the course of the trial a bill was produced.

It was obvious to me at a very early stage, without any other evidence, that this was a wholly improbable story. Here was a family intending to have a weekend together with their daughter. In the result, according to Aitken, he saw his wife for half an hour or so on the Sunday lunchtime and his daughter for half an hour on the Sunday evening. But as the story unfolded and was probed in some depth, it became increasingly clear that the story was not only wholly improbable, but plainly untrue. That became clear to me long before the final nail was driven into Aitken's coffin with the production of the airline tickets of the wife and daughter and the hire-car documents.

Apart from the improbability of the story, the next problem which Aitken had was about details of the bill. His bill amounted to some FF8000 and was debited to the account of Said Ayas. Aitken said that there was nothing said or shown to him to suggest the bill was going to be paid by Ayas. He suggested that he offered his American Express card and it was refused. According to him, when he left, leaving his wife in the room, he asked if he could have a late check-out at about 3pm and was told there was no problem. He realised that his wife would have to pay the bill, and to that end she used some dollars which he had given her. That story changed when it was discovered, according to him, that his wife had paid some FF4257, the explanation being that she was dyslexic and could not read the figures. Aitken's evidence at trial was that the balance had been paid to a Mr Abdul Rahman on the grounds that his account had been overpaid by the sum of FF3573, and that Aitken's account was underpaid by that sum.

The defendant's case was essentially a simple one. Mrs Aitken had never paid any money. The sum of FF4257 had been paid by a Madame Vidal. She had gone to pay Mr Ayas's account by cheque, found that some small expenses had been further incurred and handed over the sum of FF4257 in cash from her handbag in addition to the cheque. The description given by the Ritz of the lady who had handed over the cash did not accord with the description of Mrs Aitken.

The various explanations as to what happened in Paris, given by Aitken during the correspondence with Preston, gave rise to considerable doubt as to his credibility. The circumstances in which he had paid a cheque to Abdul Rahman were strange in the extreme, as was the fact that the bill relating to his occupancy of the room had the time of his checking out on it, which did not accord with the presence of Mrs Aitken in the room.

By about day three or four of the trial it was clear to me that Aitken was in real difficulty in relation to the Ritz. Each evening I dictated notes of the day's hearings, with various comments. I observed a number of matters. In his witness statement there had been no mention of offering a credit card; he had never asked for his bill; Rahman never in fact paid his bill or sent the money back; there was a query about the bank account on which the cheque to Rahman was paid. Further, Aitken's story to the Cabinet Secretary and the Prime Minister was not wholly consistent with what he was telling Preston. As the cross-examination continued, there were still further problems.

On the Sunday there was a telephone call from Aitken's room at the Ritz to the Hotel Bristol in Geneva, where Mrs Aitken had been spending Saturday night. It was clear from the evidence that if Mrs Aitken had arrived at the Ritz on the Sunday morning, at the time suggested, even by the speediest transport she could not have been the recipient of the telephone call in Geneva at 10.15am. It followed either that she had not come to the Ritz on the Sunday morning, or that the telephone call at 10.15am had not been made to her. Aitken's explanation was that indeed his wife had arrived in Paris at a time when she had not been able to receive the call in Geneva. It was to his mother-in-law that he had spoken.

The immediate difficulty with that explanation was that there was no mention in his witness statement of his speaking to his mother-in-law. Further, there was no witness statement from this lady that she had actually spoken to Aitken. Further, although Aitken gave evidence that his wife's stay in Paris on the Sunday was so that she could get some medical treatment on the Monday, there was nothing in his witness statement, nor in her witness statement, about it. It was only during the latter part of the trial that a document was produced relating to the bill for this medical appointment. By this time I was as sure as I could be that Aitken's explanation about the Ritz episode was quite untrue.

The documentary evidence which confirmed this view had not then been obtained, and of course no judge should make a decision on part of the evidence until the whole has been revealed. But at that stage that was my state of mind. For some reason the *Guardian* thought – and perhaps still think – that I believed Aitken on the Ritz story. Why they should have this view I know not. It is just plain wrong.

The next problem facing Aitken was the question of what his mother-in-law was doing at the Hotel Bristol on the Sunday morning. It was of course possible that she happened to be in the same room which Mrs Aitken had occupied. Alternatively, it might be that she had shared the room with Mrs Aitken on the Saturday night, and Mrs Aitken then left to go to Paris. Behind the scenes and unknown to me, the *Guardian* had managed to obtain very important evidence from the Hotel Bristol. It was detective work of the highest order. The Hotel

Bristol had closed down. All the records were in some cellar, to which it was very difficult to get access. However, the investigator persevered.

In the result, from the *Guardian*'s point of view it struck pure gold. The records which the investigator brought back showed that on the Friday night Mrs Aitken and her daughter had occupied a room and the accounts showed that she had paid by way of American Express for a dual occupancy. On the Saturday, it will be remembered, Victoria had gone back to school. The records showed, or appeared to show, that on the Saturday night Mrs Aitken had been charged for a dual occupancy, but that when she had come to pay there had been a remittance on the basis of a sole occupancy. Thus, on the face of the documents it appeared that Aitken's mother-in-law had not shared the room overnight. Further, Mrs Aitken must have pointed out to the hotel that she and she alone had occupied the room on the Saturday night in order to get the alteration to the bill.

Because there had been a good deal of reluctance on the part of Aitken to show Mrs Aitken's travel documents, the defendants had not been aware that she was using an American Express card. Indeed, it had been Aitken's case throughout that, because his wife was dyslexic and not good with cards, she normally paid in cash. The Hotel Bristol documents gave a direct lie to that and to the suggestion that it was his mother-in-law to whom Aitken had spoken on the Sunday morning. Thus, this was yet another piece of evidence casting grave doubt on the suggestion that Mrs Aitken had come to Paris on the Sunday morning.

While this investigation was going on there was of course other evidence in relation to the discrete allegations made against Aitken. While they gave rise to some suspicion of the veracity of Aitken, none was of the same strength as the evidence relating to the Ritz except for one. It was Aitken's case (which went to damages) that, while he was about to go on holiday with one of his daughters, he had been harassed by television interviewers and his daughter had been distressed. A television film of this incident was shown. It was quite clear from the video that no sort of harassment had in fact taken place. It was Aitken's case that it must have been a different occasion from that shown on the video. However, the defendants were able to blow up a picture and identify the actual occasion and the time. Aitken called his driver, who loyally in support of his employer, described an incident of harassment. However, it was perfectly clear from the film produced that no such incident as Aitken contended for had taken place, and this had the further effect of damaging Aitken's credibility.

The trial, meanwhile, proceeded. Aitken's evidence concluded and some other evidence on his behalf was called. By this time, Mrs Aitken, who had been a loyal supporter of her husband, had ceased to attend the trial. A witness statement by the daughter was prepared indicating that she had crossed with her mother to Paris on the Friday, gone to Geneva on the Saturday and then to school, thus purporting to support Aitken's case about his wife's movements.

During the course of the evidence of one of Aitken's witnesses, there was a great flurry on the defendant's side in court. Some documents were shown to Mr Carman QC. After a moment he suggested as a matter of urgency that I should look at them, releasing the witness for the time being. This I did. The documents were of two sorts. Firstly there were copies of airline tickets relating to the flight of Mrs Aitken and Victoria from London to Geneva by British Airways on the Friday arriving at Geneva some time about midday and a return ticket for Mrs Aitken, leaving Geneva on the Monday morning. This was supported by a witness statement from British Airways saying that it related to Mrs Aitken and Miss Aitken. There could be no doubt that these documents were authentic and that they related to Mrs Aitken. In one sense the defendants were lucky to obtain them, because if Mrs Aitken had flown by Swiss Air they would not have been able to obtain them by way of subpoena. That was the first additional piece of gold. The second were car-hire documents in Mrs Aitken's name showing that she had collected a car from Geneva airport at about midday on the Friday and delivered it back in down town Geneva on the Sunday evening. Thus the whole jigsaw fell into place and showed that Mrs Aitken had never been to Paris at all that weekend, and therefore the whole story of Mrs Aitken paying the bill as an explanation for what otherwise appeared to be payment by the Arabs, fell to the ground.

In those circumstances it was clear that Aitken's case had totally collapsed. I naturally adjourned the case for the day, suggesting to Mr Gray QC that he would want to consider his position. The following day I have no doubt that he discussed the matter at length with his client and decided to abandon the case, as he was bound to do. There was obviously then some discussion about costs between Mr Gray QC and Mr Carman QC, so that on the next morning when the case was resumed Mr Gray QC simply got up and said the plaintiff discontinued the case and agreed to pay 80 per cent of the defendant's costs, thus reflecting no doubt the cost of the B Marc issue on which I had given a ruling in Aitken's favour.

It so happened that the case collapsed during the course of the Lords test match. During one day that I was there I fell in with John Major and asked him about his meeting with Aitken in relation to this matter. He told me that he had had Aitken in, and he asked him whether there was any truth in the allegations. Aitken, he said, had looked him straight in the eye and said there was nothing at all in it. The Prime Minister felt bound to accept the word of a Cabinet colleague.

There was only one further matter that I had to consider – namely, whether I should report the matter to the Director of Public Prosecutions (DPP) for the question of proceedings for perjury or conspiracy starting in October 1993, and continuing off and on for the best part of a year, about his stay at the Ritz, his correspondence with Preston, his interview with Sir Robert Butler and the Prime Minister and his statement in the House of Commons. Aitken plainly had committed perjury and attempted to pervert the course of justice. But the matter was taken out of my hands by the *Guardian*, flushed with victory, sending the papers to the DPP for prosecution to be considered.

Exactly what he was doing at the Ritz that weekend we may never know. He was a very convincing witness in the witness box. He had obviously impressed his own advisors. Further, there was some suggestion after the trial that the *Guardian* had been prepared to settle the case before it started, each side paying their own costs. But the whole story of the family visit totally lacked credibility.

In June 1999 he appeared at the Old Bailey before Mr Justice Scott Baker and was sentenced to 18 months' imprisonment for perjury. Much was made of his valuable contribution in obtaining arms deals with the Arabs and of the benefit that enured to this country. It was a sad end to a distinguished political career, but he could not complain that the sentence was too severe.

10

A Legal Miscellany

When I was first appointed a judge I went to sit firstly at Birmingham and secondly at Stafford. At Birmingham I was invited to dinner by the High Sheriff. Margaret was not able to come so I went with one of my fellow judges. Sitting at the other end of the table was a young widow called Clare. She told me afterwards that she had understood that she must not talk to me, as a judge, until I talked to her, and above all she could not go the the lavatory until I had been. I subsequently rang her up and invited her to go to the theatre at Stratford called The Other Place, at which time she told me the story. After we had seen the show we went over to the main theatre to the restaurant where I had booked dinner. We had a most amusing and entertaining evening and then I asked for the bill. Along came the waiter producing the bill. I took out my American Express card. To my horror he said that they did not take American Express cards. I had no other cards in my wallet. I had not sufficient cash and I did not have a cheque book with me. So poor Clare had to write a cheque, and went away thinking 'We have got a right one here!' We have often laughed about this story and Margaret and I became firm friends with her.

One of the pleasures of going on circuit was being entertained by High Sheriffs and meeting their friends. I met a great coterie of entertaining and lively people all round the country, but nowhere better than in the West Midlands and Staffordshire, Berkshire, Hertfordshire and Buckinghamshire. Many have become close friends, whose company I much value.

20. O.B.P. High Court judge, January 1983.

When I went to Stafford, the butler who was looking after me was a lovely man called Howard Haggis. He was well into his eighties and I think had been chief steward on either the Queen Mary or the Queen Elizabeth. He laid out my clothes with some sort of disdain, enquired whether the judge wanted his suit cleaned, his socks mended, his shoes polished. But he was such an engaging figure that when I went to Reading I asked if he could come and join me there. On the first day when we were to have a dinner party he was serving lunch and he managed, because he was so shaky, to drop a potato down Margaret's front. We were terribly anxious about how he would get on at the dinner party because there was soup and soft fruit for pudding, and clearly his eyesight was not as good as it should be. It was all right when he poured out red wine, but white wine totally defeated him. He could not see how much, if any, he was pouring, and the result was that our guests either got none or the glass overflowed. Also, he was so slow in serving that we had the white wine with the beef and the red wine with the raspberries, and I don't think we ever got as far as the port. However, he was a lovely man and one could take no offence. When I was conducting the Bradford inquiry he wrote me a very touching letter about his faith and prayed for me that I would find a successful outcome to the problems which there arose.

Once I went to sit at Maidstone Crown Court in order to try a case of fraud. The ringleader had set up a simple scheme of persuading people to invest money with a rate of interest well above what was available elsewhere. At the end of the first year the investors received the interest and were naturally pleased, and some decided to reinvest. It was a bogus scheme because thereafter he never repaid the investors. A great number of innocent people got involved and lost very substantial sums of money. It is easy to be critical and observe that it must have been self-evident that the sort of returns that were being offered were never likely to be based on a sound financial basis. It was a common type of fraud. It was not a case which otherwise would have attracted any attention, or indeed required a High Court judge to try it.

However, I was sent for by the Lord Chief Justice, Lord Lane, and asked if I would do it. It was the sort of invitation a judge does not refuse. When I enquired why, I was told that one of the defendants was a member of the bar. It was therefore to be treated as a case out of the run of the mill and required a High Court judge. Accordingly I agreed to try it and read the papers.

What had happened was this. This particular villain had been in trouble before in some other sort of fraud. He had then been represented by a distinguished-looking barrister called Sir Lionel Thompson Bart. As a result of the plea in mitigation by Sir Lionel, he had avoided being sent to prison. Sir Lionel had then become a director of the man's company. No doubt he thought that having a baronet on the company notepaper would add an air of respectability to the operation. However, when it became clear that the company's activities were dishonest, not only was the villain charged but so was Sir Lionel as one of the directors of the company.

There were a number of defendants in the dock. The case was going to last for an appreciable period of time. The evidence in relation to each defendant was not identical, so that the presence of each was not necessary for every part of the proceedings. I accordingly allowed them all bail, apart from the chief villain. They were allowed to come and go in the dock and return as and when evidence relating to them was dealt with. The bar was very apprehensive that while Sir Lionel was not involved in the criminal charge he might go and appear in the next door court as an advocate. They were also greatly concerned that they might find him eating in the bar mess at lunchtime which, as a fellow barrister, he was entitled to do. Happily neither of these events occurred.

The case involved a great number of investors, some of whom were called to give evidence. It was not a case to set the blood flowing, although of vital importance to those who had lost a lot of money. However, there came a moment during the trial when there was what can be properly described as 'laughter in court'. It arose in this way. The case against Sir Lionel was that he was not simply a director in name but that he had been party to decisions which had led to the fraud. In particular he had been at a meeting, I think at Maidstone, on a particular date. In order to pursue this line of investigation a detective sergeant went to see Sir Lionel in his room in chambers. He said to Sir Lionel, 'Sir Lionel, I 'ave 'ere the minutes of a meeting what was 'eld at Maidstone on 30th July, what shows you was there and took part in the meeting.' Sir Lionel said that he was sure he was not there. In order to prove that point he went to see his clerk and produced the chambers' diary. Armed with the chambers' diary he was able to point out that on the same day as he was said to have been at Maidstone, he was in fact engaged as a barrister at Leicester Crown Court.

This caused the sergeant to scratch his head and the following exchange then took place. 'Well, Sir Lionel, I 'ave 'ere the minutes of the meeting what shows you was present at Maidstone on 30th July. You have shown me your chambers' diary, what shows you was at Leicester Crown Court also on 30th July. It's a bit of an enema isn't it?'

The judge, of course, has the statements of witnesses who are going to give evidence in front of him. I naturally assumed that what appeared in the witness statement was simply a misprint. But the sergeant gave his evidence in exactly the same way as it appeared in his statement. I hesitated to add to the fun by asking whether that could be some sort of 'variation' but judges should avoid jokes, particularly musical ones.

In the result, Sir Lionel was convicted of a minor offence, was given a suspended sentence and, I think, subsequently left the bar.

A good deal of the work I did as a judge was judicial review, done in the Crown Office. That involved reviewing decisions made by administrators, whether councils, ministers or other like bodies, and deciding in effect whether they had acted reasonably. A great number of the cases related to immigration. The volume of immigration cases was overwhelming. Cases involving asylum would not be dealt with for two or three years. There was an elaborate system of appeals. Somebody claiming asylum would apply to the Secretary of State. If the Secretary of State refused the asylum-seeker would then apply to a special adjudicator. If the special adjudicator also refused, an appeal would be made to the Immigration Appeal Tribunal. If the Immigration Appeal Tribunal also refused, an application would be made to a judge like myself, on paper, for leave to appeal. If leave were refused, an application would be made in Open Court. If leave were again refused, leave would be sought in the Court of Appeal. Thus, an asylum-seeker was given more avenues of appeal than someone charged with murder. There is no doubt that the system was regularly abused. Firstly, because the asylum-seeker was often at liberty in this country and had nothing to lose, time meant nothing. Accordingly the appeals were put in at the fifty-ninth minute of the eleventh hour. Secondly, legal aid was available in the latter stages of the appeal, and was regularly applied for and given. Most of the appeals were limited to questions of law. Most litigants and their advisors proceeded on the basis of a re-run of the facts. Legal aid was frequently granted by the legal-aid authorities without, so far as one can tell, any sensible appreciation of the legal position. Some legal advisors were happy to advise an appeal even where it was quite hopeless. The result of this was dashed hopes amongst the appellants and a great burden on legal aid.

The statistics showed that failure of the applications was very high, and simply demonstrated the hopelessness of most of the cases which came before the court. It was a disgraceful situation.

No home secretary seemed willing to address the problem, either by reducing the number of appeals or ensuring legal aid was not wasted in this way. When criticisms are made by the Lord Chancellor about how legal aid is wasted, little attention seems to be given to the vast amount spent on this part of the litigation. Recent developments seem to indicate that the government has at last started to appreciate the problems. One can only hope that a more sensible approach will be adopted so that the genuine asylum-seekers will not find themselves swamped by those whose cases are quite hopeless.

In judicial review there are strict time limits, that is to say an application has to be made promptly or, in any event, within three months. Many and varied are the excuses put forward by applicants who make late applications. The best was put forward by a Nigerian who had failed to comply with time limits, and wrote by way of explanation 'I suffered a fatal accident and I am now confined to bed'.

The High Sheriff entertained the judges when they went out on circuit, and the judges reciprocated by inviting the High Sheriff and various guests to their dinner table. Ladies on their own, whether single, unmarried, divorced or widowed, were much in demand because frequently the judges did not have their wives with them and it was customary to try and balance the table. Much time was spent on tracing such ladies. There was an occasion at Bristol when the judges asked a very attractive headmistress who arrived in her MGB GT and parked it in the drive. She had an enormously good evening and the judges thought it would be prudent to put her in a taxi so she could go home. When the MGB GT was still in the drive a week later they thought it would be perhaps more convenient if she could come and collect it. To that end, they rang up the school secretary to enquire when the headmistress would be able to come and collect her car. At this the school secretary replied that the headmistress would be delighted to know where the car was, as she had quite forgotten where she had parked it.

When the judges went out on circuit it was customary for them to take a marshall, who was usually a pupil just starting at the bar. The purpose of the pupil going out was to learn from the judge by discussion and observation how trials were conducted, how they should be conducted and to see a judge in action, having read all the papers beforehand. It was an enormously valuable experience, which seems to have fallen into desuetude because pupils now are so anxious to get on with their life at the bar that they see no purpose in spending six or eight weeks with a judge out on circuit. The marshalling system has therefore been somewhat re-jigged, in that now judges who sit in London can have a marshall during a week, discuss the case with him or her, and at the end of the day the marshall can go back to his or her own home.

My inn ran such a marshalling scheme, and I agreed to take on a young man. When he came into the room I realised at once that he was of a more mature age than most marshalls. I suppose he was in his forties. I therefore enquired how it came about that he was reading for the bar. He told me that he had been a consultant at, I think, the Brompton, but that he had got fed up with the National Health Service and resigned. He very much wanted a change of profession and had started reading for the bar. He seemed a thoroughly nice, capable man and as it happened the case I was trying involved medical negligence. He sat with me in court for the first three days, during which we had a great number of very learned professors all giving their views about the various medical issues involved in the case. I confess that I found it an exceedingly difficult case to try. It all depended on professors who were very distinguished, and they all had good reasons to justify their views. Neither side was willing to admit that the views of the other side could possibly be correct.

However, on the fourth morning my marshall passed me a note saying, 'Why don't you ask them about the – theory?' I knew nothing about the theory, nor what it involved, but it seemed a worthwhile exercise to invite the parties to consider it. I therefore turned to both counsel and said, 'I don't know whether any of your experts have considered the – theory, but perhaps you would all like half an hour for them to do that to see whether it affects their views'. The experts who happened to be in court all looked at me with increasing admiration at my apparent expertise. Counsel said that they would certainly take half an hour and they came back within that time to announce that thanks to the intervention of the judge they had resolved the issues between them. The parties therefore settled. It seemed a very good start to the doctor's career. He told me that he was going to go into chambers specialising in medical negligence and asked if I would call him to the bar at the Inner Temple, which in due course I did.

Some years later, Jonathan Hurst QC, who was the chairman of the Professional Conduct Committee, asked me if I remembered the name of the doctor. I couldn't immediately place him and Jonathan said that I had called him to the bar. It then came back to me about whom he was talking. It transpired that the doctor had gone into chambers having told them that he passed the bar exam; at the end of six months he would have been entitled to practice. Accordingly, his chambers had written to the Bar Council to get the appropriate certificate to enable the doctor to go into court under his own steam. The Bar Council was somewhat perplexed because it transpired that the doctor had taken the bar exam twice but had failed both times. The doctor had never told his chambers that this had happened, and more importantly, when further inquiries were made about his background he hadn't simply resigned from the medical practice, but had in fact, as I understand it, been struck off. I felt suitably conned. He had been a very impressive performer and I have no doubt would have done very well at the bar in medical negligence, but not unreasonably the Professional Conduct Committee decided that he must be struck off, and so he was.

Some of my time was spent doing libel work. They ranged from the spectacular such as Jonathan Aitken and Linford Christie down to local councillors who were libelled by their political opponents, people who complained about being defamed by their neighbours and other actions so trivial that it was surprising people were willing to spend their time and money on litigation. The cost of litigation is still enormously high, although the new system introduced by Lord Woolf, it is hoped, will reduce that.

I was myself involved in a libel action, in a personal capacity. I was sitting at Reading Crown Court trying a difficult murder case, which attracted a certain amount of publicity. There was in the court a silly young girl who was a newspaper reporter. She sent a report to a number of the national newspapers that I had fallen asleep during the course of this trial. Happily only one national paper printed it. Counsel drew it to my attention the next day. I asked them whether they were conscious of anything of that sort having taken place, and they all said 'no'. Reading Crown Court at that time, was in an old Territorial Army premises, and the distance between the barristers' bench and the judge was quite small. They therefore had ample opportunity to observe whether it had happened or not.

I immediately rang up Tom Shields QC to seek his advice as to how I should proceed. He suggested that I should get in touch with Geraldine Proudler, who was a solicitor very experienced in this work. She came down to Reading that evening and we discussed the matter.

She spoke to counsel involved in the trial and took the matter very much in hand.

The newspaper's first reaction was to treat it as something of a joke, and suggest it was a matter of no importance. The difficulty of doing nothing as it seemed to me, was that once that sort of cutting gets into a file it is reproduced on computer and will be repeated and repeated. If thereafter any action is taken, comment will be made that it was not taken on the first occasion. I did not consult the Lord Chancellor's department because it seemed to me that this was a private matter for me to pursue. I suspected that it would be all for keeping the matter under wraps, and in any event, it would not be funding it.

Eventually Geraldine persuaded the newspaper that we were serious, and proceedings were then issued. I suggested that the sensible approach was to get two QCs expert in defamation jointly to advise on the value of the claim, because by now the newspapers accepted that there was no truth in the allegation. While I had no particular objection to appearing in court in front of a jury, it seemed a better course, if possible, to try and agree a figure without recourse to actual litigation.

In the result, Lord Williams of Mostyn QC was appointed to act as a sort of arbitrator. I gave some short evidence before him and was cross-examined by Andrew Caldicott QC who I am sure felt embarrassed by the situation in which he found himself. He, however, did it extremely well and, in the result, Lord Williams gave an award, which was not as generous as we had hoped. However, Geraldine had persuaded the girl's employers to add something more, so that in the end I had a sum with which to buy a new car, and more importantly had prevented that sort of allegation from being repeated on other occasions. It was not however, a situation in which I particularly wished to be involved and I did not resile from my general view that litigation was to be avoided if possible.

Judges have to have fairly thick skin. As a result of the Aitken trial, the *Guardian* published a number of articles with which I would like to have taken issue, but these sort of criticisms are ephemeral. No-one pays too much attention to them and they are best ignored. It used to be thought that not to be in *Private Eye* meant that a judge was not doing his or her job properly. While it may be some satisfaction to acquire a sum of money from a publication, the apology which goes with it is usually worthless because everybody appreciates that that is simply a public relations exercise forced on the defendants as a price for settlement.

Linford Christie brought a libel action against John McVicar. Both the two personalities and the subject matter involved, namely drugs in athletics, were sufficient to ensure that there was a full public attendance and full attention by the media. A great deal of excitement and amusement was caused during the trial by my asking about Christie's 'lunchbox'. Opinion was divided as to whether this was a judge who was ignorant of the most elementary piece of knowledge, whether he was asking the question to enable the jury more readily to understand the meaning, or whether it was simply a parody of a judge's question. Occasionally, even in the most bitter litigation, a piece of light humour does not come amiss.

In 1998 Christie was, I suppose, one of the best known athletes in this country. Over 100 and 200 metres he was probably the best British sprinter there has ever been. He was one of the greatest in the world. He won a gold medal in the 1992 Olympic Games for the 100-metre sprint and his achievements were legendary.

McVicar had been a notorious criminal and spent some time in prison. A film was made about his life in prison. Subsequently he had gone straight for a great many years and had become a journalist. He wrote an article in a magazine called *Spike*, in which he was described as 'One of Britain's most wanted men – his words as hard as his reputation'. *Spike* was described by Christie's counsel as being a magazine in which there were jokes of the *Private Eye* school, and it prided itself, indeed sold itself, on telling stories that other papers would not print. The article referred to the fact that there was a campaign by journalists seeking to show that Christie had been using performance-enhancing drugs. The article made a number of serious allegations about Christie, namely that he was only able to succeed at his age by using performance-enhancing drugs. He was rich and therefore was able to afford, and did afford, these drugs, and his own character and attitude towards competition was part of the evidence to suggest Christie might be a regular user.

McVicar accepted at the end of the case that the article was intended to suggest, and indeed did suggest, that Christie actually took drugs, and was not merely suspected of so doing. To that end he called evidence to show that there was a belief that there was widespread use of drugs in the world of athletics and that there were considerable flaws in the testing system. Additionally, it was suggested that athletes on anabolic steroids become volatile and unstable (what was described as 'steroid rage') and that some of Christie's behaviour came within that definition. Christie's background was the subject of close scrutiny throughout the trial.

Until he was somewhere about 24 years old he was regarded as a good but not great athlete, and while he ran for Great Britain, he failed to get into the Olympic team in 1984. He had a job but he was not taking his athletics very seriously. It was not until his coach Ron Roddan and Andy Norman, who was a distinguished figure in British athletics at the time, took him in hand that his career started to take off. They each wrote to Christie telling him that he could be the greatest if he worked at it, but if he was not prepared to work, there was no point in bothering. Christie took these words of advice seriously and began an intensive training programme involving gym work, running, endless practising and training techniques.

There were a number of factors which enabled somebody in Christie's position to continue to be a successful athlete a great deal longer than in the old days. They were now professionals, and could keep up a high performance into their mid-thirties because they could devote their lives to it. Secondly, modern sports medicine is much better than it used to be. Thirdly, there is the possibility of training during the winter in warm countries, so that outdoor running, for instance in the cold of a winter in the UK, is no longer part of essential training. Finally, techniques to enhance the strength of the body in legitimate ways are now an essential feature of training.

One of the arguments put forward on Christie's behalf to indicate he was not a person who took drugs was to point out that he had been tested hundreds of times in his life and on only one occasion was there any criticism. The testing regime, which was the subject of considerable criticism during the trial, in theory at any rate, enabled the controlling body of athletics to test the athletes regularly. A winner of a race was always likely to be tested. There were random tests so that the runner who came third, or even last, was also liable to be tested and the testing could take place at any time at the athlete's home or his place of training.

At the Seoul Olympics in 1988 in the 100 metres final, Ben Johnson was disqualified and Christie, who came third, was promoted from bronze to silver. A subsequent test of his urine showed a tiny quantity of a substance called pseudo-ephedrin, which is on the list of prohibited drugs. It is also a substance that can occur naturally in cough medicines and in all sorts of innocent places. When Christie came before the Olympic Committee, the explanation that was given was that it had probably come accidentally from ginseng, a legal substance that Christie was taking for his health. It was suggested that the substance had come innocently through contamination of the ginseng, and given the low amount, Christie was cleared. He was told it would not be treated as positive, he was allowed to retain his medal and he was not disqualified from the games.

In another part of the article, reference was made to an occasion when he was running in the World Championships in Gothenburg. He finished sixth and was evidently suffering from a pulled hamstring. The article went on:

> After hopping off he was before the TV cameras bemoaning his injury virtually before the new champion Donovan Bailey had completed his lap of honour. However, ten days later Mr Christie was miraculously back on song, beating Donovan Bailey and any other sprinter who matters in the Grand Prix beanfeast at Zurich.
>
> Zurich is the richest of Grand Prix meetings, and besides picking up a good £40,000 Christie was on course for the 'athlete of athletes' prize of £160,000 that the European promoters of these meetings put up to spur on track-and-field competitors. Zurich was his second win in a sequence which left him with Brussels and Berlin, yet Zurich was not a slouch win: Christie recorded 10.03 seconds with a metre per second head wind, which put him pretty close to his all-time personal best of 9.9. This from a 36 year old man, who ten days previously had so dramatically pulled a hamstring.
>
> Immediately after his Zurich triumph, his face pebbled with sweat and already stripped to the waist, Christie was interviewed by ITV's lapdog Jim Rosenthal. Rosenthal asked him how he managed to recover so quickly. Christie answered, 'Well to be honest I thought I was out for the count when I came here and they gave me the best people, the best treatment, and it does seem to have done the trick. I was really surprised that I recovered so quickly.' Certainly the ten days between injuring himself in Gothenburg and winning in Zurich would have allowed Christie to recover from a slight hamstring injury, and without fear of a random test, but in seven days of intensive training, boosted by banned drugs and perhaps human growth hormone, that would give him the explosive power to run 10.03 seconds into a headwind. We do not know.

As the case proceeded, the jury heard from the doctor and two physio-therapists who had treated him in Gothenburg. They said that he was not faking and that he had a real hamstring injury which they could see and feel. It was not enormously serious but it did need treatment and he went off to be dealt with by the official doctor of the Zurich Athletics Organisation. That doctor treated him with proper legal drugs and various treatments, as a result of which he was able to run a successful race in Zurich, and therefore the suggestion that he had faked an injury and only succeeded in Zurich with banned drugs, turned out not to be accurate.

The arguments advanced on McVicar's behalf were that it was well known in athletics that performance-enhancing drugs of all sorts were used by leading athletes, that unless they did so they were unlikely to remain leading athletes, that the records showed that there had been astonishing improvements in record times, which was entirely consistent with the introduction of these drugs, that Christie's age was such that he was unlikely to remain at the top unless he were taking drugs and that the change in appearance from what was described as being a 'pole athlete' to one with substantial muscles was only con-sistent with the taking of drugs, and finally that the testing system was considerably flawed and there were occasions when Christie treated the drug-testers in a somewhat high-handed way.

There was no positive evidence from any witness that Christie had in fact taken drugs, but it was McVicar's case that that was a proper inference to be drawn from all the evidence. He pointed to a number of factors: one, Christie's sudden increase in weight; two, his improve-ment in the ratings; three, his ability to compete successfully at an advanced age; four, steroid rage; five, the events at Gothenburg; six, the events at Seoul; seven, a general allegation that drugs were used regu-larly by athletes; and finally, eight, that tests are no good because they are easily avoided.

There was indeed evidence that a number of athletes had been taking drugs. Ben Johnson was the best known. Mr Hildrith, who was himself a distinguished hurdler and had run in the Olympics three times, and was now an athletics correspondent, expressed the view that it was not possible to win unless you were on drugs, and that everybody at the top was on drugs. He elaborated on this view by saying that people couldn't go through the training which they do now unless they were on drugs, and compared the present professional system with what obtained in his day, when there was a much more amateur approach to athletics. Secondly, he observed that the improvement in results was so astonishing over the previous 20 years that the records could have only been achieved by people taking drugs.

The systems of cheating the testing process involved getting rid of one's own urine and replacing it with somebody else's urine, or simply ensuring that any testing that took place was after a sufficient period of time to allow the drugs to disappear. Strictly, the rules provided that if somebody banged on the door, one would be given an hour to produce the sample. In those circumstances, an athlete would be under supervision, and likewise being tested after a competition would prevent an athlete from beating the system in that way.

The explanation for the increase in Christie's weight was a simple one, namely that he was training very hard and weightlifting and as he put it, 'It was just bloody hard work'. As for the improvement in his results, he explained that when he was a young man he didn't put his mind to training but when he came under the wing of Mr Roddan and was training very hard, there was inevitably an improvement. Additionally, the training facilities got better and he was able to go abroad and train in the warmth. Further, he had professional advice both from Roddan and from doctors and physiotherapists.

So far as the ability to record good results at a later age, there was some evidence that somebody like Christie who was a late starter would do better later, and because of the professionalism which has crept into athletics, that frequently happened. There was conflicting evidence as to whether people in their thirties were still at the top of their profession but a number of examples were given. Mr Hildrith didn't accept that and suggested that what Christie was able to achieve at 33 was wholly indicative of drug-taking.

It was clear that Christie was not very favourably disposed towards journalists or those who were required to test him. There was some evidence that on occasions he treated those who had to test him with something less than enthusiasm. There was a particular occasion when some testers came out to Lanzarote, where he was training. The incident did not reflect very much credit on Christie and he was reproved by the authorities for being less than co-operative.

Christie was giving evidence chiefly about his background and he was starting to tell the jury about a letter he received from Roddan when he burst into tears in the witness box. He was asked by his counsel 'Are you able to tell the jury why you felt unable to speak just then?' and he said:

> The reason is, I sit here and I think, why am I here, what am I guilty of? I go out and do my best to make people feel good about themselves, I sit there for many years – nobody in Britain especially sprinting writers are doing anything at all. When they play the National Anthem and I sit there and I look, there was no British National Anthem. When I got the letter from my coach and Andy Norman, I thought why me? For those two people to take interest in me I decided I was going to work so hard to try and make people feel good when they hear an anthem, it has to be British and make them feel good about themselves. I trained hard and I have to sit here and have people accuse me of cheating. What did I do wrong? I get so emotional about athletics.

McVicar suggested that was either an act by Christie to impress the jury or showing in some way that he was volatile.

There was a general attack on homeopathic medicine and Dr Bedot's treatment came in for a good deal of criticism. He was the Swiss doctor who was the team doctor of the Swiss national football team and was appointed doctor of the International Zurich Athletics Meeting. Dr Bedot had been recommended by a member of the anti-doping control. He had treated other distinguished athletes. There was simply no evidence either that there had been falsification of the injury or that Dr Bedot had given him an injection of a banned drug, or that Christie knew that the way he was treated involved injection with a banned drug.

McVicar relied on the events of Seoul. Christie took part in the Seoul Olympics in 1988 and competed in the 100 metres, the 200 metres and the relay race of 4 x 100 metres. The team stayed in Japan to train before going to Korea, and while he was there he bought some ginseng. He felt it was doing him a lot of good and he took it with him to the games. He took some before the 100 metres and after the 100 metres; he then took part in the 200 metres. In the 100 metres final he finished third, which he didn't expect to do, and became the first European to beat 10 seconds.

Ben Johnson won. He was tested for drugs. He was found positive and accordingly Christie was upgraded to second. He was tested for the 100 metres and nothing untoward was found. He took part in the 200 metres final, came fourth and was tested again. Subsequently he was notified by the team manager, Dr Turner, that they had got a letter to say that he had been tested positive. It was a random test. He filled in a form, saying among the other substances he had taken was ginseng. He was invited to attend a meeting of the IOC Medical Commission and was told that pseudo-ephedrin had been detected.

At the meeting he attended with a lawyer. The commission then wrote to Christie as follows:

> Following such a meeting the IOC Medical Commission deliberated and after a lengthy discussion decided your client should be given the benefit of the doubt and warned regarding drugs containing Ginseng. As far as IOC is concerned the situation is quite clear. The results of both analyses made on your clients urine samples were indeed positive and under the Olympic Charter could have resulted in sanctions such as disqualification ... In your clients case, his previous record was certainly considered as a positive factor and contributed to the decision under which he was to be given the benefit of the doubt and warned regarding products containing Ginseng.

Christie was annoyed at the suggestion that he was getting the benefit of the doubt. He said he had never knowingly taken any prohibited substance before or during the games and he thought the benefit of doubt was not good enough. Before he had appeared before the commission he had been rigorously cross-examined by Mr Watson and Mr Palmer, who was the chief of the team. They said they were not there to defend the indefensible but they concluded that although he had taken something which appeared to be prohibited it was not done deliberately. It is clear from the evidence that there was a great dispute before the commission between those who wanted to ban anybody using drugs and those who were willing to listen to a sensible explanation.

The jury decided that the allegation which McVicar made was an allegation that he was taking drugs, not that he was reasonably suspected of taking drugs. McVicar did not seek to justify saying that was true. In addition to suing McVicar, Christie had sued the printers, publishers and distributors. They agreed to abide by the result of the action between Christie and McVicar as to whether the allegation was true. Their defence at law was more limited. If the jury had found in favour of Christie against McVicar, it would normally have been their responsibility then to decide on the amount of damages which McVicar should pay.

However, the other parties had between them paid into the court a sum between £45,000 and £50,000. This gave rise to two arguments. Because Christie thought that sum was sufficient to vindicate his reputation, he saw no point in continuing to pursue McVicar, who had conducted the litigation on his own, and did not appear likely to be able to pay that sum as well as the costs of Christie's trial. There would also be an argument that the sum paid by the others was in any event sufficient, and accordingly even if the jury had made an award against McVicar it would not have been worthwhile to have pursued McVicar for his money. Accordingly, Christie agreed to waive his damages against McVicar.

This gave rise to an application by Mr David Price on behalf of McVicar, that as Christie had not got any damages from McVicar, Christie should not get any costs from McVicar. I declined to accede to that surprising submission because it was quite clear to me that Christie would have got a substantial award from the jury from McVicar, and that the waiving of that claim was a sensible exercise. To describe the waiving of the claim as in effect, a decision against Christie, was nonsense. McVicar went to the Court of Appeal and did not persuade it otherwise.

As mentioned earlier, a defendant in an action can put money into court, the amount of which is unknown either to the judge or jury. If a plaintiff gets less than the sum put into court the plaintiff has to pay the defendant's costs from the date of payment in. It is a safeguard for a defendant against an exaggerated claim by a plaintiff. In this case one of the parties, Johnson News, had at early stage paid £2500 into court, which was part of the global sum of £45–50,000. It had not been taken out earlier, but was now part of the settlement between the defendants and the plaintiff. Johnson News argued that as it had put money into court at an early stage, which was now accepted by the plaintiff, it should have all its costs paid after the payment in, which was the normal practice. Christie's counsel argued that as it was all part of an overall settlement and that as substantial sums had been paid in by other parties in recent days, it would be unfair that he should have to pay the costs of Johnson News after the date of payment in. It seemed to me that the ordinary rule should apply and accordingly I ordered that Christie would have to pay the costs of Johnson News after their offer of £2500 in October 1997. Thus, Christie would have been somewhat out of pocket because he would be unlikely to get his costs of his action against McVicar, and additionally he would have to pay the costs of Johnson News for a period of time. However, he seemed, publicly at any rate, unconcerned about that, and was happy to have vindicated his reputation.

On 23 May 1999 the *News of the World* published an article alleging drug-taking by Lawrence Dallaglio. On 30 May 1999 the *News of the World* published a further article, and on 30 June the *Mail on Sunday* also published an article making further allegations against Dallaglio. Dallaglio was at that time the captain of the England rugby football side. As a result of the articles, an inquiry panel was set up under the distinguished chairmanship of Sir John Kay, the High Court judge, now Lord Justice Kay, and two members of the Rugby Football Union (RFU) Council, Mr Rodgers, a solicitor, and Mr Stevens, a retired senior police officer. Their remit was to enquire into the allegation that Dallaglio had taken drugs with others on the Lions tour of South Africa, and had sold drugs for financial gain. It was within the inquiry panel's remit to make recommendations as to possible disciplinary charges.

In the result, the disciplinary charges that were brought were that in July 1997, while a member of the British Lions tour in South Africa, he took ecstasy tablets and a quantity of drugs in the presidential suite of the Intercontinental Hotel in Johannesburg; further, he had claimed that two other members of the British Lions party, namely players A and B, had been involved in drugs together with him.

None of the other matters which were contained in the newspaper articles were the subject of the disciplinary proceedings. The panel had rejected some of the allegations and decided that some of the others had no relevance to their particular inquiry.

The story started sometime in April 1999, when a bogus sponsorship deal was offered to Dallaglio involving a payment of £1 million over four years. It was a subterfuge. There never was such a sponsorship scheme and Gillette's name was taken in vain. The first meeting between Dallaglio and the two reporters occurred on 22 April, and involved meetings at the Kensington Hilton, then at Langham's restaurant and finally at the London Hilton, where video cameras had been set up to record the occasion. Nothing of significance to the disciplinary proceedings there occurred.

On 21 May 1999 a photo-shoot was arranged to take place at the Conrad Hotel in Chelsea. Photographs were taken employing a number of Gillette products by a cameraman who was a member of the *News of the World* staff. After the photographic session the video camera and microphone which were in position were set to run. Thereafter, the two reporters from the *News of the World* were left with Dallaglio and remained there talking into the early hours of the morning for perhaps four hours. Some five bottles of champagne were supplied to the room.

After about an hour-and-a-half of this conversation the transcript records:

> Taylor [reporter]: 'So what age did you give up your wild ways then?
> Dallaglio: '... probably about twenty.'
> Taylor: 'What, you have taken nothing since then?'
> Dallaglio: 'No.'
> Oswald [reporter]: 'Not even coke or anything like that?'
> Dallaglio: 'I tell a lie actually. I know I can tell you things in confidence. After the Lions tour in South Africa we had just won the Test series and we had just finished the third Test and we had a massive party, an all day party. Halfway through the party player A [whom he identified] came over to me with three Es and popped one straight into my mouth and one for player B [whom he identified], one for myself and one for him, and dropped an E, had a couple of wraps of coke and we celebrated the test series in South Africa and we got absolutely mullered and we had a suite in the Intercontinental Hotel overlooking Johannesburg and we had a jacuzzi in the top room. It was a fantastic room. It was the Presidential suite ... and we got absolutely mullered and we had a bit of lively party back there and celebrated winning the series in some style.'
> Taylor: 'My God.'
> Dallaglio: 'I woke up as the sun was coming up in Johannesburg.'
> Taylor: 'Fantastic.'

When players A and B gave evidence before Sir John Kay they both denied either having taken the drugs alleged or having seen any drugs being taken. Dallaglio gave evidence about his movements after the third test. He denied taking drugs. There was supporting evidence from a number of witnesses that they had been with Dallaglio at various moments and had seen no drugs. The panel's inquiry was then directed to the suggestion that this had occurred at the Intercontinental

Hotel in Johannesburg. The team had in fact been staying at the Crown Plaza outside Johannesburg. Dallaglio denied ever having been to the Intercontinental Hotel, and both players A and B also denied it.

However, enquiries at the Intercontinental Hotel showed that presidential suites did exist. They had a jacuzzi. Of two presidential suites, one was not occupied and the other occupied by a test cricketer. Further enquiries revealed that the third presidential suite was let out to airline hostesses employed by Virgin Atlantic, who the panel referred to as Miss X and Miss Y. It seems likely that they were part of the crew due to fly the main Lions party back to London on Monday 7 July. Miss X was traced and was seen by Mr Stevens. She was a friend of player B. She knew Dallaglio and had attended Wasps games.

She said she had met some of the Lions players on the Saturday night and told Mr Stevens that a number of them had returned to the presidential suite at the Intercontinental Hotel with her, including player B and Dallaglio. There was a party where a great deal of alcohol was drunk, but she was trained to recognise those who were affected by drugs. She said she had seen no drugs taken and she was satisfied that Dallaglio had not taken drugs. Eventually the players left and returned to their hotel. When Dallaglio was asked how he could make up a story about a hotel in which he had never been and come up with the detail which was accurate, namely that it had a jacuzzi, he said he had stayed in Intercontinental Hotels in other parts of the world many years ago and that might be one reason why the Intercontinental came to mind. His father was in the hotel business and therefore his knowledge of how the system ran was quite extensive. But he said he would be surprised to learn that the hotel in Johannesburg existed, let alone had the feature to which he had referred, and said it must have been a mere coincidence.

The panel concluded:

Mr Dallaglio's explanation had been that it was a mere coincidence that he had actually described a suite in an hotel of which he had no knowledge. That had seemed unlikely but the additional information suggesting a link between the very suite and the hotel where he and the other players were staying seemed to us to stretch coincidence too far. We concluded that the Disciplinary Panel considering this evidence might very well conclude that Mr Dallaglio's account and explanation to us were not true. This is in stark contrast to his protestations at his press conference on a later occasion that although he had told lies to reporters he was telling the whole truth about these matter now.

And, said the panel, 'Our assessment that he was not telling the truth seems to be borne out by evidence gathered since'. And they referred to the evidence of Miss X. 'The only sensible conclusion therefore sadly is that Mr Dallaglio told us lies about these matters, which he must have appreciated were very important to our inquiry.' And, said the panel, 'Records of phone calls by Miss X to player B on the Sunday were consistent with the story which Miss X told.'

The panel concluded:

> In any event consideration should be given to disciplinary charge under rule 5.12 in respect of Mr Dallaglio's admitted conduct in speaking to reporters in the way that he did whether or not the apparent admissions are true or lies. There can be little doubt that his conduct has been prejudicial to the interests of the Union and the game and anyone considering the Report is likely to be conscious of the volume of adverse publicity attracted to this matter in the media. For the person entrusted by the RFU with the captaincy of the national squad to make claims true or false to almost complete strangers of highly dishonourable conduct relating to such a sensitive subject as illegal drug taking while trying to secure substantial financial rewards for himself is, we consider, a matter of the most grave concern. Its potential effect by someone who acknowledges his acute position as a role model for the young is clearly grave. It is greatly aggravated in our view in his involving two other Lions players, particularly if, as he now claims, that was entirely without foundation.

Accordingly, the RFU set up a disciplinary tribunal, of which I was invited to be the chairman. The other two members of the tribunal were to be John Spencer, the distinguished old international, who had himself been part of the Lions tour when they beat the All Blacks. He was now a solicitor, and a good after-dinner speaker, to whom I had had the privilege of listening at a cricket dinner in Harrogate. The other member of the tribunal was to be Keith Plain, a farmer from the west country who was a member of the council. On the Sunday before our meeting he was reported in the *Mail on Sunday* as having made some inappropriate remarks as to how the matter should be dealt with. It was clear to me that if the tribunal was to have any credibility he could no longer continue to sit. However, the matter was taken out of my hands by the board itself which, notwithstanding Mr Plain's protestations that he had been misreported, persuaded him that it would be inappropriate for him to sit. Accordingly, Chris Tuffley, a naval captain and in charge of the Navy rugger was appointed in his place.

The inquiry panel had taken a little time to prepare its report, necessitated by the difficulty of obtaining evidence from witnesses and pursuing various lines of inquiry. Thus, it was not until the end of July that they were able to report. In the light of the forthcoming World Cup, which was due to start on 1 October, it was essential in everybody's interest that our tribunal should sit and resolve the charges as soon as possible. To that end I held a preliminary meeting with the solicitor for the board, with leading counsel for the board and with Dallaglio's solicitor. He had written a number of letters about the necessity of the board fully proving the allegations made by Miss X, which were at the heart of the board's allegation. When I suggested that the hearing should take place almost immediately, I was told that Dallaglio would rather wait, even it if meant not being available for the World Cup, in order that Mr Carman QC, who was on holiday, should be available to conduct his case. Accordingly, a date was set which accommodated all the parties, and two days was set aside for it. There were apparently difficulties in getting Miss X to repeat her evidence, and steps were therefore taken to obtain an affidavit from Mr Stevens about what she had told him.

Unknown to me, but shortly to be revealed, Dallaglio had told Mr Carman that he had indeed been at the Intercontinental Hotel and that the reason that he had lied to the panel was in order to protect players A and B. This information Mr Carman communicated to Mr Lissack QC, who was conducting the case on behalf of the board. Subsequently Carman rang me up to tell me this and also to tell me that in the light of this information the board had decided not to proceed with the charge of actually taking drugs. He was to be acquitted of the serious allegation of taking drugs.

It was no part of my responsibility to decide whether this was a correct approach or not. Judges in criminal cases are entitled to express their views to the prosecution who decide to drop a charge, though they actually have no power to do very much about it. But these were proceedings brought by the board. It was a decision made, no doubt after due consideration by the board, and whatever Mr Lissack's own feelings may have been (which I know not) he was not now required to present a case of actually taking the drugs. A number of newspapers expressed some surprise at what happened, but it was no part of our responsibility and we therefore had to deal with the matter as it was presented to us.

Carman did a fine plea in mitigation, as one would expect. When he said he didn't believe that Dallaglio was guilty of bringing the game into disrepute by privately telling the *News of the World* reporters that two fellow players had taken drugs, we had to point out that the inquiry panel's view was one which we fully supported. We also said that the lie to the inquiry panel reflected very much on his conduct and cast doubt on his judgment as an England captain.

There was no doubt that he would have suffered substantially so far as his finances were concerned. His marketing value as England captain was now greatly depreciated. His reputation had suffered, and whether he would again acquire financial support from sponsors was a matter of doubt. His powers of leadership were self-evident. Mr Melville and Mr Crane gave powerful character references. In the light of the loss of the England captaincy, the public humiliation, the loss of the tour of Australia, the nightmare of the past three months and the fact that his opportunities for endorsements were now likely to be severely limited, we took the view that a comparatively modest fine would be appropriate.

Our powers in fact varied from a suspension, which would have necessarily involved the World Cup and the Five (or Six) Nations, down to doing nothing at all. Because he had lied to the Panel and caused the board to incur additional costs, we took the view that some part of the punishment should be a contribution to the board's expenses. In the result, we fined him £15,000 and made him pay £10,000 towards the board's costs. Thus he was now free to take a full and active part in England's World Cup preparations and in the World Cup itself, which he did with enormous skill and was probably the outstanding player in a disappointing series.

It would not have been possible, publicly at any rate, for a High Court judge to condone taking drugs if that had happened. But when I stand back and look at the excitement and euphoria which must have obtained after winning a Lions tour, it is perhaps fair to ask if it would have been a hanging offence if, on this one-off occasion, in fact it had occurred. Though one could never say so publicly, I very much doubt it. In the event we were not faced with the problem, but it was certainly a matter to which I gave some considerable thought when I first read the papers.

In May 1996 Rupert Allason was an MP. He was better known as Rupert West, the well-known writer and expert on intelligence affairs. He brought an action against Alastair Campbell, who had been the political editor of the *Daily Mirror* and the Mirror Group, claiming damages for malicious falsehood. It was heard by Mr Justice Maurice Drake. Allason had recently won a substantial sum of damages for libel. Employees of the Mirror Group conceived the idea of creating an early day motion to persuade Allason to donate his damages to Mirror Group pensioners. A question arose (among others) during the trial of Campbell's involvement, and there was a dispute by George Galloway, Labour MP for Glasgow Hillhead, as to whether Campbell had handled the draft EDM.

In resolving that conflict, Mr Justice Drake said:

> I did not find Mr Campbell by any means a wholly satisfactory or convincing witness ... quite apart from these and other matters on which it seemed to me that Mr Campbell was less than completely open and frank; he did not impress me as a witness in whom I could feel 100 per cent confidence.

Subsequently, the case went to the Court of Appeal and a new trial was ordered. Thus I came to try it on the second occasion, and I heard much the same evidence and came to much the same conclusion about Campbell's credibility.

He was by now the Prime Minister's spokesman at No 10 Downing Street. It is a rather sad reflection on modern political life that in the face of these findings he should have been offered and accepted that position. Autres temps, autres moeurs.

11

Employment Appeal Tribunal

In 1985 I was invited by the Lord Chancellor to be president of the Employment Appeal Tribunal (EAT). I had already sat as a judicial member under the presidency of Mr Justice Waite, as he then was. The tribunal was set up in 1976. It was the successor of the National Industrial Relations Court, which had been set up to deal with the problems arising out of trade-union activities presided over by Sir John Donaldson, as he then was. It had been ill-received on the union side, and the court regularly received hostile criticism to such an extent that quite unfairly its reputation as an independent body suffered greatly. It was quite unjustified but in the result, the EAT was set up together with industrial tribunals.

The EAT consisted of a number of judicial members presided over by the president, with members appointed from either side of industry. The tribunal sat as a body of three. Mr Justice Phillips was the first president, and he and Mr Justice Browne-Wilkinson, as he then was, succeeded in laying down substantially the framework for the future. It heard appeals from industrial tribunals, which consisted also of a legal member who was either a full-time or part-time chairman, again with two industrial members. Essentially, an appeal from an industrial tribunal to the EAT was only on a point of law. It was essential because of the number of industrial tribunals and the fact they operated separately all over the country that the EAT should lay down some sort of guidelines, and this Mr Justice Phillips and Mr Justice Browne-Wilkinson did with very great skill.

The guidelines which they laid down have been the framework for the decisions of the EAT in industrial relations and have been in existence now for some 21 years. Mr Justice Phillips published an article in 1978 at the very beginning of the EAT's existence, in which he said:

> The practical question therefore very often is whether the Appeal Tribunal in a case where it disagrees strongly with the views of the Industrial Tribunal on such a question can say not only that it disagrees but that the decision is wrong in law. It was quite possible in almost all such cases to say the question is one of fact and therefore unappealable. We have not adopted that approach and to do so meant we could not do what we considered to be an important part of our task, namely to try to introduce in the decisions of something like over 60 Industrial Tribunals up and down the country dealing day after day with a question of this kind, something in the nature of a uniform approach. While there is no doubt a long way still to go we believe that a beginning has been made in the establishment of a coherent body of practice, perhaps it may be called law, prescribing the correct approach in a very large number of standard situations such as fighting, commission of offence, breaches of discipline, falling off of performance, insubordination, participation in trade union activities, clock offences and so on.

This was in reference to unfair dismissal cases which certainly initially formed a very large part of the work before the tribunal.

Certainty and consistency in practice was necessary where the waters were uncharted. It was an essential part of the EAT's function to guide industrial tribunals and more particularly those who were engaged in industrial relations so that they were more easily able to arrange their affairs so as to avoid wherever possible having to resolve their disputes by litigation.

At the very beginning of an industrial dispute was the opportunity of recourse to mediation at the Advisory, Conciliation and Arbitration Service (ACAS). This body, with its enormous experience of industrial affairs, played a major part in reducing the friction which undoubtedly existed in large part in industrial affairs between unions and employers in the 1970s and 1980s.

It was originally intended that cases going to the industrial tribunal and to the EAT be dealt with simply and as expeditiously as possible and without recourse to lengthy arguments on points of law and the involvement of lawyers. Sadly, this well-intentioned idea speedily fell into disarray. It became clear that what seemed a simple question of fact gave rise quite often to difficult points of law. Again, what seemed quite simple matters of fact were not always easily resolved by a witness on one side saying white and the witness on the other side saying black and leaving it to the tribunal to say which was right. Thus, while initially there were quite often litigants in person in front of industrial tribunals putting their case forward, gradually on one side they were represented by unions and on the other side by employers' organisations. Thereafter, as the law grew increasingly more difficult, lawyers appeared, either solicitors or barristers, on the one side or the other. What had been hoped to be a speedy, cheap and lay-orientated procedure became an expensive and lengthy contest between lawyers. The matter was not helped by European directives, which gradually assumed more and more importance in industrial relations and whose language was often so delphic that no one decision seemed to agree with another.

The strength of the system was simple. At industrial-tribunal level the permanent chairman was an experienced barrister who had probably previously been a part-time chairman and either by way of practice or by sitting, had acquired industrial relations experience. On either side of the chairman sat an industrial member, one from the employee's side and one from the employer's side. They were not there as representative of their particular side but to give the tribunal the benefit of their industrial experience. They were an immensely talented body, vastly experienced and able generally to act judicially. Having come from a background of confrontation, it always seemed to me to be remarkable that when they sat on a tribunal they were able to put aside their historical background and view the cases with enormous detachment.

The same applied to the EAT. When I first sat and did not know the members, I deliberately did not look in my papers to see which side of industry they represented. It was astonishing at the end of the day to learn the background of each member. It was very frequently the case that the employee's representative would be highly critical of the way the union behaved in a particular situation; on the other hand, often the employer's representative was equally critical about how an employer had behaved in another case. In my time on the EAT, a period of some two-and-a-half years, I can only think of one or two members who did not seem to find the function of impartiality always easy to attain. These were rare occasions and I was surprised that the matter occurred so very infrequently.

Unfair dismissal cases were the bread and butter of industrial tribunals' work. However, the general decline in industry during the 1970s and 1980s started to give rise to a great number of cases of redundancy. These were always difficult cases both for the parties involved and for the tribunals, because to decide that one person should stay and another should leave really required the judgment of Solomon and could readily be perceived as unfair. Although various guidelines were laid down and codes of practice were issued, like the application of all principles, while it was easy to set them out they were sometimes difficult to enforce in practice.

Another feature of industrial relations in the 1970s and 1980s was the increasing number of mergers and takeovers of companies, and questions arose as to what was to happen to the contracts of those who had previously been employed by company A and were now employed by company B. The Transfer of Undertakings Regulations covered this situation. They were based on directives from Europe and gave rise to an enormous quantity of litigation.

Another fruitful field of litigation were cases relating to race discrimination and equal pay. In simple terms, they ranged from a person complaining that they had not got a particular promotion because of their race or sex to the very complicated cases of equal opportunities, namely equal pay for equal work and discussions of what constituted equal work.

We were frequently asked what the purpose of the EAT was. Although a great number of the cases that came by way of appeal to the EAT were really questions of fact dressed up as law, there were from time to time very important and difficult questions of law that had to be resolved, and more importantly it seem to me that it gave the opportunity for an unsuccessful litigant before an industrial tribunal to have the opportunity to air his or her grievance. As it has been said, 'A grievance expressed is a grievance redressed'.

In order to avoid an expensive and lengthy hearing of appeals which we identified as being likely to be pure questions of fact, John Waite had introduced a system whereby we had a preliminary hearing with only the appealing party present to see whether there was anything in the alleged grievance. In most of the cases we found that there was not and the appeal was dismissed. Occasionally we found that what appeared, on paper at any rate, to be a hopeless appeal had something to be argued, and we gave leave for it to more fully argued. It was always difficult to explain to a litigant, and particularly a litigant in person, that the finding of fact by an industrial tribunal was usually unappealable and that the question of law that was sought to be argued simply did not arise. But at any rate it gave the litigant an opportunity to have his or her say. Our system of preliminary hearings worked marvellously well in John Waite's day and in my day. It saved a lot of time and expense and was welcomed generally by the practitioners.

I was succeeded by Mr Justice Wood as president. For some reason the Lord Chancellor, Lord Mackay, took exception to this particular practice. I confess I never really understood the basis of the objection. It saved expense and it speeded up the appeal procedure. There was always pressure on the tribunal to get through its work with great expedition, and this the preliminary hearing procedure certainly facilitated. However, the Lord Chancellor took objection to this procedure, which had been operating then for at least eight or nine years without criticism, and conducted a correspondence with Mr Justice Wood, which got more and more fractious. What had started with 'Dear James' and 'Dear John' ended with 'Dear Lord Chancellor' and 'Dear Judge'. It finally concluded with the Lord Chancellor writing to Mr Justice Wood suggesting he should consider his position. This gave rise to very great offence, as might be imagined. Eventually the matter, not through Mr Justice Wood, got into the public domain, and as a result questions were asked in the House of Lords about what the Lord Chancellor had in mind. The Lord Chancellor's somewhat feeble explanation that he wasn't intending to put pressure on Mr Justice Wood but was simply asking him to reconsider the matter did not go down well in the House of Lords. It was a strange incident.

The work that ACAS did can be illustrated by the fact that in my time there were something like 36,000 applications for industrial tribunals, and it in fact heard about 11,000 of them. The EAT heard about 1000 appeals and there were about 25 cases from us to the Court of Appeal. In my day we sat two courts regularly. Now something like four or five courts sit and the volume of work has increased enormously.

The premises which the EAT occupied until about 1989 were in St James's Square. It was a house which had belonged to the Astors and it had at sometime been used as some sort of criminal court – there were cells in the basement. It was an enormously rambling house, singularly ill-designed to be used as a court, but it was. The president's court sat in what I think had been the dining room of the original building, and the other court sat in what was the original ballroom. The president's room was apparently Nancy Astor's sitting room and when I took over from John Waite was full of lovely pictures. His taste and mine were not entirely similar and so I got in touch with the Property Services Agency (PSA), which provides pictures for government buildings. I was invited by a nice lady to go down to its premises on the Embankment where its pictures were kept in order to choose something to my taste. I marvelled at the lovely pictures that were available and was in the process of selecting some seventeenth and eighteenth-century masterpieces when I was quickly informed that what I was looking at was for government ministers only. The president of the EAT was well below the salt. She told me that if I followed her I would no doubt find a lithograph that would be available to me in accordance with my rank. In the result, what I was allowed to have on loan was sufficiently attractive to enable Nancy Astor's room to be restored to some sort of glory.

I was approached by the Astor family to enquire whether it would be possible to have a party in the building on the occasion of the unveiling of a blue plaque by Margaret Thatcher commemorating Nancy Astor's presence in the building. There was a female organisation known as the 300 Group devoted to the proposition that half the members of parliament should be women. They had prevailed on the local authority to provide the blue plaque and had invited the Prime Minister to come and unveil it. We readily assented to the idea and arranged to keep the morning free for this exercise. There arrived before the official unveiling a great number of the Astor family, who walked round the house and recalled with great pleasure and amusement the activities of their elderly relations, in the ballroom on the stairs and elsewhere. Margaret Thatcher came along and gracefully unveiled the plaque and attended a very bibulous morning, where the Astors entertained the members of this women's organisation. It was an amusing, entertaining and convivial morning and I suspect that the EAT behaved with unwonted benevolence in the afternoon.

It so happened that the building which we occupied was next door to the Libyan Embassy. I was not present during the siege and shooting of the woman police officer, but the building had to be evacuated and some of the members of staff, and the industrial members I believe, escaped over the roof. Thereafter, for an appreciable period of time the Libyan Embassy remained unoccupied.

The building, though perfectly agreeable to work in, was ill-suited for continued use by the tribunal because of the condition of the roof, which required a very expensive refurbishing. As a result, enquiries were put in hand as to where a suitable building could be found. There was such a building on the Embankment, almost opposite HMS *President*, which had been vacated by a government department and elaborate plans were drawn up to enable the tribunal to move there. While I was party to the plans, which involved the president having a large room overlooking the river, I was unfortunately not still in office when the move took place. One immediate advantage of the move was in relation to the cooking facilities. In St James's Square we had on the books a lady who did the cooking, but because it had never been sanctioned she was I think classified as a cleaner. While she undoubtedly did her best with the inadequate facilities that were available, no-one I think would have described it as being a very great gastronomic experience. Matters have improved somewhat on the Embankment.

It was our custom from time to time to invite those interested in industrial affairs in government, in opposition and among trade unionists and employers' organisations, to come and have lunch with us to meet the members and find out how we operated, and above all for us to pick their brains about future industrial legislation and industrial affairs. It was not as successful as I had hoped, because there seemed a certain lack of enthusiasm to come and visit us, though it did give an opportunity from time to time to learn from Whitehall what they had in mind.

There was not only a president of the EAT in England but also a president of the EAT in Scotland, where a similar tribunal sat. We sought to have a uniform approach if we could, but inevitably from time to time there would be judgments of each court which appeared to differ. Indeed, there were sometimes contrary judgments of different divisions of the EAT in England. They occurred usually because each tribunal was unaware of the decision of the other. One of the happier features of the system was that from time to time the president of EAT in Scotland would come and sit in London, as would some of the Scottish members, and I would go and sit for a fortnight or three weeks in a year in Edinburgh with Scottish members and hear appeals there.

I have to say that the experience was enormously valuable, because the Scottish approach seemed to me to be pragmatic, down to earth and without frills. The members, too, made a valuable contribution. Secondly, the practitioners were much less concerned to take per-nickety legal points and got on with their cases with a refreshingly robust approach. There is no doubt that the Scottish connection was a valuable one.

One other valuable exercise which I performed was to seek to visit industrial tribunals around the country. It was of course impossible to visit every single one. But chairmen of areas were immensely helpful and invited me to meetings of their members and sometimes to dinners where I had the opportunity to meet the industrial members and to explain the workings of the EAT. No-one who has sat on a tribunal or in court ever likes to be overruled by an appeal court; industrial tribunals were no different and they were not unnaturally displeased if they found that the EAT had overruled them, particularly if they thought it was a question of fact upon which they were the experts. This position was enormously understandable.

I explained to them that they were not the only ones aggrieved by pointing out that from time to time the Court of Appeal overruled the EAT on what we regarded as our function and from time to time the House of Lords overruled the Court of Appeal. At one meeting the members were enormously pleased to find that a decision of theirs which had been overturned by the EAT had been allowed by the Court of the Appeal, so honour had been restored. These were immensely valuable visits. From time to time I was accompanied by some indus-trial members of the EAT who had the opportunity of adding their words of wisdom to the industrial tribunal members. It was a very important way to keep in touch with the thinking of industrial tri-bunals and to get a feedback from them about how they saw the EAT and themselves operating.

The input of the industrial members to the EAT was of enormous value. There were very many cases in which what we used to describe as industrial common sense gave the answer to the problem. They saw immediately that what appeared to a lawyer to be the right conclusion could not possibly be correct, because of the effect it would have on the workplace. And likewise, for the industrial members I believe the judicial approach was of value to them, both in analysis of a problem and above all in the ability to see both sides of an argument. I like to think that those who only had a picture of the stereotypical judge went away realising that there was a kindly, intelligent and sympathetic person behind the façade.

There were moments of humour even in the dullest cases. There was an appeal from an industrial tribunal where the complaint was that one of the members of the tribunal had fallen asleep. In order to test this allegation I wrote to the chairman of the tribunal concerned to enquire as to whether there was any truth in the allegation. I got a letter back from him in which he accepted that indeed one of the members had fallen asleep during the course of the hearing, but added that 'She had taken a full and active part in the discussions in the retiring room afterwards'. Needless to say, we had to allow the appeal.

One of the other difficulties was that sometimes in complicated cases we would have on one side a layman, either a litigant in person or a union official, and on the other side a distinguished QC. Ensuring that the balance was properly kept was not always terribly easy. There were additionally some organisations which held themselves out as being some sort of advocates. They were not legally trained but had some experience of industrial relations. Their presentation and their preparation was quite inadequate, and because they were not proper legal representatives we had no power to make them pay the costs that were thrown away by their incompetence. They did their clients no good and they often cost the opposing side a lot of money. It was a difficult situation which we were never able to resolve, and I suspect that it has not been resolved even now. While generally the level of competence among the advocates was good, this was an unhappy situation.

We set up what was described as a user's committee, because from time to time I would receive complaints from individuals or firms about the listing or some other administrative detail. It seemed to me a good idea to have a group of those most frequently appearing before me to meet up from time to time in an informal way to sort out problems which arose and which if left unresolved tended to fester and cause resentment. It was a useful exercise. A user's group has been adopted in other spheres of litigation, namely the official referees court and certainly in the Crown Office.

I had two-and-a-half immensely interesting and enjoyable years with the EAT and made a number of friends. I learnt a great deal about industrial relations and was grateful for the opportunity to preside over the EAT. When I left the members generously gave me a cheque which I used to buy garden furniture for our cottage in France. It was customary for retiring presidents to present members with photographs of themselves in somewhat solemn form, to hang up in the members' room as a memento of their presidency. It seemed to me that it would be appropriate to show the membership the use to which I had put their generous cheque and there therefore appeared in the members' room a photograph of me in relaxed mood and clothing holding a glass of champagne and sitting at their large table in my garden.

12

Murder

Most members of the public think that criminal courts are concerned only with cases of murder and all have the excitement of Crippen or Neilson, and that there is some sort of glamour attached to a celebrated murder trial. Nothing could be further from the truth. Most murder trials are sad affairs. They are often in a domestic context. Some are of a variety of 'I killed the deceased but I am not guilty of murder because of … ', and the other type are those where the accused denies having done the killing. In the first type of case there is room for a verdict of manslaughter by reason of provocation or lack of intent, and cases of diminished responsibility where the accused's mental condition is in issue. The second type of case is of the nature of a 'whodunnit' and often involves complicated forensic evidence linking the accused in some way with the deceased, both as to opportunity and motive.

I was involved in a good number of criminal trials of both types both at the bar and on the bench, but there were two which I tried as a judge which attracted a good deal of attention at the time and were something of general interest to the public.

The first case involved an allegation against a mother of murdering her six-year-old son. The body had been laid out naked in a wooded area not far from the mother's house and positioned carefully with the arms and hands and legs spreadeagled in a symmetrical way, which the prosecution alleged had some connection with the occult.

Mrs Neeve was the accused. She was 27 at the date of the trial. She was a mother of four children. There were three girls aged 10, 5 and 18 months at the date of the trial and a son, Rikki, who was aged 6 in 1994 when he was murdered. There were two fathers of the children. In addition to being charged with the murder of Rikki, Mrs Neeve was charged with cruelty to the other children, to which she pleaded guilty.

In 1992 Mrs Neeve and her then three children had moved to the Welland estate at Peterborough, where they were living at the time that Rikki was murdered. The story began on Monday 28 November 1994. Mrs Neeve called the police on a 999 call at 6pm to report that Rikki was missing from home. It was the prosecution's contention that that was simply a device to cover the fact that she had already murdered him. The police went to see Mrs Neeve, and were struck by the fact that she did not seemed concerned and had not contacted the school to see if he had been there. The police conducted a search of a number of places where he had previously turned up when he had gone missing. They also conducted a search with dogs in part of the wood where he was eventually found. It was a very cold and foggy night, and although the searchers resumed in the early hours of the morning a complete and thorough search was impossible and nothing was found.

About lunchtime on 29 November the body was found naked in some woodland, laid out in the curious way that has been described. The police officers found at Mrs Neeve's home a large number of books on mysticism, divination and prophesy, as well as books about unsolved murder cases. These documents were strongly relied on by the prosecution at trial as indicating that there was some element of mysticism involved in the way the body was laid out. There was no sexual interference and no evidence to suggest that he had been physically assaulted, save that he had clearly been asphyxiated. He was killed by having his own clothing pulled up and twisted around his neck, in such a way that the zip from his anorak left its imprint in the neck at the top, which acted as a ligature. The tapings taken from the neck matched fibre fragments from his anorak. It was the pathologist's view that he must have been held in that position for at least half a minute before the body would become limp and lifeless.

It was Mrs Neeve's case that she had not seen Rikki since he left for school on the morning of 28 November, and she insisted that she had not been out in the afternoon when she expected him home, apart

21. Trial of Mrs Neeve. James Hunt QC prosecuting; Mrs Neeve front left.

from going briefly to a near neighbour to check if he were there. The prosecution called a witness called Sarah Turner, who had observed Mrs Neeve walking near the bottom of a walk near her home about 15 minutes before the 999 call was made. Mrs Neeve denied that it was she who had been seen by Sarah Turner, but the prosecution suggested that she was lying about not having been out, and attached importance to it.

The prosecution also attached great importance to the way that the children had been treated by Mrs Neeve and by the general set-up in Mrs Neeve's household. There was a volume of evidence that it was Mrs Neeve's practice to use violence against the children with whom she couldn't cope. There was ample evidence from the Social Security authorities that on a number of occasions she had asked them to take charge of the children, and one of the criticisms in the case was that Social Security authorities had not taken seriously her suggestion that she couldn't cope with the children, and that if something was not done she would kill Rikki.

One method she used to deal with Rikki was to seize him by the neck and then hit him, sometimes lifting him off the ground by the throat or more specially by his clothing, which rode up around his neck. Sometimes she used to lock him out of the house, and one December at about 10.45pm he was found screaming and crying on the doorstep wearing only his pyjamas, having been shut out. On another occasion she was seen holding him by his ankles upside down over the edge of a bridge with a 15-foot drop to the water below. The cruelty to the other children was equally serious and was well known to a number of witnesses.

Dean Neeve was a man who came and went in the life of Mrs Neeve. He was the father of the two younger children, but not of Rikki. Mrs Neeve was obsessed with Dean. Sunday 27 November was their third wedding anniversary, and in the afternoon he left the house and did not come back, although he promised to do to celebrate the anniversary. He went to another girlfriend and stayed there. Rikki and Dean hated each other, and it was the prosecution's case that Rikki's presence was a stumbling block to the continued relationship between Dean and Mrs Neeve.

There is no doubt that on the Monday morning Rikki had set off for school, but he never went there. He was seen at various points during the day, and the last sighting was at about 3.30 in the afternoon by some workmen working near his home. From the pathologist's report it was clear that he had taken some Weetabix about an hour before he was killed. That fact again led the prosecution to suggest that he must have gone home and had Weetabix to the knowledge of Mrs Neeve sometime during the day, and shortly before he was killed. She said that he always turned up for food. It was clearly not consumed at breakfast time and Mrs Neeve said that normally he got home at 3.30 or 3.45pm. Weetabix was a regular meal for him at home and there was no evidence that he had broken into somebody else's house to get the Weetabix, or indeed that he had been fed it by anyone else.

The naked body found in the copse was described as being like Vitruvian man, and like a drawing of Leonardo da Vinci which was a naked man in a cosmic circle.

There was evidence from a number of witnesses that somebody who was said to be Rikki was seen at 6.30 or 7pm, i.e. after Mrs Neeve's telephone call. The prosecution did not accept these sightings, and indeed Mrs Neeve was heard to say that all the 'so-called people' who had seen Rikki wasn't true. She also said, 'The poor little sod had got his walkman stolen from him that morning'. When she was asked how she knew this when her account was that he hadn't been home, she replied that it was obvious or they would have found it.

After she was arrested she was bailed to a number of hostels, first in Leicester and then in Liverpool. To a number of them she denied being responsible for the murder and blamed various people, including Dean Neeve. On one occasion she showed another inmate a letter in which she had written that she had killed Rikki but said it was a mistake, and she made a number of statements to various people in which she had said various things that might have been construed as some sort of confession. She denied, however, ever admitting having committed the murder, and that was the position she took up at trial.

Her case was a simple one. Although she had undoubtedly been cruel to Rikki on occasions, she had not seen him after he had left in the morning. He did not return home before she rang the police. There was no forensic evidence to indicate that he had been murdered in the house or elsewhere. The connection between the way the corpse was laid out and Vitruvian man and her interest in mystic was very far fetched. There was simply no evidence as to how the body had got to the scene which involved her. Additionally, there were a great number of witnesses who purported to see somebody who was either Rikki, or resembled Rikki, after she had made her telephone call. There were people in and around the area of the woods the next morning who in some way might have been involved.

However, the single and most vital piece of evidence upon which she relied came from a police officer. Police Constable McNeill was one of the officers involved in the search. He had been at the community centre sometime after 7pm on the evening of 28th November and sometime after 7.35pm he began to search through the area beginning at the rear of the houses. He had what he described as a dragon lamp, which was a powerful hand-torch. He was looking for a live boy and was shouting Rikki's name. He went directly into the woods and he found a track and followed it through the woods along to the end. He was asked if he had seen the area where Rikki's body was found. He replied that yes, he had. 'Did you go past it?' Answer: 'Yes I did.' 'He wasn't there when you were in the woods was he?' Answer: 'No, not all. No, there was no body there.' 'And this was half past seven?' 'Yes my Lord, it was.' He accepted that the mist did not start to come down until about 8.30pm and he could see clearly.

Although the prosecution sought to call a senior officer to suggest with the help of a video that the tracks were nothing like as clear as they appeared, Police Constable McNeill's evidence was unshaken. The jurors themselves were taken to the scene of the incident and could make up their own minds. Of course it followed that if PC McNeill's evidence was right, namely that at 7.30pm on 28 November 1994 the body was not there, Mrs Neeve could not have committed the murder. She had rung the police at 6pm that evening, it was inconceivable therefore that thereafter she might commit the murder, having told the police that he was missing, and in any event she was under observation effectively thereafter, either by the police or by neighbours.

PC McNeill's evidence was of course the bull point in the defence case. Mr Rumfitt QC pointed out that however strong the evidence of motive was, however unlikely someone else had killed this child and undressed it and left it in the way that it was left, nevertheless the jury should simply not convict, because PC McNeill's evidence could not be set aside and had to be accepted. Mr Hunt QC, for the prosecution, set out all the points which he said led inexorably to the conclusion that it was Mrs Neeve that could have done it and nobody else. As far as PC McNeill's evidence was concerned it would have been perfectly possible for an officer, however dedicated, at 7.30 at night on a disagreeable November evening looking for an upright child, simply to have missed something lying on the ground.

The jury was out for an appreciable period of time but, in the result, came back and found Mrs Neeve not guilty of murder. The end of the trial caused a good deal of uproar, because Rikki's father and his family were incensed both at the result and also at the way that the Social Security authorities had behaved. There was subsequently, I believe, a full inquiry into the Social Services, and a number of people were severely criticised. The police indicated that they had no intention of pursuing any other line of inquiry into the murder.

I then had to deal with Mrs Neeve for the allegation of cruelty. It was quite clear that she was an inadequate person, that she was frequently on drugs and that she and her husband were part of what is called the 'drug scene'. However, it seemed to me to be one of the worst child cruelty cases that I had come across, and notwithstanding the fact that she had had to undergo a jury trial for murder and had pleaded guilty to the charges of cruelty, I sentenced her to a term of seven years in all.

What actually happened will never now be known for certain. Counsel very kindly took me out to dinner afterwards and there was much speculation as to what might or might not have happened. I have my own views.

The second murder case of interest which I tried was unusual in that the body of the victim was never found. David Martin and Colin James were business partners. They were primarily involved with helicopters. The business partnership had not gone well and it was suggested that James owed Martin £140,000 and may well have been ripping off Martin. Solicitors letters had been exchanged, and Martin had gone to the extent of taping conversations between himself and James.

In December 1992 Martin lived at a house in Naphill near High Wycombe. On 29 December 1992 he was seen at his house somewhere between two and four o'clock in the afternoon. He had a girlfriend called Kate Turner, with whom he was on the friendliest terms. Later that afternoon she tried ringing him unsuccessfully. When she arrived about half past ten in the evening she found that both he and his BMW car were missing. The burglar alarm was not on, some of the locks were not secure and the house was untidy. She thought this extremely curious because Martin was a man who was obsessive about tidiness and security. Being anxious she rang up James, who told her not to worry.

But on the morning of 30 December she rang the police, who now became involved. In the workshop adjoining Martin's house were some very valuable old cars. The floor was extensively covered with traces of blood. Unfortunately, although the police had been into the workshop on 30 December, the marks aroused no sort of interest and were ignored. It was not until 1 January that Kate Turner's son observed what was self-evident: that there were numerous marks on the floor which were highly suggestive of blood. Efforts had been made apparently to mop it up. A print from one of James's shoes was found on the floor. The scientific evidence called on both sides was rightly described as difficult, unclear, poorly recorded and presented, and very lengthy. On the prosecution case it was submitted that the blood was that of Martin, that it was comparatively recent, that an attempt had been made to clear it up, that James had left a footprint in the blood while he was trying to do so, and that as James had left the company of Martin at about 4pm and had not been seen since that it was logical to assume the blood was that of Martin and that James was involved.

The defence case was that in the light of the late discovery of the blood and the fact that the police officers had not noticed it for days, there was nothing to link James with the blood. He had been a frequent visitor to the house and it was just as likely that his footprint had been on the workshop floor before the blood was spilt. There were difficulties about the nature, position and causation of the blood, and the defendant's expert tended to suggest that not only was the blood spilt after the footprint was made, but that it may well be that footwear had not been in contact with blood at all. The way the tests were carried out were subject to great criticism and it has to be said that the scientists did not distinguish themselves.

James told the police that he had left Martin's house at about 4pm, had driven his green Citroën motor car to his workshop at Whitehall Farm, Watton. He had stayed there working on a helicopter until about 7.30 in the evening and then driven to his house in Mill Hill, arriving at about 8.25pm.

When the police made some enquiries they discovered from one of James's employees, Mr Wilkie, that James had not gone home then. According to Wilkie they had gone to Leavesden airport in north Watford in James's green Citroën. At Leavesden, Wilkie was told to drive James's green Citroën to his Mill Hill address, where James would rejoin him. James drove home in another car which Wilkie never saw.

When James was interviewed on 5 January and confronted with Wilkie's version of events on 29 December, he told the police that he had got the days mixed up and said that the car he had collected from Leavesden was a white Citroën owned by a man he knew called Raymond. That too turned out to be a lie.

It was the prosecution case that the car which James drove from Leavesden back to his house was in fact Martin's BMW. One of the strong points in the prosecution case was that at no time was James prepared to say whose car it was that he had driven from Leavesden. One of the mysteries of the case was what was the purpose of visiting Leavesden and how the BMW, if it were the car, had got there. Leavesden is a private airport, and it may have been one of the thoughts going through the jury's mind, given that James was a helicopter pilot, that a helicopter might have been used to dispose of the body. But there was simply no evidence about that or of a helicopter taking off without anyone's knowledge, and how and where Martin's body was disposed of will never be known for sure.

Although the prosecution alleged that Martin was not seen alive after 4pm on 29 December, there was some evidence from neighbours of movements in the house later on in the evening. More particularly, a lady in a nearby garage who knew Martin well gave evidence that some days later she had served him. She was plainly a totally honest witness and it was of course a very important piece of evidence from the defence point of view. In the result, the jury must have taken the view that she had simply made a mistake. It was perhaps a good example of a totally honest witness making a genuine mistake.

To prove that somebody is dead without a body being produced is not a very easy task. Martin's GP spoke of a fugue state where a person in a dreamlike condition takes up a new identity somewhere else. He described past episodes during which Martin had suffered some mental illness, when he had been hypomanic and had undergone treatment on and off until 1988. There was, however, a good deal of evidence that he had appeared to be happy, although there was some worries about his job. He had enquired from a local newsagent as to whether there would be newspapers on 1 January. He remained firm friends with Kate Turner, although they had decided not to marry. She discounted any question of suicide, and there was no dispute that since 29 December people had written to him and received no reply. He had made no use of his bank account nor of his credit cards or his telephone. No-one who knew him had heard a word from him: Kate Turner in particular would have expected to do so, and there were others. Financially he was in a good position, and his estate when wound up was worth over £900,000, with a tax liability of some £55,000.

Raymond was interviewed and gave evidence that he did not own a Citroën car, nor did he arrange for a car to be collected from Leavesden. Further, he said that James had told him to say, if anyone asked, that he had lent him, James, a BMW car and that the car outside James's house was his and not Martin's. This conversation was denied in interview by James. James did not give evidence himself and much play was made by the prosecution about the fact that there never was an explanation as to who owned the car driven from Leavesden, save to suggest that there was some sort of dodgy deal which indicated that the car might have been stolen.

Martin's BMW was last seen by James at Martin's house at about 2pm on 29 December. It was eventually found outside Martin's London flat in Lancaster Drive on 7 January. It had been there for some days, badly parked with a smashed side window. It was the prosecution's case that Martin would not have left his car outside the flat, because the flat was not really habitable, whereas James might have done so, not being aware of the flat's condition. There was the further coincidence that the nearest tube station to the flat was Finchley Road, which was where James said in interview that he had taken Raymond's white Citroën the day after collecting it from Leavesden. He said that he was proposing to buy the white Citroën that he had picked up at Leavesden which belonged to Raymond, and which he had driven to Mill Hill. Accordingly, he parked it overnight at Mill Hill and then changed his mind about buying it and in the result, drove it the next day to Finchley Road tube station, where he left it with the keys up the exhaust pipe for Raymond to collect, thus linking the position of the Citroën with the position of Martin's car where it was eventually found.

The jurors took a very keen interest in the whole case. They visited the house where this had all occurred and spent an appreciable amount of time looking at the marks in the garage. Various tests had already been carried out by the experts. Tests called Kastle-Meyer had provided a number of positive results, and fucian dye tests had also been carried out. The effect of this was to enlarge the spots of blood and to give a somewhat distorted appearance of the whole garage being covered in blood. The jury was singularly unimpressed by the failure of the police to notice the blood marks until Miss Turner's son pointed them out, and equally the evidence of the scientists was not very well received. The jury clearly rejected the idea that he had either committed suicide or taken himself off somewhere and hidden himself, or that he had been alive after 29 December.

In those circumstances the evidence against James was overwhelming and his explanations in interview were clearly wholly unsatisfactory; he was convicted of murder. I do not believe that his failure to give evidence assisted his case. Quite clearly, if he had given evidence he would have faced a number of questions, the answers to which would have placed him in even greater difficulties. His case was very well conducted by Mr Marshall Andrews QC, now an MP, who had sought to exclude the interviews on the ground that because the police had reasonable ground to suspect that he was guilty of murder they should have cautioned him and complied with the provisions of the Police and Criminal Evidence Act. I had ruled against him on this and the Court of Appeal upheld my decision. And as it said, the truth was that there was an overwhelmingly strong case against this appellant. How did Martin come to be killed? Firearms were collected from James's house but they were not linked to Martin's death. It is almost certain that a knife of some sort must have been used, because of the amount of blood found. How or where the body was disposed of is still a mystery. Why James went to Leavesden and how Martin's car got to Leavesden in the first place is a great mystery.

Altogether it was an absorbing and fascinating case, in which justice was plainly done. The result reflected little credit on some of the police officers involved, and the experts made a miserable showing.

13

Parole

In September 1985 I became a member of the Parole Board, of which Lord Windlesham was then chairman. It was customary for there to be a number of High Court judges on the Parole Board and the senior one became, in due course, the vice-chairman. We served for some three years. The parole system was not one with which I was enormously familiar, save that I had had experience on the Aarvold Committee of advising the Home Secretary on the release of prisoners who were confined to mental institutions after having committed a criminal offence.

That committee was so called being named after its first chairman, Sir Carl Aarvold, who was recorder of London. A patient had been released into the community and subsequently poisoned a victim – which was what he had done in the first place – which necessitated his being sent to a mental institution. Naturally there was a public outcry. As a result, Carl Aarvold was asked to advise the Home Secretary on how best the release of patients could be achieved. The Aarvold Committee was thus set up consisting of two lawyers, both queen's counsel, two specialist doctors, a member of the Probation Service and a member of the Social Services. We used to meet regularly once a month. Each patient whom we were considering was interviewed by a member of the board and we dealt with some six or eight patients at each meeting. The visits by members necessitated going to Broadmoor, Rampton or Liverpool, spending the day discussing with staff and the nurses the background history and behaviour of the particular patient, and interviewing the patient. It was wholly absorbing, highly educational and very demanding.

Our responsibility was to advise the Home Secretary whether a particular patient should be released from a top-security institution either straight into the community or usually into a less-secure environment. It was a great responsibility, because if we were to release somebody who subsequently committed a crime of a similar nature, which was naturally very serious, the public outcry would be enormous, great harm would have been done to a victim and serious damage to the release system. Forecasting how people whose habit it was to strangle women where sex and drink were involved were likely to behave in the outside world, to which they had not been exposed substantially for some 12 to 15 years, was self-evidently not an easy process. No-one wanted to keep a patient in a place like Broadmoor or Rampton any longer than was necessary, but the potential consequences of an untimely release were always present in our minds. Even for the professional staff at the institutions and the professional doctors on the committee, whose insight into the mentality of the patients was absolutely vital to our deliberation, the decision could never be more than an educated guess. But decisions needed to be made, and we did the best we could. Generally our efforts proceeded without any particular disaster during my time, for which we were all profoundly grateful.

Thus, when I came to sit on the Parole Board I was not entirely unfamiliar with decisions relating to prisoners sentenced to life imprisonment, whose position was not dissimilar to that of patients under the Aarvold Committee. However, the system of parole and its effect relating to 'non-lifers' was not one with which I was generally familiar. It can be traced back to the eighteenth and nineteenth centuries as a result of transportation. After a certain number of years those who had been transported were, if they behaved themselves, granted a 'ticket of leave'. It enabled them, subject to certain regulations, to work on their own account and to have a substantial measure of freedom within the colony to which they had been sent, although it did not enable them to go elsewhere until the end of their sentence. The Select Committee of Transportation of 1837 said, 'This indulgence on the whole has a very useful effect as it holds out hope to a convict if he behaves well and is liable to be re-assumed in case of misconduct'.

When penal servitude was introduced in the middle of the nineteenth century for those serious offenders who had previously been sentenced to transportation, the idea of the ticket of leave was also introduced so that those sentenced to penal servitude became eligible for release on licence, on the serving of a certain proportion of their sentence. Those subject to penal servitude were released on licence while those subject to ordinary terms of imprisonment had by the turn of the century had one-third of their sentence remitted. In 1948 this resulted effectively in a system being adopted whereby all prisoners who behaved themselves were entitled to release without any kind of licence after serving two-thirds of their sentence. There were some exceptions to this rule, but that was the general practice. The only other substantial change was that in July 1987 those serving sentences of 12 months or less were entitled to a remission of half.

In April 1968, as a result of the Criminal Justice Act 1967, a parole system was introduced. The effect was that a prisoner was eligible for parole after serving one-third of the sentence. One of the anomalies which arose related to the minimum qualifying period. A prisoner would not be granted parole until at least 12 months had been served after sentence, with the result that prisoners serving sentences of less than two years had to stay in custody until they had served two-thirds of their sentence, whereas many of those serving three or four years were getting out on licence after one-third of their sentence. In the 1982 Criminal Justice Act (what was known as a section 33) the minimum qualifying period of 12 months was reduced to 6 months.

One of the effects of this particular provision (section 33) was that there was a parole rate of some 75–80 per cent for those serving less than two years, so what had originally been conceived as some sort of privilege was now being treated as an entitlement. The other problem was that distinction between sentences was being nullified, because most prisoners sentenced to different periods of between 9 and 18 months were coming out on exactly the same day, 6 months after sentence.

The Parole Board consisted of a chairman, vice-chairman, judicial members, both High Court and circuit judges, and distinguished members representing different disciplines. We had little or nothing to do with the section 33 cases. They were dealt with by local review committees, whose expertise did not in any way compare with the Parole Board. Secondly, particularly with the cases of short sentences with which they were substantially dealing, the amount of information available to them was limited, partly because of resources and partly because of the time element.

Prisoners who were sentenced to a short sentence had their application for parole put in the pipeline at an early stage in their prison career when not all the necessary information had been gathered or collated, or indeed available. That may well have been one of the reasons why a very high proportion of those section 33 cases were released, as it appeared to the public, 'on the nod'. Another reason why the section 33 cases attracted severe criticism was that the Home Office and the Parole Board had proposed in the section 33 cases that there should be a presumption in favour of parole.

I confess that I found the whole concept of parole at that time somewhat difficult to come to terms with. The Parole Board have an annual conference. In September 1986 it was held at Cumberland Lodge, and I was invited to give a talk which I did and described it as a 'A judge's view, a culture shock'. I there expressed the culture shock that I felt when the first case that I attended at the Parole Board was of a man sentenced to three years for burglary. Substantial sums of money were involved, and there were a number of burglaries. It was not a case of a man on an impulse breaking in; it was a series of well-planned professional offences. He had previous convictions, he was in his mid-thirties and he was typical of a large number of cases with which the courts regularly had to deal. He had been sentenced to a term of three years' imprisonment by an experienced judge, no doubt after everything by way of mitigation had been said on his behalf. He had behaved well in prison and had a wife and children who were much distressed when he was in prison. He was much distressed at being in prison, and was determined when he came out of prison not ever to re-offend, and he had a job to go back to. When he came before the board he had done a year of his sentence and to other members of the board he appeared to be an ideal candidate to be released and indeed released on parole he was.

The difficulty I had was that, having received a perfectly proper sentence, he would if he behaved himself be entitled to a one-third remission and would come out after two years. I asked myself what it was that had happened in his year in prison which had in effect enabled him to halve his sentence.

A cynical view sometimes expressed was that this was simply the executive's way of ensuring that the prisons did not get overcrowded. The idea of building more prisons was of course anathema to the more liberal minded members of the public and in particular to the Treasury. But it seemed to me that if parliament thought the sentences passed by the court were too high, the remedy was perfectly simple, which was to reduce the maximum sentence for any particular offence – thus, it would have a substantial effect on sentencing. Courts of course are not allowed to take into account the effect of parole on sentence, although a judge, having passed a sentence of three years, knows perfectly well, as does the accused, not only that the accused would be eligible for parole after a year, but also that the accused would be likely to come out after a year. Thus, the general public was wholly misled. Victims were sometimes somewhat surprised to find the author of their misfortunes, whom they expected to remain in prison for an appreciable time, wandering the streets after a short time, because of being released on parole coupled with time spent in custody for trial.

My criticism of the way the parole system was operated, both generally and in relation to section 33, was not enormously well received by other members of the board, who enquired in effect, if that was my view then what was I doing on the Parole Board? It did however seem to me that someone from the sharp end of criminal law should be free to express their views about the anxiety and distress the system was causing. In effect, a body of people, although no doubt distinguished, were subsequently 'second-guessing' the decision of a judge appointed to pass sentence, who was assisted by tariffs laid down by the court of Criminal Appeal. In effect, the board was re-sentencing without perhaps as much information as the trial judge had. A trial judge, particularly after a plea of not guilty, has a much better assessment of the seriousness of a crime and the criminal involvement of the accused than any other body could possibly have.

It seemed to me also that there was everything to be said for a system of parole which avoided a prisoner simply being let out into the community without any form of support. Prisoners who did not succeed in getting parole were simply let out after serving two-thirds of their sentence, without any support. I therefore suggested in my talk that it would be sensible for all prisoners when released to be subject to some form of parole. It would not only assist the prisoner but more importantly it would be a help to the public. The anecdotal evidence that appeared about the supervision that occurred, particularly with the section 33 cases, was that probation officers, who were overworked and underpaid (they still are), were not able to give the attention and supervision which was required, and although they had the power to recall a prisoner who did not fully co-operate, the will and ability to supervise these particular parolees appeared to be somewhat lacking.

As a result of a great number of criticisms, in July 1997 the Home Secretary announced that he was going to set up a committee to look not only at the parole system but at the whole relationship between sentences passed by the courts and time actually spent in custody. The committee was chaired by the Right Honourable Lord Carlisle of Bucklow QC, who had had a distinguished ministerial career, was a well-known advocate and was at home in the corridors of power. He chaired the committee with consummate skill, bringing together disparate views from experts in their field, who expressed their views forcibly and with conviction. That at the end of it he was able to produce a report for the Secretary of State to which all members assented says as much for the skill of the chairman as for the willingness of the members to acknowledge the depth of feeling which other members had on particular subjects.

I cannot remember being on a committee which expressed such sensible or formidable arguments with such little rancour and with a flexibility which enabled members to change their mind after hearing argument on many of the subjects. We had two members who might be described as from outside the criminal law world. One was Nicolas Hinton CBE, who was director general of the Save the Children Fund. He died at a young age, but was an immensely valuable contributor, bringing experience of the outside world and common sense, and always testing arguments which lawyers took for granted but needed probing. The other was Martin Laing, who was chairman of John Laing plc. He came to the committee, I suspect, with a total absence of knowledge of the criminal system, was astonished at some of the things what occurred, made a great number of sensible criticisms and suggestions and was a most valuable member of the committee.

The other members were more familiar with the criminal system. David Atkinson was a retired prison governor and Navnit Dholakia JP, was a member of the Lewes Board of Visitors and an officer for the

Commission of Racial Equality. Dr Roger Hood was director of the Oxford Centre for Criminological Research. Mrs Jenny Roberts was Chief Probation Officer for Hereford and Worcester. His Honour Judge Sir David West-Russell had been a criminal practitioner and was a circuit judge and Peter Wright CBE was Chief Constable of South Yorkshire. Thus there was a wide breadth of experience, both of the criminal system and outside, to consider the very difficult topics before us. We had as our secretary William Fittall and his assistant secretary Joe Langdale. As the chairman said:

> Their cheerfulness, tolerance and willingness to do anything asked of them never failed. They conducted a great deal of research and put in a lot of hard work. They arranged interviews, visits, and above all prepared clear and sensible documentation for each meeting and afterwards constructed a report to which eventually we were all able to put our signatures.

A particular problem was that in 1983 Leon Brittan, who was then Home Secretary, said:

> ...that prisoners serving sentences of over 5 years for offences of violence or drug trafficking would be granted parole only when release under supervision, for a few months before the end of a sentence, is likely to reduce the long term risk to the public, or in certain circumstances which are genuinely exceptional. In future there would have to be the most compelling reasons before I would agree to parole being granted in such cases.

This announcement of policy, 'the restricted policy' as it became to be known, was the subject of a good deal of criticism by a wide variety of bodies.

We first met as a committee in September 1987, and in October 1988 Mark Carlisle was able to write to Douglas Hurd with a copy of our report. Given the difficulties of the subject, the vast amount of evidence and the necessity also to consider comparative systems external to the UK, it was a remarkable effort. We held 18 meetings in all, including two at conference centres, and additionally there were a great number of visits by the committee, either individually or as a group, to prisons, youth custody centres, probation services, judicial seminars, special hospitals, to the parole boards for England, Wales and Scotland, and the Scottish Parole Review Committee. One group of the committee visited Canada and another visited the US. In Georgia there was a visit to the Parole Board and to a correctional institution. In Tennessee there was also a visit to the Parole Board and meetings with the chairman and staff of the State Board of Paroles, and to the Tennessee State Penitentiary. In New York we observed some parole hearings and visited the Hudson Correction Facility, and in Minnesota we had meetings with several people concerned with early release schemes, supervision and prisons, and visited Oak Park Heights.

In addition a visit was paid to Otisville, a Federal Correctional Institution and a series of meetings were held with senior officers in the Federal Parole Commission in the Federal Bureau of Prisons, the Federal Sentencing Commission, the Federal Probation Service and we also met the Deputy Associate Attorney General.

These were very rewarding visits. The Americans had been in the forefront of the parole systems because they had as we understood it no appeal court to deal with sentences. In addition, a lot of their sentences were of the 5–15-year type and release therefore depended a lot on good behaviour. In some states there was a structured sentencing policy by which a prisoner's sentence could be calculated by reference to various criteria laid down by the state.

There was a generally accepted view by the committee that our system as it stood was illogical, unfair and indefensible. The immediate question was what should be put in its place. It was agreed that a parole system was necessary and that to let prisoners out 'cold' was quite unsatisfactory. The question then arose: at what stage should parole be available? Should it be automatic? How long should supervision be for, and would supervision in fact be effective?

There was a good deal of evidence before us suggesting a certain lack of enthusiasm among probation officers to take on the role of supervising serious criminals. The first objection raised, a substantial one, was the lack of resources. And the second, which seemed to be an objection in principle, was that the probation service culture was not geared properly to supervising those who had been convicted of serious offences. The whole object of parole and supervision would be lost if prisoners simply turned up as and when they liked at probation centres and effectively continued in their old ways without the authorities having any real control. It did require a whole new approach by the probation services, whose representatives were not all in agreement.

We had seen in the US that a number of parole officers were effectively policemen by another name. They had guns and their job was in a disciplined way to control the parolees under their charge. However, at the end of the day the probation services were persuaded, provided sufficient resources were available, that they would be in a position to deal with the effect of our recommendations. Another problem which divided the committee was the effect of sentences by the judges. It was clear a number of members of the committee were seriously critical of the length of sentences and the number of people in prison. They were keen therefore to get the length of sentences reduced in some way and thereby reduce the number of people in prison.

There were, as one would expect on any discussion about sentencing, 'hawks and doves'. Our final conclusions as to length of supervision and length of licence necessarily reflected a good deal of give and take between those two groups.

The main recommendations were that those sentenced to more than a year but less than four should automatically be released after serving half the sentence and should be subject to supervision up to three-quarters and on licence until the full duration of their sentence was reached. Thus, a four-year sentence meant serving two years in custody, being subject to supervision for one year and on licence for the remaining year. Thus, during the two years a prisoner was in the community, he or she could be recalled for failure to comply with the terms of supervision, which was for a year, but was on risk if he or she committed any further offence during the whole period of the sentence. Those who were sentenced to over four years were eligible for parole after serving half of their time, but that was to be discretionary and decided by the board, with the sole criterion being risk of re-offending. As to the restricted rule, we recommended abolition. Those serving over four years when released would be subject to supervision up to three-quarters of the sentence and on parole until the the full duration was reached and thus again were at risk if they committed any further offence for the whole of their sentence. Remission for these prisoners remained the same.

Another recommendation made was that there should be greater openness in providing prisoners with information as to why they have been refused parole. This had given rise to a number of challenges by way of judicial review by prisoners – on the grounds either that they had been unfairly treated or that the reasons given by the board were insufficient, or that in some way the decision was unreasonable. Not many of these cases had been successful, but there was no dispute that greater openness about decision-making was much to be encouraged – not least when a person's liberty was at stake. There was considerable discussion that the changes which we were proposing did not go far enough and that anyone who was refused parole should as a matter as of principle have a right to appear in person before the board, just as they had the right to be present when the judge sentenced them or when a board of visitors considered disciplining them for a prison offence.

While a majority understood the desire of prisoners to have the opportunity to present their case in person, the question was whether the additional benefits were likely to be such as to outweigh the major practical problems that a hearing system would involve. Clearly they would have to be held in the prisons, and the Parole Board would have to be peripatetic and meet wherever a particular prisoner eligible for parole happened to be located. In June 1987 there were prisoners in some 88 different prisons who were serving sentences of more than four years. The logistical problem of going to each and every one of those prisons at the material time would be enormous. Additionally, there was a doubt whether the sort of people who the committee wanted to see serving on the Parole Board would be available to travel around to the extent that would be required.

Some of the penal-reform groups were critical of the report, and it was suggested that we were not able to be radical because of the imposed terms of reference. But the fact that some of the papers suggested that the government was unhappy, and other reports suggested that the penal reformers were unhappy, inclined us to the view that we got it just about right. We were not asked to express any view about sentencing. It was not within our terms of reference. The views that were expressed were done without any observations being sought from the Lord Chief Justice or other judges or without any evidence other than anecdotal evidence being put before the committee. Sensibly, the judges took no notice of this part of the report.

14

The MCC and the Bailey Affair

I became a member of the Marylebone Cricket Club (MCC) in 1951. There were then and still are two ways of getting into the MCC. The first is to put your name on the waiting list and wait. Currently the waiting time for those on the list is 25 years. In 1951 the waiting time was less and in the 1970's the membership rose from some 7000–8000 to some 18,000, with the result that those who happened then to be on the waiting list became members within two or three years. One of the disadvantages of the sudden increase in membership was that there was no sort of control over who applied. There was little or no vetting and as a result a number of people were able to join whose interest in cricket was minimal. Whether that has resulted in causing some of the turmoil at AGMs over the last decade must be a matter of speculation.

The other alternative was to play 10 games for the club over two years, and in the event that you showed that you were a comparatively promising cricketer you were likely to be elected. Thereafter there was an obligation to play for the club in out matches. One of the ways that the MCC encourage cricket is to play against schools and clubs all over the country. Now there are some 400–500 out matches, so the spirit of the game is taken to all parts.

In those days the match managers were somewhat elderly, rather stuffy and not themselves particularly good cricketers. I played my first qualifying match against Epsom College the day after we had won the university match in 1949 when, not surprisingly, I was on a high, full of a certain amount of the arrogance of youth and unreceptive to advice from an elderly captain for whom I had little or no respect. I managed to run myself out when I was on 49 and was reproved by the captain. I did not regard his criticism as either justified or sensible and with all the brashness of youth told him so. Happily he had enough sense not to put a black mark against me, and after my 10 games I was elected in 1951 to the MCC.

Apart from playing some games for the club, thereafter I took little or no interest in the affairs of the club. One day in the robing room John Stocker QC, who subsequently became Lord Justice Stocker and was a keen cricketer, asked me if I would be prepared to add my name to a number of others who had written to *The Times* about the forthcoming South African tour. It has to be remembered that in the late 1960s and early 1970s sport in South Africa was a nasty word, and it was not politically correct to suggest that strengthening the sporting ties with South Africa might be beneficial rather than detrimental.

Whether the letter persuaded anyone to the contrary I very much doubt. It was one of those arguments where views were set in concrete. However, out of the blue came an invitation from the MCC Committee to stand for the committee. In those days it was customary for the committee to 'star' those which it supported, and as a general rule those who got the committee's nod got elected. And so it turned out. As a result, in 1971 I went on the committee. I was appointed to the General Purposes Committee, on which I sat until 1988 and of which I was chairman for a short period. Combining that with practice at the bar was never easy, and after I became a judge, was almost impossible. The General Purposes Committee used to meet after lunch on the same day as the Main Committee. But getting to the meetings at 2pm, or more importantly, getting there in time for 12.30 lunch was well-nigh impossible. Lunch was an important part of committee and sub-committee work because it enabled people to have full discussion about all sorts of matters which were not necessarily on the agenda but were vital to the welfare of the MCC.

In 1971 the committee was very large, and it was not until 1983 that, as a result of a working party, its membership was slimmed down considerably. Up to 1968 the MCC had been effectively responsible for domestic cricket in the UK, with the responsibility for selecting the touring sides to go abroad. Further, by providing the secretariat and chairmanship of the International Cricket Board (ICB), it had a strong part to play in international cricket. English teams abroad played as England in test matches and as MCC in state or provincial games. The MCC was and still is responsible for the laws of the game. Its members rightly considered that they controlled cricket, that there was no other body that could affect their rights and privileges, and although they were described as a private club with a public face, nevertheless they expected the MCC to be recognised throughout the world as the cricket authority of the UK.

All this changed in 1968 when the MCC accepted that a private club should no longer be seen to be running a national game and accordingly, the MCC voluntarily relinquished its implicit though largely undefined authority. Three bodies were created. The Test and County Cricket Board (TCCB), which was a fusion of the Advisory County Cricket Committee and the board of control for test matches, themselves bodies set up by the MCC, would in future be responsible for the organisation, administration and promotion of first-class test matches and one-day internationals in the UK. The National Cricket Association (NCA) would administer what came to be called 'the recreational game'. A body initially called the MCC Council (thereafter the Cricket Council) was the game's new governing body comprising the MCC itself, the TCCB, the NCA and the Minor Counties Cricket Association (MCCA).

By 1983 the Cricket Council had become a poodle of the TCCB which could command a majority in the council. The membership of the TCCB consisted of the MCC, each of the 17 first-class counties and the MCCA. For the time being the MCC continued its worldwide role by providing the chairman and secretariat of the International Cricket Conference (ICC), though by the 1990s that of itself changed. Although the first chairman of the ICC was Colin Cowdrey, Lord Cowdrey, a chairman outside the MCC was thereafter appointed and a new secretariat was set up, with David Richards in charge. This recognised the reality of world cricket, which previously had been dominated by England and Australia and gave much-needed support to the aspirations of cricketers throughout the world, both among the developed and undeveloped nations.

Initially relations between the MCC and the board were comparatively happy, as was the relationship between the board and the Test Match Ground authorities (TMG). The test-match grounds apart from Lords were Old Trafford, Nottingham, the Oval, Edgbaston and Headingley.

In staging major matches the board had to act through the TMG. Difficulties arose because these clubs were autonomous, composed of members possessing rights and privileges within the rules and regulations of those clubs which were likely from time to time to conflict with the wishes of the board in relation to the staging of matches.

What the board did was to allocate the major matches, to lay down the playing conditions and the system of distributing the surplus of revenue, and to begin with there was little interference from the board. However, things changed. Money became an essential part of the cricket scene. Sponsors who put substantial sums of money into cricket did not wish to negotiate individual packages with each test-match ground, but with the board. Given that sponsors were putting a large amount into cricket, the board naturally wanted to provide them with as many facilities as they could, such as boxes, advertising sites and blocks of seats. This necessarily brought them into conflict with the TMG where the boxes for instance, particularly at Lords, were a privilege enjoyed by members who saw no reason why a sponsor should have a box when they did not, or a sponsor should have parking space when it was almost impossible for members to get their cars into the ground. Additionally, the board needed to provide hospitality for official guests, as did the MCC, and this again caused difficulty.

Because there was now a commercial approach to cricket which was new both to the MCC and the other test-match grounds, again there was a conflict because the board wished to sell publications and souvenirs, whereas it had been the practice of the MCC to produce its own brochure for matches played at Lords. Advertising too, which had now become a major money-spinner for test-match grounds, was another area of conflict. The MCC wished to arrange its own advertising and take the revenue, whereas the board wanted to have a national scheme for perimeter advertising – and more particularly, the board wanted to have a central policy for selling the tickets while the MCC wished to retain control of its own arrangements.

To begin with the MCC secretariat serviced both the club and the TCCB but by 1974 it was clear that the conflict of interest between the two bodies was such that the administration needed to be separated. Over the years thereafter there was a constant source of tension between the two bodies, the board seeking to exercise its authority over the test-match grounds while the MCC, and other test-match grounds and in particular their members, insisted on preserving the rights and privileges of the membership.

In 1983 a working party was set up to examine the workings of the MCC and it recommended that control of what happened at Lords should always be directly retained by the committee and its employees, and this was adopted by the members. A good deal of sterile argument existed between the board and the MCC as to the overall and ultimate responsibility for major matches. Quite clearly some flexibility was required, and there was also agreement that, consistent with the board's overall responsibility the test-match grounds should stage the matches in the best interests of the board as a whole. There was a dispute as to what should happen in an emergency and thereafter there was a growing frisson between the MCC and the board. There were threats by the board to take major matches away from Lords. It even reached the stage that the secretary of the MCC and the secretary of the board, who were both housed in the pavilion within walking distance of each other, communicated by letter.

The president of the MCC set up a Joint Liaison Committee so that the board's Executive Committee and the MCC Committee could meet from time to time, but the board withdrew its support because of its belief that the Secretary of the MCC was reluctant to co-operate. During the spring and summer of 1986 the only effective link was personal liaison between the president of the MCC and the chairman of the board.

The board had written to say that its authority was to deal with the MCC in a way that was consistent with that which they exercised on all test-match grounds. It was not its policy to interfere with the running of all major matches unless it was deemed to be in the interests of the board, and it would act in a reasonable manner in its dealings with the MCC. Thereafter, it was hoped that the board and the MCC would settle by agreement all matters relating to the staging of the matches. One of the matters which had given rise to dispute was that the board decided to charge members for the privilege of coming into the ground. As membership of the MCC entitled a member to come into the ground free, this gave rise to a good deal of upset. The committee took the view that in the interests of cricket it was a sum which had to be paid, although there was a strong view that the board's bluff should be called and the threat of taking a match away from Lords nailed forever. However, it was pointed out that this money was to be ploughed back into cricket, that the MCC got substantial revenue from the test matches and that the MCC should take a broad and not an insular view of the new situation. In the result, the MCC decided that it would pay the sum out of the members' subscriptions. The argument resurfaced during the World Cup.

What was quite clear was that for the members, and for some of the committee and secretariat, the loss of authority went deep and it was not possible for them readily to accept the new situation. Every suggestion by the board was treated as an incursion by the board into the rights and privileges of the members, to be fought to the bitter death as a matter of principle.

Thus, the scene was set for what became known as the Bailey affair. Jack Bailey had been appointed as assistant secretary in the 1960s and succeeded as secretary when Billy Griffith retired in 1974. He had a distinguished cricket career. He played for Oxford University, which he captained in 1958, and then for Essex. Initially, as assistant secretary he was responsible for public relations and promotions and the John Player sponsorship was secured. He played an important part at the international conference and in particular made a substantial contribution to the very difficult period arising from the Packer affair.

David Clark was at this time treasurer. The treasurer is not responsible for the finances, as the name might suggest, but is really the right-hand man of the president, being elected for some five years, and therefore the link between the membership, the committee and the president. He and the secretary are vital parts of the administration. The treasurer is almost a permanent fixture, while the president in those days came and went at yearly intervals. Clark had immense experience, having been on the committee since 1959 and served almost continuously since then. He was president in 1977, became treasurer in 1980 and a trustee in 1985. Apart from his cricket connection with Kent, he had managed MCC sides overseas with success; he was a deep thinking, sensible and balanced farmer who had made a contribution, not only to the MCC, but to first-class cricket, both as a player and administrator. It was their enthusiasm to protect, as they saw it, the rights and privileges of the membership, which led them into eventual conflict with the committee and their ultimate resignation.

Messrs Halsey, Lightly and Hemsley had been the club's solicitors for some 50 years. While by no means a sinecure, until the Packer affair blew up there had been little necessity for serious legal advice. In 1984 and in 1986 the secretary and the treasurer instructed Halsey, Lightly and Hemsley to obtain opinions from counsel on the extent to which the committee should consult the membership and about the question of conflict of interest. The seeking of the opinions was not authorised by the committee, which did not know about it at the time, and indeed copies of the opinions were not seen by the committee until sometime in December 1986.

The allegation of conflict of interest centred essentially around George Mann and Doug Insole. George Mann had been an outstanding captain of Middlesex and of England, and in 1983 he was chairman of the TCCB. In the autumn of 1983 Mann was re-elected to the MCC committee (topping the ballot) and at the same time retired as chairman of the TCCB and was succeeded by Mr Charles Palmer. Although Mann had retired as chairman of the board, he continued to be a member of the Executive Committee. In early April of 1984, Alex Dibbs, the outgoing president, nominated Mann as his successor. The right to nominate a successor is given to the president. Although entitled to make the choice without consultation, it is customary for the president to do so to ensure that the incoming president, secretary and treasurer and the chairman of finance can work together, and that the incoming president is likely to be acceptable to the committee. There was no question that Mann would make a good president, but the treasurer made it clear to Dibbs that he might be forced to resign. He felt that because Mann was then a member of the TCCB Executive Committee he was not an independent person for the purposes of the ICC or the MCC in the context of the negotiations with the board. Secondly, this was the first occasion apparently when a president had not consulted either the treasurer or the secretary about a proposed nomination.

Doug Insole had captained Cambridge and Essex and played nine times for England. He had been Mann's vice-captain in South Africa, had been a member of the Cricket Committee since 1953 and on the committee since 1956. He of course wore an Essex 'hat', and he was also on the board. Many of the MCC Committee wore several 'hats', because they had either played for or were on the committees of county sides. It was because of their vast experience of the world outside the MCC that they were such valuable members of the MCC Committee. Colin Cowdrey, Hubert Doggart, Peter May, Gubby Allen, Colin Ingleby

McKenzie, Mike Smith, John Warr, Ted Dexter and many others had much to contribute from their cricketing experience elsewhere, and to have a committee with no outside expertise would have been futile.

Conflict of interest, of course, normally arises where a financial interest is involved, but although the lawyers waxed long about the dangers of conflict of interest, in the cricketing context there really was absolutely nothing to it. The advantage of having someone on the committee who was involved with the board was self-evident. They could speak for the MCC at the board and they could speak at MCC Committee meetings about the attitude of the board and the reasons why the board took a particular view. This was cross-fertilisation of a most important nature.

Mann in fact retired from the Executive Committee of the board before he became president of the MCC. At no time that I was on the committee was there any problem about the commercial interests of members of the committee having a conflict with their county club or the board, and it was in my view a total red herring. However, it gave rise to a good deal of ill-feeling, primarily because members simply could not accept the situation that the board was now in charge of cricket, and any weapon with which to beat the board was worth using.

In October 1985 Mr J. G. W. Davies became president of the MCC. He had played cricket for Kent. He was a well-known rugger player and when at Cambridge had bowled Bradman out. He was a very jovial man, highly intelligent and an immensely able negotiator. Apart from meetings of the Joint Liaison Sub-Committee of the MCC and the board, Davies had negotiations with the new chairman of the board, Rahman Subba Row, on a person-to-person basis. Subba Row had been up at Cambridge with me – he had managed to run me out in the university match, which subsequently occasioned much hilarity between us. He was a first-class businessman, a deep thinker and sensible. As I have indicated, the meetings of the sub-committees were not a success. The board indicated that it would prefer the secretary not to be included as a member thereafter. The board felt that the secretary's influence was an obstacle to harmonious relations between the two bodies, and although assurances had been given by the board to principles that had been set out in 1983, the committee was not at all certain that the secretary was willing to work in a co-operative manner with the board.

There was no doubt that Bailey had at the forefront of his mind the view that the position of the members was at all times to be protected against, as he saw it, the encroachment by the board of the club's authority at Lords. He regarded every concession as a sign of weakness. His attitude was undoubtedly wholly motivated by a desire to protect the interests of the members. It was, however, obvious to the committee that what it regarded as a somewhat inflexible approach was now quite inappropriate if harmonious relations with the board were to be re-established. It was quite impossible that the MCC and the board (of which the MCC was a member) should conduct their affairs at arm's length without give or take. It was neither in the interests of cricket as a whole nor indeed of the members in particular.

In August 1986 matters came to a head. There was a meeting between the treasurer, the chairman of finance, Colin Cowdrey and the president with representatives of the board, including Subba Row. There was no particular agenda, and the discussion drifted from point to point. There was obvious hostility from the board, which was sceptical about assurances given to it, and while it accepted the legal position with regard to ownership, it was not happy about the interpretation of overall responsibility. There was some sort of threat about the bi-centenary match not taking place at Lords and the board said they would not negotiate terms until the MCC committee convinced them that the situation was under control and it had got control of the secretary.

On 26 August Subba Row had written a letter to the president complaining about the lack of co-operation from the MCC secretariat over recent years, and suggesting that the committee was largely unaware of the extent of this non-co-operation. Additionally, he said that it was up to the MCC to convince the board that it had control of its secretariat and ending up by saying, 'that if the board remained unconvinced that the MCC does not mean business I regret to say that the board cannot pursue any of the matters outstanding between us'.

This letter, not surprisingly, was not very well received by the committee when it met on 3 September, and the committee was somewhat incensed at what it regarded as a threat that the bi-centenary match might be taken away from Lords.

Meanwhile, it was agreed that no letter should be sent to the board until the committee had drawn up guidelines for the secretary as to his role for him to consider and say whether they married up with the points raised by him. Accordingly, guidelines were prepared by the MCC without the board having any input to them. In September 1986 Colin Cowdrey succeeded Davies as president. In October he had to write to Bailey to point out that the committee was disappointed that the guidelines which had been set out in such a way as best to accommodate him had not received ready acceptance. At the meeting in October, the committee regarded the guidelines as a perfectly reasonable set of requests and conditions, and expected the secretary to comply with them. Additionally, an official warning as to his future employment was given.

On 30 October Bailey wrote to the president, observing that he was seeking clarification of the meaning of the guidelines, and was therefore somewhat surprised that he had received an official warning and asked that it should be suspended until the situation was resolved. He then suggested a number of guidelines which should be given to the secretary. On 4 November the president replied, pointing out that prior to giving him the letter of 24 October the contents had been spelt out and the president had made it clear that the committee had lost confidence in the manner in which he was conducting their affairs. He further asked that the secretary give an assurance that he would abide by the guidelines which the committee had approved.

On 7 November the secretary wrote to say that he confirmed that as instructed he would use his best endeavours to carry out the agreement entered between the immediate past president of the MCC and the chairman of the TCCB as contained in their correspondence, and to work to the draft guidelines which he was assured had been approved by the committee. He ended up by asking that the formal warning should be withdrawn pending that review.

Although the secretary took the view that he had given unreserved acceptance to the guidelines (though he had reservations about them which he would like to reconsider after the year), the president thought that he was not giving unreserved acceptance to the guidelines. The matter therefore came before the committee again on 19 November. At that meeting the secretary addressed the committee. He deprecated the necessity for any warning to be given and said he was willing to carry out the wishes of the committee in accordance with the guidelines. He explained that his letter of 7 November 1986 meant that although he did have some reservations about the guidelines he would do his very best to carry them out, but at the end of the year he would like the position reviewed.

The president raised three specific matters of lack of co-operation by the secretary. It was pointed out to him that it was a pity that those complaints had not been put to the secretary. The treasurer observed that the secretary had given the committee the assurances that were being requested, the review was reasonable and that the way relations with the board were developing was unknown, and therefore not only the secretary but maybe the committee would require a review in the light of experience. The treasurer also asked that the warning should be withdrawn because it would be difficult for the secretary to operate with a threat hanging over him.

It was pointed out that the president had lost confidence in the secretary and there was no hope of peace and quiet if the matter was swept under the carpet. There was continuing disagreement with the TCCB, and although broadly the secretary had done a good job in the 12 years and worked in the interests of the MCC, the club was not now being well run. A number of the committee expressed the view that confidence had gone and that the presence of the secretary was affecting good relations with the TCCB, that the club was not being particularly well run and that there were a number of dissatisfied members. Other members of the committee took the view that there had not been unqualified acceptance of the guidelines. Among a number of members of the committee, the view was that the secretary's way of defending the club had been misplaced. They thought that there had been constant battles between presidents and the secretary and that if the matter continued it was unlikely the secretary's view would change.

David Clark, the treasurer, said he could not support any suggested sacking as there were no grounds, and it would cause difficulty in any year but particularly so in the year of the centenary. He did not think the secretary would resign, but if the matter were handled with tact and generosity he would accept early retirement and that was a better way of approaching it. In the result, there was a resolution that the secretary should be invited to take early retirement or resignation, at immediate date, due to the loss of confidence in him by the committee. The trustees did not vote, but the resolution was carried *nem con.*

On 3 December, having received the minutes of the meeting, Bailey wrote a personal letter to me complaining, perfectly reasonably, that a number of matters about which the committee spoke had never been addressed to him, that he had had no opportunity of replying and that they provided scant basis upon which they had invited him to resign. He explained in detail what had happened in relation to the particular criticisms raised at the committee meeting. He pointed out that no opportunity had been given to him to deal with them, that there was a feeling of a pre-organised coup signed, sealed and delivered before the meeting took place, and that he felt that he had been very harshly treated. On 19 December 1986 Halsey, Lightly and Hemsley revealed for the first time that the secretary and treasurer had taken advice from leading counsel on a number of occasions, and the committee was now provided with a copy of those opinions. They were unrelated to the position of the secretary save that it strengthened the committee in its view that there was a lack of trust and confidence from the committee when the permanent officials sought counsel's advice without informing the committee of that fact or of the contents of the advice received.

Discussions then took place between the president and the secretary about the terms of his retirement. The secretary had gone to Australia, and it was agreed there should be no press announcement until his return. Unfortunately the secretary had been unwell while in Australia, which delayed his return. There had been pressure from the Australian press to publish a story that the secretary had been dismissed and accordingly a press statement was issued which read as follows:

> It was announced from Lords today by the president of the MCC, Mr M.C. Cowdrey, that the MCC committee had formerly accepted the request made towards the end of last year by Mr J.A. Bailey to take early retirement from his post as secretary to the MCC. Mr Bailey was appointed secretary in 1974 having been an assistant secretary since 1967. 'He has served the club with total commitment over a long period', said Mr Cowdrey, 'and on behalf of the committee and the members I wish to express their warm appreciation for the service he has given to the club'. Lieutenant Colonel J.R. Stevenson will become acting Secretary of the MCC and ICC.

At the same time Clark felt that he ought to resign. He had worked closely with the secretary in defending the rights and privileges of the members. He thought it was unnecessary for the committee to take the step that it did, and he did what he considered the only honourable thing at the time, which was to resign.

It was a very sad occasion. Both men had served the MCC with distinction and acted as they thought best in the interests of the members. That the secretary had lost the confidence of the committee was one of those matters that occur from time to time, however well run an organisation is. It has to be said that Bailey behaved with very great dignity after resigning. He continued to take an active interest in the cricket world. He came back onto the General Purposes Sub-Committee in 1995 and has now been elected a member of the full committee. To lose two important members was a sad blow, but in view of the continued frisson between the board and the MCC, looking back I think it fair to say that some such resolution was almost inevitable given the personalities involved. Whether it was very well handled, on reflection I have some doubt.

Unfortunately, that was not the end of the unhappy saga. Although the president wrote to all the members in February 1987 seeking to explain as best he could how the matters had arisen, it was not easy to set out fully the extent of the difficulties of relationship between the MCC and the board or to create in writing the atmosphere which had developed between the two bodies. The club's solicitors having obtained the opinion of counsel about the conflict of interest, the sterile argument as to who had the ultimate responsibility for managing matches at Lords continued to concern the solicitors. It was a totally sterile argument because in the end it was a matter of pragmatism. Lords owned the ground and exercised control over it. The TCCB had the responsibility for staging the matches. If a conflict arose and could not be settled by negotiation, no amount of saying who had the ultimate responsibility was going to determine it. Either the MCC said, if you insist on that condition you have to go and play your game elsewhere, or the board could say, if you will not accept our condition we will take the match away from you and play it at the Oval. Both of these scenarios were extreme and unlikely to occur, and what was needed was not a discussion about the semantics but getting down to the particular problems which arose and sorting them out as and when they did arise.

Thus, an assurance that the MCC recognised the overall and ultimate responsibility of the board gave nothing away, because if the

MCC Committee decided that a condition which the board wished to impose was such that it could not commend it to its members, the committee would say so and the board would have two alternatives, either to withdraw the idea or go elsewhere. Nevertheless, much time and energy and no little heat was generated by argument about ultimate responsibility leading up to the AGM. The solicitors continued to be concerned about Mann and Insole's relationship with the board and the MCC. The conflict of interest argument was equally sterile, in my view. There were no commercial interests involved and what was needed was members of the committee to come from every background. It mattered not whether they were members of the committee or trustees – they were independent people who would give their advice without fear or favour. This too generated a good deal of heat and occupied a great deal of wasted time.

In addition Colin Cowdrey, who was president of the club, was chairman of a TCCB committee and had some anticipation of being chairman of the board. This gave great concern to the solicitors but in truth it was a matter which need not have occupied so much time and trouble.

It was pointed out that the elimination of everyone with any other interest would leave the MCC in splendid isolation. As for the trustees, they did not have a vote in committees except in relation to certain property matters. As the board had no interest in these property matters it was difficult to see where a conflict of interest would arise.

The AGM was due to take place on the afternoon of Wednesday 6 May. In the morning there was a meeting of the committee together with the solicitors. The solicitors were anxious to draw the members' attention to the distinction between overall responsibility and ultimate responsibility. There was a general feeling at the meeting that the issue was greatly overstated, and anxieties were expressed about the solicitors' suitability to answer questions, since it was clear that they had been fully behind the line taken by the former treasurer and secretary. The solicitors expressed a view that it was not for them to have an opinion either for or against the committee, but it was their duty to bring to the committee's attention any views they held as to anything incorrect either in the report or in accounts.

The meeting held in the afternoon was extremely ill-tempered and loutish. It was not helped because it was held in the banqueting and conference centre. The communication system was not at its best and the members were still in a somewhat angry and bemused state about the resignation of their secretary and treasurer. One member raised the question of whether the club's solicitors were prepared to support the annual report. Meyer, on behalf of the solicitors, said that he had raised reservations about the annual report and referred to the question of the responsibility of the board and the conflict of interest of the trustees. I had to point out that under the constitution we were members of the board, and I also pointed out again that the argument about the ultimate, overall or supreme responsibility had been going on for some five years, was perfectly sterile and had got us nowhere. I also pointed out that the conflict of interest was a non-runner and that members would wish to elect those who had interests outside the confines of Lords.

The members found it extremely difficult to understand the relationship between the MCC and the board, and believed that if we simply said that we had absolute control over everything that happened at Lords all would be rosy in the garden. The membership were obviously of the view that in some way their rights were being reduced, (though in what way no-one ever said specifically) and accordingly voted against the annual report, and likewise the accounts.

The president then outlined the problems which the MCC had had with the board. Davies, who had recently retired as president, summed up the relationship in this way:

> In its treatments of the Board the MCC has really had a choice between two main policies. To polarise them I shall describe them in rather extreme terms. Policy A which is along the lines of adopting a mainly defensive stance, conceding as little as possible beyond what is statutory, keeping the board's officers at a distance, preserving all the manifestations of MCC's independence and former privilege, relying on MCC's ownership of Lords as leverages of that policy... Policy B is the obverse, it would recognise that power has shifted decisively to the Board from MCC, we should maintain close and regular communication with its representatives, be prepared to make concessions as long as members' rights are not seriously impaired, promote MCC's influence in cricket and do so largely by diplomatic means. The secretary was convinced, and he is a man of very strong convictions that something not too far removed from policy A was in the best interests of the club and its members.

As a result of the refusal by the membership present to approve the annual report and accounts, a special general meeting (SGM) now became necessary. The solicitors sought to be helpful by undertaking to negotiate with the board and with the author of a resolution at the SGM. At its meeting in March 1987 the committee considered the various suggestions that had been made by the solicitors to assist, and decided not to accept them. It was agreed that an SGM be called for 30 July. During the meeting it was agreed Messrs Simmons & Simmons should replace Halsey, Lightly and Hemsley as the club's solicitors. It was agreed that a document should be prepared for circulation to the members setting out the necessary background, and in the result, at the SGM on 30 July 1987 the reports and accounts were re-presented and accepted. Thus ended one of the most unhappy periods in the history of the club. I am still firmly of the view that it was a storm in a tea cup, and the differences between the committee, the members, the secretary and the solicitors could all have been resolved given some flexibility among the various individuals concerned.

The matter has now resurfaced. When the English Cricket Board (ECB) was designated by the World Cricket Board to run the World Cup in England, it was inevitable that the arrangements which obtained at Lords on the previous occasion (in 1975) were unlikely to recur. On that occasion, interest in the World Cup had been very limited and the members had been allowed to come in using their passes. The worldwide interest which was now overwhelming simply did not then obtain. On this occasion it was abundantly clear to me as president that if matches were to be staged at Lords, which holds about 30,000 people, the idea that the 18,000 members would be entitled to come into the ground free was simply laughable. The worldwide demand for tickets was such that the public either in this country or overseas would simply not stand for it. The money for the World Cup was substantially to be raised by the selling of the television rights. Lords, which has the largest capacity and is therefore the greatest money-spinner when matches are arranged, was favourite to be the host for the final. The world at large, however, could not be really less interested as to where the final took place provided they could see it on television.

In anticipation of the World Cup the club spent something over £12 million of its own money in building a new grandstand and was in the act of spending something over £5 million on a media centre

270

to which NatWest made a substantial contribution. It would be unthinkable from the MCC's point of view that we should not host the final and indeed other matches. It was vitally important financially and in the best interest of the members that the final should not be taken elsewhere. The idea that our members would have the greatest proportion of tickets simply did not have any basis for reality.

In the summer of 1996 I had a discussion with the secretary of the board and the marketing manager in general terms about how the matches at Lords were to be staged. The ECB had clear instructions from the world cricketing authorities. Although it had indicated that the final was likely to be at Lords, until the package of arrangements had been put in place no firm contract had been entered into, nor would one be entered into until the final details had been agreed.

What the ECB said was that it was quite impossible for the same situation which obtained in 1975 to recur, that the public would not stand for the members having the vast proportion of the tickets and that there would be an allocation of tickets for the membership. That number was, I believe, some 8000. This was substantially above what I had in mind that we would be likely to obtain for our members. There was no question of negotiation. It was take it or leave it. Members were to be charged. The same conditions applied to all grounds. Nothing was said about what would happen if the offer were rejected. But it was clear, to me at any rate, that any idea of the whole membership asserting their rights and privileges was absurd. No games would have been played at Lords. Thus, the first question seemed to be that, if we were to get 8000 tickets for our members and a guarantee of the game at Lords, was that a good deal as opposed to the match being taken to the Oval and our members having to watch it on television? There would have been a loss of revenue from the catering, publicity, souvenirs and so on, which a match at Lords provides. It took me no more than 30 seconds to agree, as the alternative was too awful to contemplate. It did not seem to me a matter which needed consultation. It was a very simple issue.

The demand for payment by members affected not only MCC members but members of county grounds, and no doubt they also felt upset about it. Nevertheless, the object of the exercise was to raise money worldwide for the benefit of cricket, and it would have been quite wrong to take a narrow, parochial view of members' rights, even if there had been an alternative – which there wasn't. The question then arose as to whether the member who applied for a ticket should pay for it directly or whether it should be paid for out of club funds, so that those who either did not apply or those who applied and did not get tickets should subsidise those who did get tickets. Again, it seemed to me that this question admitted of only one answer – namely, those who did not get tickets should not be required to subsidise those who did get tickets. No doubt we should have consulted the members as we promised in 1977 – but as the decision was so clear, it really didn't matter.

However, when the membership learnt of this all hell let loose, and continued up to and including the AGM in 1999, when a concerted attempt was made to disrupt the whole meeting; it was raised yet again in 2000. It succeeded, no business was done and a further meeting had to take place at some expense in July. It was clear to me that the AGM in which a small number of dissident members can cause total chaos cannot any longer be supported, and that all important decisions at the AGM would in future have to be decided by postal ballot like a company meeting. Nobody wants to stifle debate among the members, but the yobbish behaviour and loutish attitudes which prevailed reflected very poorly on the membership of the club.

15

Imran Khan and Barry Wood

In May 1977 I chaired the Appeals Committee set up by the Cricket Council to hear an appeal by Sussex Cricket Club in the case of Imran Khan.

Khan had been registered with Worcester Cricket Club and now wished to join Sussex Cricket Club. Worcester objected to this. The rules were quite simple. Under rule 3 governing the qualification and registration of cricketers, 'the cricketer only qualified for registration (a) for the county of his birth, (b) [the county] in which he is residing and has been resident for the previous 12 consecutive months and (c) the county for which his father regularly played'.

Khan did not come within any of these categories so far as Sussex was concerned. By rule 4, which was special registration (a),

> the requirement of residents under Rule 3 may be wholly or partially waived by the board and a cricketer can be specially registered should the board conclude that it would be in the interest of competitive county cricket as a whole to do so. Either the county, the cricketer or the board, may request an independent tribunal to investigate and report on an application made for such waiver.

And by rule 9, appeals from decisions of the board may be made to the Cricket Council. The Registration Sub-Committee of the TCCB had refused to allow Sussex County Cricket Club to register Khan specially. Thus, the matter came before the Appeals Committee on 24 May.

Khan had been born on 25 November 1952 and in 1971 he joined the Pakistan team. He had discussions with Worcester, and Worcester arranged for him to go to the Worcester Royal Grammar School where in May 1972 he took his 'A' levels. He played some cricket for Worcester second eleven in 1971 and 1972, and in October he went to Oxford University and lived at the school. During the 1973 vacation he played for Worcester and stayed there for about eight weeks. In June 1974 he played for Pakistan, and didn't play for Worcester in 1974 except for a Gillette cup match. His first full season with Worcester was 1976. He lived by himself, and one of the points he made with Worcester was that he wanted decent accommodation because he wished to stay in a place where he felt at home. None of his friends from Oxford or school were at Worcester.

In April 1976 he started by sleeping on the floor in Mr Turner's flat and then moved to the Great Western Hotel, where he stayed for about six weeks and was pretty uncomfortable. He then moved to a friend's house. He said he was very lonely in Worcester, there was only pub life and he was a teetotaller. He had no friends there, he was very miserable and there was no way he was going to be happy.

In September 1975, the secretary wrote offering him re-engagement for the 1976 season and enclosed a contract. Khan signed the contract, but he wanted it to be noted that his accommodation should be subsidised as the rent was high. In February 1976 he wrote to the secretary asking him whether the club had found any accommodation for him, and saying what he wanted was a decent place at a reasonable price. The secretary replied by saying they were looking for suitable accommodation and hoped they might be able to rent a house where three or four of the team might be housed.

In August 1976 he was offered terms for re-engagement. The club was aware of Khan's accommodation problems. At the end of August Khan met with the secretary and explained that he was unable to accept the new contract as he was unable to live in Worcester. He emphasised quite unequivocally that he had no grievance with the club or with the way it was run or with the terms offered, explaining that he was quite well off at home. He had no quarrel with his fellow players, it was just that he did not like living in Worcester. He had no friends with the same interests, he did not like standing in pubs all night and he had no social life. The meeting ended with Khan agreeing further to consider the matter.

In September, he wrote to the secretary, 'provided I make up my mind to return to Worcester next year, of which I am still pretty doubtful, I would like the following terms, (a) £4000 basic salary, (b) free accommodation, (c) full return air fare'. He also wrote a letter saying, 'after a considerable amount of thought I have finally made up my mind that I would not like to renew my contract next year'. His substantial complaint related not to the quality of the accommodation that was offered, but to the fact that he didn't enjoy living in Worcester. As he said, 'I am sad that the major cause of my decision is not poor accommodation, although it did help to make life pretty miserable, the fact is I just couldn't face life in Worcester'. In November, Khan wrote to the secretary having made up his mind not to return and said, 'I honestly don't think I can spend another 6 months of my life in such a stagnant place ... it is certainly nothing to do with finance ... I've realised no matter how much I get paid I can't face life in Worcester'.

The county began to get suspicious that perhaps he had been approached by another county and that that was at least partly responsible for his restlessness and desire to move. In January 1977 he sent a postcard to the secretary saying he had decided not to come back to Worcester, and asked for Donald Carr, the secretary of the board, to cancel his registration, and in February it was cancelled.

On 7 February 1977 Sussex, which had been in correspondence with Worcester in 1975, gave notice that it was intending to approach Khan to see whether he was interested in joining its staff. Worcester was naturally concerned that Sussex may have been in some sort of prior arrangement with Khan which was the reason why he wished to leave Worcester, and expressed its view forcibly in a letter of 16 February 1977.

In April Sussex wrote to say that it had agreed terms with Khan and asked Worcester to complete the registration application form and to add any comments it wished to make. On 15 April Worcester wrote to Carr and to Sussex, expressing very great concern as to what happened. It said that it was anxious to retain Khan's services for 1977 and that the granting of special registration would be harmful to the whole structure of county cricket.

In September 1975 Khan had written to Tony Greig, who was then captain of Sussex, saying,

> It seems as if there is some doubt about my registration at Worcester for next season and I wondered if you and the Sussex committee would consider the possibility of taking me on the staff if I cannot play for Worcester next year.

My two reasons for choosing Sussex are (a) the availability of overseas registration and (b) the young age group of the team. I would be most grateful if you could let me know firstly the chances of getting a contract and secondly the terms that would be offered.

The secretary of Sussex spoke to the secretary of Worcester in October 1975, observing that Worcester was appealing against the findings of the Registration Sub-Committee at that time, which related to the temporary registration of Khan, and suggesting in the event of Worcester's appeal being turned down that Sussex would be grateful if the committee could agree to its approaching Khan. In the result, as the Worcester secretary pointed out, as Khan was fully qualified for Worcester under two sections of rule 2, their appeal was likely to succeed and in effect telling Sussex to keep 'hands off'.

That was how the matter stood when the appeal came before us. Khan himself gave evidence before us in a quiet dignified way. The independent tribunal had concluded that he had a genuine feeling about not continuing to live in Worcester. Ted Dexter, whose contribution to cricket, both as a test player and as administrator, had few rivals, gave evidence on behalf of Khan. He said that he couldn't see what harm there was in Khan being specially registered with Sussex in that it was better that he should continue to play first-class cricket than sit about on the sidelines. He understood that the rule was to prevent counties poaching a player and having an easy transfer system, but he didn't think it applied in the instant case. Khan was a young, unmarried man, and Dexter didn't think that any good would be done by refusing the registration.

Mr Vokins, who was the excellent secretary of Worcester, also gave evidence. He pointed out that Worcester had been exceedingly generous to Khan in the early days. He had joined them in 1971. His schooling had been arranged by Worcester; they had advanced him money; they subsidised his tour fee when on the Pakistan tour. Although he alleged he was unhappy about living in Worcester, at no stage had he spoken to the captain or officers of the club. The committee was a new committee, the chairman had made himself available and he expressed surprise that Khan had been unhappy in 1975, since he hadn't he said anything about it then.

Vokins said that they found it difficult to believe that the only reason was social and the absence of his countrymen, and asked rhetorically if an Englishman would be allowed to leave. He observed that if this registration were allowed it would lead to a simple transfer system that was undesirable. Worcester had treated Khan with very great sympathy, the reasons given were quite unacceptable and above all there was loyalty involved. If this were allowed the rules would be abused, it would open the floodgate to unsettled players and other counties, players and committees, were fully in support of Worcester. Carr observed that loyalty was fundamental to the whole structure of English cricket and that there were 12 other cases where players had been specially registered without objection.

Having heard arguments from both sides, we then had to come to our conclusion. Both parties had accepted the report of the independent tribunal. We observed that Khan's letter of 10 September 1976, in which he asked for a substantial salary, weakened the force of the argument that he was totally unhappy at continuing to live in Worcester, but we agreed with the tribunal that this was a genuine feeling. We accepted that there had been difficulty about his accommodation and that had continued for some time, but were quite unable to come to a concluded judgment on the merits of that dispute.

What we had to consider was whether it was in the best interests of county cricket to allow the requirements of residence to be waived and special registration to occur. We observed that the purpose of this rule, which we fully supported, was to prevent the development of an easy transfer system, and that loyalty to a club was one of the foundations of the strength of county cricket. It was clear to us that Worcester had treated Khan exceedingly generously since he arrived in this country in 1971, by encouraging him academically, giving him financial assistance and advancing his cricketing talents. We were concerned that the sort of explanation about unhappiness, which is easy to advance and difficult to disprove, could be misused to increase applications for movement of cricketers from one county to another.

However, we took the view that his unhappiness was genuine and that there was on the evidence no financial motivation in his movement, and that it was in the best interests of competitive county cricket that he be allowed to play in county cricket but not immediately. We allowed the appeal to the extent that he could be specially registered for Sussex with effect from 30 July 1977.

Thereafter, he had a remarkable career, which culminated in leading Pakistan to victory in the World Cup. I confess that we had a good deal of sympathy for Worcester after all the time and trouble they had put into looking after Khan. We were particularly concerned that the transfer system which obtains in soccer should not apply to cricket. On the other hand, to hold cricketers to a life with a club which they do not enjoy and where they do not make a full contribution was not a situation which had much attraction. In the result, because of a change in the law, a sort of transfer system has now been brought into force without any of the disastrous results which its opponents anticipated.

The next appeal we had related to Barry Wood. He was what could be described as a 'bits-and-pieces' player. He batted a bit, he bowled a bit, he fielded with enormous enthusiasm and was a valuable player, both for Lancashire and on a number of occasions for England. One of the financial incentives to a county cricketer is the benefit. Although it is not written into a player's contract, where it would attract tax, it is generally understood on the cricketing circuit that after 10 years or so as a capped player, a cricketer would receive a benefit. The system goes back quite a considerable way. In 1923 the Inland Revenue challenged the idea that it should be tax free. The revenue lost, it being decided by the House of Lords in Seymour vs Reed 1927AC that, as a cricketer's benefit was a spontaneous gesture by supporters to a cricketer who was now in the last year of that person's career and except in very special cases was not granted more than once, the benefit was not subject to tax.

Not every cricketer's benefit was a financial success. George Geary, our coach at Charterhouse, told me the story of his benefit. Before the war the committee allocated him a county match which Leicester were playing at home, in which he was to receive all the gate money and all the money taken on the ground, but was to be responsible for the expenses. In the result, it rained almost continuously, and his expenses outweighed all the sums taken in the match. When he was asked if he would like to have another benefit, he observed that he could not afford it.

After the war, however, it started to be organised not simply by the county club to which the player was attached, but by a benefit committee. Cyril Washbrook was perhaps the first to acquire a sum of some proportions, which was in the order of £14,000; gradually, with better organisation and more generous support, players started to get not merely five-figure but six-figure sums. The amounts received did not necessarily reflect either the ability of the beneficiary or what contribution had been given to the county by that player, but rather reflected the efficiency of the organising committee and its ability to generate funds. There was one particular cricketer from Sussex who injured himself on the first day of the season and scarcely played thereafter. However, he got one of the largest benefits in Sussex because he was able to be physically present at a great number of events, which necessarily increased the amount of his benefit. Nothing now could be less spontaneous than a benefit. Players also started to get a second benefit, so that the idea that it was a farewell had rather fallen by the way.

In 1979 Barry Wood's benefit amounted to £62,300, which was not an insubstantial sum even at that time. He had previously registered for Yorkshire, which was the county of his birth, but had played for Lancashire from 1966 until 1979. At a committee meeting held on 11 July 1979 the committee offered him a further contract for two years, in 1980 and 1981. He was to receive a basic salary together with other bonuses. The terms were conveyed to Wood in December, together with a copy of the contract. When the secretary returned from his holiday on 21 January he was told by the cricket manager that the player was looking for something more, plus a further benefit if he played for another eight years. The salary offered was the same as his fellow senior-capped players, and he was told by Mr Bond, who was the cricket manager, that he would not recommend any increase in that offer.

On 23 January the secretary spoke to Wood and said it was doubtful that the committee would increase the offer already made; Wood said that he would not come down from his figure. There was to be a committee meeting scheduled for 30 January. Wood wanted a decision sooner than that, as he was anxious to have the matter concluded. He was seen by Bond on two separate occasions and stated that he would get better terms elsewhere in the region of his figure and wanted more time. He was told that the committee was not prepared to give him more time. He said that he was anxious to captain the county and had ambitions towards further representative honours, and that his ambitions could be best furthered with another county. And it was Bond's evidence that Wood was not prepared to come down below his figure.

As a result, Wood declined to sign the contract and the offer was withdrawn. When he was interviewed on 3 February he suggested that his figure was a negotiating figure, and that although the terms had been offered on 12 December, he really had not sufficient time in which to consider them.

On 18 March he asked that his registration with Lancashire be cancelled forthwith. On the same date, the secretary of Derbyshire wrote to Carr saying they were intending to register Wood. He had been offered a contract not just as a player but as vice-captain, he was going to receive a basic salary plus bonuses, with appearance money etc.

The objection by Lancashire was not based on any irregularities by Derbyshire. Their committee felt that the facts surrounding his application should be brought to the notice of the registration committee because it felt that he had brought the game as a whole into disrepute, and had certainly done a disfavour to his fellow professionals. It was anxious about the general feelings of members of the public towards benefits hardening. Further, it thought he had attracted unnecessary attention towards the benefit system. All in all, Lancashire complained that he had acted in a manner that was not in the best interests of cricket or cricketers. The secretary expressed his view in this way:

> If a player comes to us and says that he is not happy with the terms or whatever, wants to go elsewhere, I do not really think we would stand in his way. We don't want to keep an unhappy employee, whether it be a player or any other member of staff, we would say off you go. But in the light of the benefit cheque, a sizeable one in fact, the reaction generally in the county has been quite unbelievable. I am certain the committee thinks that if this is the way cricketers are going to react then it is going to have a great deal of bearing and influence on future beneficiaries and we have found this already.

Derbyshire expressed the view that it had had a situation itself where one of its players had moved immediately after a benefit and it had indeed signed on another player who had had a benefit two years before. And, said the secretary, 'We felt that Barry would be the ideal person to become vice-captain at Derbyshire. We very much believe in Englishmen and because he was vice-captain he would become a member of the cricket management committee, selection committee and the cricket committee as a whole.' He went on to say that if there was some moral objection to somebody leaving after getting a benefit it must continue forever and a day and that there had been precedents. It was pointed out that if Wood had gone a year later feeling would possibly have been slightly eased, and certainly one more year would have made a difference.

On 9 April 1980, the Cricket County Appeals Sub-Committee upheld the decision of the Registration Sub-Committee of the TCCB by a majority of 4–1. The majority took the view that to grant the application would not be in the best interest of competitive county cricket as a whole and said:

> The most important feature taken into account by the committee in reaching its decision is the fact that the 1979 season was Mr Wood's benefit year granted by Lancashire CC. The benefit system remains a very important one for a large number of players and for county cricket generally. The tax free nature of benefits for county cricketers is also most important. Anything which brings a system into disrepute will do a disservice to cricketers, counties and competitive county cricket generally. It is in this connection desirable as a general principle that players granted benefits should be prepared to remain in the employment of their counties if so required for a period following their benefit year. This is undoubtedly the expectation of the general public and the supporters of the county cricket club.

Lancashire Cricket Club said that Wood's action had already resulted in functions for the 1980 beneficiary being cancelled and it would have a detrimental effect on the eventual cash sum for the beneficiary. The committee took the view that the offer by Lancashire in relation to his contract was a reasonable one, though the dissenting member thought that Lancashire had contributed to the problem, first by its method of dealing with the renewal of players contracts, and second by its refusal to grant Mr Wood's request, first for a seven-day and then for a 24-hour extension of time to consider the club's offer.

The committee was anxious not to encourage the development of a transfer system and in the result, the committee decided to refuse the application for Derbyshire to register him. There was then an appeal over which I presided.

In the result, we agreed with the view expressed by the Registration Sub-Committee. However, representations were obviously made to the board by the Players Association, and I suspect by lawyers, with the result that the board overruled our decision. I protested in the nicest possible way to Carr, and while I could appreciate the board's reluctance to be involved in legal proceedings, and wholeheartedly supported a desire to keep good relations with cricket association, I did just wonder whether a severe blow had not been done to the whole system generally. In the end Wood went to Derbyshire, and I believe had another benefit. I have to say that I do not think the episode reflected very well on him.

16

Lottery at Lords and 'Pie in the Sky'

Over the years the MCC showed itself most imaginative and forward-looking in bringing the buildings at Lords up to date. The Old Tavern stand went to be replaced by a brand new building. Subsequently the Allen stand, in honour of Sir George Allen, was put up. The Warner stand replaced an out of date building. Boxes were installed both in the Tavern and Allen stands, an indoor school was built and the whole of Lords architecturally buzzed.

The Mound stand was out of date, gloomy and probably unsafe, and a blot on the landscape. Thanks to an imaginative design a new Mound stand was built, incorporating a large number of boxes, built on time and at cost. It was a brave and successful venture. There was a view that the Mound stand should be extended round the nursery ground, where the Edrich and Compton stands now are. Objections were raised in a number of quarters that it would block off the trees which are a special feature of the ground, and in the result, the idea of extending the Mound stand was abandoned. It was, I think, a pity because the Edrich and Compton stands, which turned out to be something of a white elephant because of the delay in construction, really were not architecturally of the same quality. There were generous contributions by well-known benefactors for the indoor school and for the Mound stand, but for the rest of the building the money had to come from the members. Thereafter, in October 1995 a new indoor school was opened by His Royal Highness the Duke of Edinburgh, and in October 1995 building of the new offices for the TCCB began and the

ECB now have spacious offices on the nursery ground. The whole face of Lords now has a new look.

In 1994 Dennis Silk, who was then president, suggested that we should investigate the potential redevelopment of the existing buildings around the perimeter of the playing area to establish the maximum number of spectators who could be accommodated with unrestricted views of the playing area. There were two views about building at Lords. One was to develop the ground so as to be able to accommodate the greatest number of spectators. That was sometimes called the stadium approach; the other was to build as and where necessary, but retaining the essential cosiness of the ground.

The committee commissioned two architectural practices to investigate the practicalities. They looked at the Tavern stand, the Allen stand, the Warner stand and the grandstand. It was possible to increase the Tavern stand by some 2000 seats and another four boxes and the Warner stand by some 870 seats, whereas in the Allen stand there would be a drop of seat numbers but an addition of three boxes. The cost of the work per seat in the Tavern stand was just over £1000 per seat, in the Warner stand some £890, compared with £940 for the Mound stand.

The committee had to consider its priorities. It was bound to commence the offices for the TCCB and if a new grandstand were to be built for the World Cup in 1999 a start date of September 1997 would need to be achieved. There were two problems facing the committee in relation to building a new grandstand. Firstly there was the question of planning and secondly the question of financing. Westminster City Council was our planning authority and were immensely helpful. The architectural team appointed was Nicholas Grimshaw & Partners. They had won a host of international awards. Among their best known buildings were the British Expo building at Seville; the Waterloo International terminal; the *Financial Times* press in Docklands; the *Western Morning News* building at Plymouth and the RAC Communication Centre at Bristol.

The initial anxiety in 1995 was that, although the grandstand itself was not listed, an application might be made to list it as soon as it became apparent that we were applying to demolish and rebuild. Apparently it is open to any person to apply to place a building on a list without notifying the owner. The owner has no rights in the matter and the building can be listed entirely without the knowledge of the owner. Accordingly, the secretary and I had discussions with various departments of state and with English Heritage, which was very supportive of the scheme. The next problem was the various amenity societies in the area and the members in general. The old building was immensely attractive. It had been designed by Sir Herbert Baker, who was a very distinguished architect. His buildings included government buildings in Pretoria, some buildings in Capetown and government buildings in New Delhi. He was an associate of Lutyens and was highly regarded in architectural circles. There was a Herbert Baker Society, which naturally took an interest in the suggestion that one of his great works might be demolished, particularly when to the outside world the building was a marvellous piece of architecture and had been an integral part of Lords since 1926.

Unfortunately the building had now become a white elephant. When it was built it provided 3904 seats and 17 boxes. Unbelievably, of those seats some 1700 – 43 per cent – had restricted or impaired view, either because in the upper stand a wall obscured the view to left or right, or because in the lower tier the height of the balcony above prevented upward vision. Conditions there were very unsatisfactory and claustrophobic. The boxes were uncomfortable and out of date, as were the dining facilities. In addition, the reinforced concrete frame began to show signs of deterioration as long ago as 1928 and this had increased ever since, so parts of the concrete frame had detached themselves. This was believed to be due to lack of cover and subsequent corrosion of the reinforcing bars.

The layout and orientation of the stairs providing access to the seats and boxes was extremely unsatisfactory and inefficient, causing confusion and therefore dangerous congestion. In addition, it did not comply with the requirements of the Guide to Safety at Sports Grounds Act, and the council required Lords to take steps to deal with congestion in the concourse area under the stand. This would inevitably result in a decrease in the number of seats. In any event, because of this and deterioration, unless the stand were to be demolished, the repairs and alterations required would themselves cost some £4 million. Thus, while the stand when observed from outside was very attractive, its real problem was the failure to fulfil the promise for which it was intended. Sir Pelham Warner commented in his book, *Lords in 1787 –*

1945, 'Never in the history of cricket has so large a stand held so few people'.

How it came about that such a distinguished architect as Sir Herbert Baker could design a stand in which 43 per cent of the seats had a limited view is absolutely incomprehensible. It was not designed as a monument, it was designed as an area from which people could view cricket. How the committee of the day, the equivalent of the Estates Sub-Committee, could have allowed the plans to go ahead again is incomprehensible, unless it was so overwhelmed by the status of the architect that it failed to observe that the emperor had no clothes.

Plans for a new stand were first submitted in 1923, although it wasn't until 1925 that they were acted upon. On 30 July 1923 the Finance and Property and Works Sub-Committee reported combined meetings held at Lords on 18 and 23 July respectively.

> Mr H. Baker's plans for increasing accommodation had been considered, Mr St. Leger being present to explain. The plans were divided into 5 separate schemes. No.2 scheme (Old grandstand) to provide 2,000 more seats at a cost of about £29,000. The treasurer said he couldn't recommend No.2 scheme unless approved by a General Meeting of the club. It had been decided to postpone No. 2 scheme.

At the AGM on 6 May 1925 it was announced that 'the plans submitted by Mr Baker in 1923 embodying the rebuilding of the present grandstand had not been lost sight of. By this scheme the accommodation of this side of the ground would be increased by 3,200 seats at a rough cost of £33,000.' On 25 May 1925 the committee decided to recommend, subject to the concurrence of the Finance Sub-Committee, that the scheme for increasing the stand accommodation over part of A stand and on the north of the Mound stand, as well as rebuilding the grandstand as detailed by Mr Baker in his letters of 13 July 1923 and 8 October 1924, be carried out. It was seen therefore that Baker was responsible not merely for the grandstand but for other buildings in the ground.

On 8 June 1925 the Finance Sub-Committee decided to recommend for submission to an SGM that the committee be empowered to elect 200 additional life members, each paying £200. Baker's plans for the new stand were to be explained at this SGM of the club, at which it was decided it was expedient to increase the seating accommodation, both for members and the public. To help meet the cost the committee was empowered to elect in priority of entry 200 candidates at £200 each as life members, and it was announced that of this number 132 had accepted the offer to date. The total gain in seats, irrespective of those in boxes, would be approximately 3000, and the works were being carried out by Messrs Trollope & Coles at a cost of £45,000, exclusive of seat fittings and fees.

The SGM was held on 13 July 1925, and there was apparently a long discussion and some opposition. But the following resolutions were carried with a majority prescribed by the rules: one, that it was expedient to increase the seating accommodation at Lords, both for the members and the public; two, to meet the cost the committee should be empowered to elect in priority of entry 200 candidates at £200 each as life members.

On 20 July the secretary reported that the architects had asked for a date when the contractors might begin operations in connection with the new stand accommodation and it was decided that the work might begin on 2 September, and that there should be a penal clause in the contract in regard to the date for completion, and only British Empire materials should be used. On 19 October 1925 it was agreed that the contractor should complete the whole of the works on the new stand by 1 June 1926, and the stand was in fact completed in time for the Australian visit.

None of the records indicate that anyone raised the question of seats with limited views and today it remains as much a puzzle as it did then as to how that came about.

Baker's grandstand replaced the old grandstand which had been finished in 1867. It was designed by Maurice Allom's grandfather, Arthur Allom. Maurice Allom was a distinguished international cricketer and president of the MCC between 1969 and 1970. His grandfather was the first president of the Architectural Association. A contemporary account says of the grandstand:

> The committee may congratulate themselves on the successful completion of a most useful and ever necessary addition to the comfort of the many ladies and gentlemen who admire the national and manly game of cricket. The architect, Mr Arthur Allom, may be complimented on the lightness and elegance of the structure. It has given universal satisfaction to the numerous patrons to the game of cricket.

Given that situation, all the amenity societies readily lent their support to the scheme and no application for listing was made. In addition, both the Department of the Environment and the Department of National Heritage, which were both concerned in the aspects of demolition and rebuilding, were enormously helpful.

The rebuilding was to take place in two separate years – the first tier going up one year and the second the second year. The idea was that the first tier should be up by the summer of 1997 and the stand completed for summer 1998, so that there could be a year's trial and work-out before the World Cup in 1999. There really was no doubt that if Lords were to host the final of the World Cup there needed to be put in place a grandstand which was worthy of both the occasion and the crowd. The design attracted a good deal of publicity and appreciation and while there were a number of problems during construction, it was an enormously successful venture. The initial estimate for the building was £12.7 million. While it was an enormous sum, particularly with regard to the limited increase in capacity for the public, nevertheless there really was no alternative.

The next and most immediate problem was how that figure was to be raised. The club simply did not have that money. We therefore decided to apply for a grant from the lottery. It was, or ought to have been, self-evident that the World Cup in 1999 was likely to attract enormous publicity. It was a world event. Lords, regarded as the home of cricket in England, had to provide the very best facilities available. Lottery money was poured into a great number of other ventures, the importance of which certainly seemed less persuasive than the argument for supporting this grandstand. What we sought was £4.9 million from the lottery and that application was made in December 1995. It had to be channelled through the TCCB. In March it was rumoured that all applications from first-class cricket clubs were likely to fail, either because there was a lack of a national development plan for cricket, or because priority was being placed on participation rather than spectating.

On 5 March 1996 the Sports Council issued a press notice deferring applications in relation to major cricket schemes. It observed:

> There is no overall development plan for cricket in this country and the long awaited ECB scheme due to begin operations in January of

this year is still on the Governing Bodies' drawing board. Thus we have no overall structure within which to assess these particular applications no matter their merits and weaknesses. What is apparent is that the number of events requiring such spectator accommodation is limited, moreover the lack of strategy gives us no clear indication about how additional money generated by increased spectator accommodation will be reinvested at the sports grass roots level ... the Sports Council is aware of the importance of these issues particularly at county level and leading up to the 1999 World Cup, we want to be sure the sports governing bodies are clear in which direction English cricket is going.

It was astonishing that the Sports Council couldn't understand the importance of having proper facilities for the World Cup final and thought that the absence of a development plan was relevant to our application. In this aspect it was living in a world which was unreal. It was, to say the least, exceedingly disappointing. However, after further discussions they were persuaded that the absence of the national plan was irrelevant to our particular application. There was also a directive from the department which suggested that there was no problem with lottery money being given for spectator seating.

The next obstacle that was raised was that because we were a private club which didn't have women members our application for lottery money for the grandstand could cause difficulties. We observed, which was self-evident, that the lottery money was not to be used for the benefit of members of the club but for the public, who would have unlimited access to the grandstand. The guidelines were exceedingly unclear. Some of them suggested that the organisations were eligible provided the recognised activities were permitted by their constitution and there was public access to the facility, others that there should be a commitment to use by all sections of the community regardless of gender, race, religion and disability.

There was a further direction stressing that the need to ensure that monies distributed for projects promoted the public good, in contrast to the other part of the guideline, which said that open access applied equally to the applicants of the projects as well. If the Sports Council really was of the firm view that we were ineligible because of the absence of women members, there was no reason why it should not have said so when it received our application. Instead of this, a considerable amount of time and trouble was spent visiting government offices and the Sports Council trying to explain to it what the MCC's contribution to the community was. One matter which suddenly emerged in our discussion with the Sports Council was that it had become concerned about aspects of the project – 'Technical design and financial'. No details were ever given to us about this or why it was suddenly raised at the last moment.

On 19 June the Sports Council wrote again saying that at the time of the application, planning permission had not yet been received, but as that was now being provided it was not a matter of concern. However, it continued to express doubts about the design of the stand and the placing of the scoreboard. Quite why the Sports Council should be concerned with the design was impossible to understand, given the quality of our architectural team. The letter continued:

> The project essentially is about providing increased spectator accommodation with a net gain of 2,000 seats at an estimated cost of £12.9M. Clearly we recognise the improvements to the other 4,000 seats currently available. In terms of added spectator accommodation this represents £6,450 per seat with £3,500 from the Lottery Sports Fund for a facility which annually would be used relatively infrequently. Clearly a judgment ultimately has to be made in respect of value for money for the project itself and on a comparative basis with the many other projects submitted. The Council's role is to assist in projects which provide for community benefit and further clarity would be needed on this issue in relation to the project proposed, particularly the availability of tickets to the general public.

On 21 June the secretary and I met with the Sports Council to reassure its members as far as we could about the importance of the grandstand for cricket as a whole, and pointing out again that because women were not allowed in the pavilion it had nothing to do with what happened in the grandstand. On 2 July 1996 the Sports Council wrote rejecting the application. The first ground for refusal was its concern about the value for money in return for the lottery investment; the second, the non-acceptance of women into membership of the club. It went on to point out that the Sports Council was jointly funding a study to examine the facilities and needs of cricket which would include the provision for test-match cricket. This was of no value to us because of the tight schedule for construction that was about to begin.

The Sports Council issued a press statement saying:

> Currently there is no overall strategy for cricket at county or national level. The ECB is yet to be established and if public money is to be invested in cricket via the lottery sports fund, certain fundamental issues need to the addressed, both by the TCCB and the clubs themselves. Community benefit and open membership are fundamental criteria for lottery funding as is value for money. Like all cricket supporters we are looking forward to the World Cup in 1999 and want the very best facilities for the matches. However, we believe we cannot overturn our long established practice of granting aid only to those organisations which operate open membership policies and practices.

The Sports Council may well have been looking forward to the World Cup in 1999 and wanted the very best facilities for the matches, but went a very curious way about it. Quite how it thought the very best facilities for the World Cup would be provided by the old stand is difficult to understand. While I have no doubt that it was a well-meaning body, it was clear that political correctness was an important factor, and I am afraid that its members merely succeeded in making themselves look inept. A number of people who disliked and were jealous of what happened at Lords rejoiced in our discomfiture, which reflected no great credit on them because what we wanted to do was not provide a bonanza in any way for our members but to provide facilities for the World Cup which would be a credit to the nation. The government was not willing to provide money, nor was the board. Thus, it was left to the committee to pick up the pieces and see whether it was possible in some other way to build the grandstand out of our own resources.

There were various ways of raising the money. There was a debenture scheme for the seats on the balcony of the new stand and the sale of boxes to commercial companies, regardless of whether or not they were MCC members. The board agreed that the additional improved seats would be included in the board's seat scheme, which meant that the club would be able to retain the extra sales revenue generated from those seats. In addition, the club owned some property which it was agreed could be applied towards the cost of the stand and some of the club's investment portfolio could be sold.

However the most controversial suggestion was that there should be a one off admission of some 250 additional members, out of turn, they being admitted as life members on payment of £10,000 each. This caused a certain amount of upset among the members because it was said, rightly, that rich young men could buy their way in and get ahead of the queue. The current waiting list was in the order of 25 years. However, this system had been used on five previous occasions to fund major building projects, and in the result, the membership approved of it. Additionally, life membership was offered to current members based on age, and this proved to be exceedingly popular. In the result, well over a thousand members became full life members and although we did not quite get the 250 candidates, there were sufficient to provide the balance to enable us to pay for the new grandstand.

The new grandstand was universally recognised as a very great architectural feat and provided a marvellous setting for the World Cup games and for the final. No-one could have contemplated allowing the World Cup to be played at Lords without the new building, and it was a great pity that the Sports Council took a narrow, insular and parochial view about supporting a building of such enormous importance to the prestige of this country in the cricketing world.

Shortly before I became president I had a conversation with Tony Lewis, the well-known cricketer and commentator, about the facilities for broadcasting from Lords. I was aware of *Test Match Special*, which was housed on the very top of the pavilion in what can only be described as a tiny hut, but where the broadcasters were apparently happy to remain. The same was not true of the television broadcasters. They were housed in the Warner stand in a small, very cramped, somewhat airless room holding four commentators and their equipment, with a small table at the back, where the commentator not on call could sit and relax. Tony enquired whether I was aware of the dreadful conditions in which they operated. I had to confess that I wasn't, and accordingly I went and had a look. I was absolutely horrified at the squalor of the conditions and the lack of space. Tony told me that when the South Africans had been over their commentators had to stand in one of the lavatories because there had simply been no room for them.

He pointed out that in 1999, when the World Cup was to take place, the conditions for the broadcasters would be totally inadequate, and unless some urgent steps were taken soon there was a very serious risk that the ICC might take the view that Lords was not at all suitable to be the venue of a World Cup final.

I regarded the matter with great seriousness and we had a long discussion in the committee. In February 1995 it was agreed that we should have a new media centre. Various sites were considered, but it was quite clear that the only acceptable site was behind the bowler's arm at the Nursery end. The ideal position would have been at the top of the pavilion, but that was regarded as quite impossible: firstly, because the planning authorities were unlikely to give us permission, and secondly, because it would deprive the members of their seats. There was an argument that because the television broadcasters had their monitors it was unnecessary for them to be behind the bowler's arm, and to some limited extent that applied to the journalists who were presently housed in the Warner stand, where they certainly weren't behind the bowler's arm. In addition, there was a strong argument that if the facilities were up the Nursery end there would be difficulty in interviewing players, who presently went up to the top of the Warner stand, which was easily available from the pavilion. It was said that there would be difficulties in getting interviewees to the Nursery end. As there plainly was no other site except between the Edrich and Compton stands, a decision was made that that was where it should be.

To that end it was agreed to hold an architectural competition, and four architectural practices were selected. Initially the gross cost had been put at some £2 million. The timetable provided for completion by April 1997, and the architectural practices were to present their concepts in June 1995. The architects were instructed to work on a construction budget not to exceed £1.5 million. In the result, two schemes were considered, one by Future Systems and the other by David Morley Architects. David Morley's scheme could fairly be described as a classical design, whereas the Future Systems, which is now what is in place, I christened 'pie in the sky'. The 'pie in the sky' exceeded the budget, whereas the more classical design was closer to the budget.

I confess that I regarded 'pie in the sky' as an unattractive option, and very much hoped that both the Estates Sub-Committee and the Main Committee would take that view. At one meeting the Estates Sub-Committee was asked simply to consider the matter on an aesthetic basis irrespective of cost and of facility. To my chagrin, the committee voted almost unanimously in favour of 'pie in the sky' on its aesthetic quality.

I determined therefore to take the matter to the committee, in the confident expectation that the committee would agree with my view.

I introduced the matter by saying, 'We have two options. One is this marvellous classical design which is nearly within our budget and the other is this "pie in the sky" which is considerably in excess of budget. I leave you, members of the committee, to make up your own minds.' Such was the power of my advocacy that apart from one or two members they all voted in favour of 'pie in the sky'!

I have to admit now that I was wholly wrong. I consider that what we now have is the most marvellous building of which we can be enormously proud.

Unfortunately the 'pie in the sky', which was adopted by the Estates Sub-Committee and the committee, greatly exceeded budget. It had the further disadvantage that only one firm, Pendennis, tendered for it; this was a boat-building company down in Southampton. There was considerably anxiety about this, because having only one tender meant that we were at great risk in respect of any difficulties which might arise. Pendennis had never built anything of this sort before. It was quite rightly described as a futuristic building involving aluminium cladding, which was an entirely new concept and considered 'avant garde'. The committee gave its approval to proceed with the Future Systems design, but was reluctant to endorse the development until there was some proposal about how the project was to be funded. It was intended that a good deal of the building should be prefabricated at Pendennis's premises, and then installed as and when it fitted into the programme at Lords.

By April 1996 all the design work had been completed, and the Chief Planning Officer at Westminster City Council was enthusiastic for the concept and a planning application, it was agreed, should be made in May. By February 1996 the cost had risen above the £3 million mark, and during that year the marketing committee set about seeking a sponsor. By 5 September, negotiations with NatWest had been successfully completed, and members' approval needed to be sought. The sponsorship from NatWest was generous, but unfortunately because of the continuing rise in the cost the club needed to find a substantial sum of money from its own funds. There was a good deal of urgency because it was essential that there should be a season to test the running of the media centre, and the ICC had made it clear that it was unlikely the World Cup final would be held at the ground unless there was a media centre in place in 1999. The committee was anxious that the matter should go ahead, and in the result, an SGM was held on 3 December 1996. A planning application was submitted on 9 December 1996. The membership voted in favour of the new scheme, though with a number of reservations – particularly about the cost.

In February 1997, Brian Thornton, chairman of the Estates Sub-Committee, wrote to me with his concern about the escalating costs. He suggested that there had been errors and misjudgments on the part of the quantity surveyor. Originally the figure had been put at just over £2 million, it had risen to £3.7 million and then up to £4.2 million and by February 1997 it was up to £4.5 million. This figure included a contingency of £500,000 because there was concern about the high level of risk involved in the building of this entirely new type of structure. Thornton decided that he would give up the chairmanship of the Media Centre Working Party and ask Mr De Rohan to replace him because of the time pressures. By now the target completion date which had been for the beginning of the 1998 season was July 1998, but because of the vast escalation of cost the committee had to consider the whole position and decide whether it would still go ahead with the project.

Pendennis at Falmouth did not complete the tender documents until April 1997. There was also considerable criticism of the failure to control the design team and of the quantity surveyor properly to estimate the cost. Meanwhile it was necessary to keep NatWest in the picture, because it looked as though there would be delay which would adversely affect its sponsorship. By April 1997 it was clear that completion could not be expected until the NatWest final in 1998. There were problems over the ordering of the aluminium, and by April the cost had got up to £5 million.

In the result, although the programme of construction envisaged the shell being completed by 1 May 1998 and the interior fitting by the end of September 1998, this was not to be. The building was not in fact completed for use until April 1999. It was thus impossible to have a year in which to get rid of any of the snags. The only advantage of the shell being in place in 1998 was that it enabled the general public and the members to get used to the nature of the building. Although there were some criticisms, in general it was regarded as a marvellous piece of architecture, and the committee was much congratulated on the foresight and courage which it had shown in pursuing the venture in spite of the horrendous problems which arose in 1997. Much credit goes to Brian Thornton and to Maurice De Rohan for successfully dealing with the hundred-and-one problems which arose, and above all to NatWest, which is much to be congratulated on their sponsorship. I have no doubt that the picture of the NatWest Media Centre will be used as part of its logo throughout the world and bring much kudos, and no doubt financial reward for its bold decision in providing sponsorship.

After the official opening the NatWest Media Centre was brought into full use for the World Cup, and proved a magnificent contribution to the architecture of the ground and a splendid position for the media from which to report on the cricket. The absence of serious criticisms by hard-bitten reporters speaks volumes about the success of the venture.

17

Reflections

It is now just over 50 years since I was first called to the bar, and this is a good moment to reflect on the changes, both for better and for worse, that have occurred in the legal system. When I came to the bar the number of barristers practising was around 2500. It was a very close-knit community where everyone tended to know everyone else. Sets of chambers were comparatively small, and discipline was firmly exercised by the circuits.

Sets of chambers then varied in size from three or four to a dozen, but scarcely any were bigger than that. There was usually only one queen's counsel per set of chambers, and lots of chambers did not have any. Many chambers existed on a shoestring, and in a good number the clerk's remuneration was pretty small. The organisation was still Dickensian. Fees were entered into large tomes by hand. Much of the litigation was conducted by managing clerks, and partners were a rare sight. Those who practised in the provinces and wanted to take silk were required to take up chambers in London. Some circuits had a rule that those who had taken silk could not live on the circuit or appear at a circuit town unless they had work, and for a good many years there was very considerable risk in taking silk. A number of very eminent juniors with large practices simply vanished into the air. The hurdle of having to come to London with a new clerk, a new set of chambers and starting effectively a new practice, was truly frightening. Those who did succeed made a tremendous mark. They always brought a breath of fresh air and a businesslike attitude to their work and often made their London contemporaries look somewhat pedestrian.

22. O. B. P. at work.

The discipline exerted by the circuits was very important. The Oxford circuit was a small circuit. There were probably no more than ten silks practising at any one time and the members of the circuit would meet regularly, both at quarter sessions and the assize. Proper behaviour is taken as read among the profession, but for the general public it is one of the most important aspects of litigation. It is easy for a member of the bar to play a particular trick on an opponent or to deceive a judge in a particular case for the benefit of his or her client, and no doubt the client is enormously grateful. But once a member of the bar gets a reputation among his or her peers for sharp practice, that is effectively the end of that person's career. A barrister's reputation among his or her contemporaries is as important as, if not more important than, his or her reputation among solicitors. It may seem strange to the outside world that barristers are bound to refer to an authority against the proposition which they are putting forward when their client is interested only in winning the case, but that is their duty.

Sadly, the disappearance of the assize system, and of quarter sessions sitting at regular intervals, has to a very large extent destroyed the circuit system. That system had the added advantage that with a particular judge going round in succession to eight or ten towns where a member of the circuit regularly practised, that judge had the opportunity to get to know, and more importantly, to form an opinion about, individual members of the bar. Likewise, it was to the immense benefit of a mem-ber of the bar to have appeared before a particular judge, so that his or her worth could be properly evaluated.

The importance of this judgment was vital for the Lord Chancellor in appointing silks. The system has been frequently criticised as being elitist, secret and open to abuse. All selections of course attract criticism, but it would not be possible to have a public debate about the relative merits of those applying for silk. When I started at the bar there were few candidates for silk because of the risks involved. There were probably no more than 20–30 applications. Now it is no secret that somewhere over 500 apply. To a limited extent of course that reflects the growth in the size of the bar from the 2500 at the start of my career to the present number of over 10,000. But the system operates on the basis of views expressed by those who best know the particular individuals. If you have been against an opponent for 10 or 15 years it is possible to form a very good judgment about his ability, judgment and honesty. No amount of academic input into this exercise could possibly compare with years of experience as an opponent. Those who suggest that there should be an appointments committee headed by an independent person simply fail to understand that this is necessarily a somewhat subjective exercise anyway. Years of experience count for more than a half-hour interview. Of course, there were and no doubt still are anomalies. Some faces may not happen to fit, some may not get before a number of High Court judges, some may be more favoured because some judges carry more weight than others. But these factors are inevitable in any selection procedure. By the time the Lord Chancellor has canvassed several hundred people, ranging from the House of Lords, the Court of Appeal, High Court judges, circuit judges, other members of the bar and heads of the various different bar associations, he is likely to get not only an accurate assessment of suitability but also an assessment which is likely to ensure a measure of approval for the system. From time to time there have been some whose appointment has caused some surprise in the Temple and others who may have been the subject of positive discrimination. It does them no favours if that is how they are perceived by their contemporaries, nor does it increase confidence in the system.

In the same way, there is a constant attack on how judges are appointed, particularly to the High Court bench. Again it is suggested that there should be a judicial-appointments system with an independent chairman, and indeed there has been some suggestion that MPs should be involved. One only has to look at the calibre of some of the MPs and their judgment, and in some cases their extreme views, to realise just what a disaster that would be.

The experience in the US of judges being subjected to a barrage of questioning from the legislators is one not to be repeated in this country. The track-record of all those who are eligible to be High Court judges is well known, and has been monitored over 30 years. No interview of 30 minutes can possible replicate that experience. The constant criticism that it is done in secret is laughable. Archbishops, generals and medical consultants do not go through that process, and neither should High Court judges.

The other charge about High Court judges is that they are 'elitist'. In the sense that they are especially chosen, that is true. In the sense that they should be intelligent, have had a broad education and have judgment, it is also true. The particular school, college or university to which they went is irrelevant, save in the sense that they need to have acquired the particular qualities necessary to make a good judge. As for the constant criticism that they do not live in the real world, 30 years at the sharp end of a barrister's practice – or indeed time spent on the lower deck – is no bad training to be a judge.

The increase in the size of the bar has had a very marked effect. It is not all that long ago that the Lord Chancellor required a set of chambers where there were likely to be four silks to split, so as to ensure that there was not some form of monopoly. Nowadays there are some chambers of over 70-strong where there may be as many as 20 silks. It is seen as a matter of strength to be big. Whether bigger is better is a question difficult to answer. But certainly it has had an adverse effect in loyalty to chambers. In my day, for someone to move their chambers, or for chambers to split up, was an event which reverberated around the Temple. Nowadays there is constant movement, and successful barristers are poached by other chambers. The idea of loyalty seems completely to have disappeared. This is, I think, a sad feature. It has turned the profession with high ideals into a business of self-aggrandisement. It may be that that is how the modern world exists outside the Temple, but it is nevertheless regrettable. It is an inevitable consequence of commercial pressure.

The introduction of modern, efficient business methods has been nothing but a benefit to the bar. Buildings have been modernised. Out has gone the quill pen. Managing clerks have more or less vanished, and junior partners now control litigation. The old-fashioned, traditional east-end barristers' clerks who identified particularly with the solicitors' managing clerks have been replaced by office managers and trained executives who are running what is now a multi-million pound business. A more efficient and professional approach has resulted in a much more friendly approach to solicitors. In our day touting was totally forbidden for members of the bar. It was left to the clerks to chat to their opposite numbers in solicitors' firms over pints of beer, extolling the quality of their members of chambers. Nowadays, public relations is the 'buzz word'. Smart brochures are produced, advertising in all its forms is encouraged, and solicitors now mark sets of chambers not only for their expertise but for the personal relationships.

One further loosening of the disciplinary control has been the upsurge in sets of chambers opening in remote areas where the circuits may not be able to exercise their discipline as they used to. Members of the bar still require a clerk, but it can be their spouse. Members can operate from home, and with modern technology those who are not involved in litigation can spend their time more usefully in front of their computer in their study at home without ever setting foot in their inn.

The rules against touting in our day were somewhat archaic. It was forbidden to entertain solicitors, certainly publicly. The idea of any form of advertising was frowned on. To go to a solicitor's office was regarded as a breach of etiquette, and it has to be said that those who were scrupulous obeyed the rules but those who were unscrupulous did not. All in all, these were rules which needed to be scrapped and have been scrapped. Members of the bar regularly take the opportunity to bring their practices in one way or another to the attention of influential solicitors.

There has been a constant struggle ever since I was at the bar to maintain the independence of the bar and of the judges. There is a constant 'drip, drip, drip' by the media and by the civil servants to seek to dumb down the legal profession. The independence of the bar, which is absolutely fundamental to our judicial system, enables barristers to exercise their own judgment and to give even-handed advice to their clients. Even when legal aid was introduced so that the paymaster was at the end of the day the crown, it did not affect the independence of the bar. The administration of legal aid was substantially in the hands of the legal profession. It had many critics, particularly in relation to criminal law, because of the financial limitations. But broadly it was an enormously valuable service to the public, and meant that the criminal-justice system in this country was widely admired for providing a service to the community.

All this is changing. The Lord Chancellor's department, fearful of the independence of the bar, has sought to put constraints on the use of legal aid, using the expense as an excuse. Thus, in ordinary murder cases queen's counsel are not to be employed. The limits on fees to be charged have been disastrously lowered. A public defender's system is to be introduced, where no doubt those who do not get the seal of approval of the government will find that they do not have work. Thus, the independence of the bar is being seriously undermined. The effect is likely to be catastrophic to the community. The criminal bar is the poor man of the legal profession. It has never been overpaid, save in one or two high-profile cases, and it depends on having a pool of advocates willing to go to distant crown courts at a modest fee to defend very unlovable characters. The present system seems designed to reduce the quality of service which is to be provided, with disastrous consequences to the criminal law.

In 1972, when quarter sessions were abolished and crown courts set up, civil servants took over the job of clerks of the court. The consequences were immediate and predictable, namely due to their lack of knowledge of legal procedure, cases now began to take three or four times as long, with the consequent increase in costs. The present proposals of the Lord Chancellor will inevitably lead to the same result. Inadequate presentation and inefficient advocacy will simply increase the costs of trial, increase the costs of appeal and reduce public confidence in the whole system.

One favourite target of the media and indeed of the civil servants are the judges' lodgings. The picture which is always given is of judges living in large houses with a butler and housekeeper, entertaining all their friends at public expense and drinking excessively. The provision of judges' lodgings of course goes back to the days of the assize when the judge went round from county to county administering justice, and was often put up in a house provided by the High Sheriff, who was responsible for the judge's safety in the county. The practice of staying in a private house continued in some places until comparatively recently, but the Lord Chancellor found that it was more economical either to build, or to buy, houses where the judge could lodge.

When a judge goes out on circuit he or she takes along a clerk, male or female. When out on circuit the judge requires a certain degree of accommodation, for instance a bedroom, a dining room, a sitting room and a study with a library of books where he or she can work of an evening, either writing judgments or preparing a summing-up or reading the papers for the next day. Additionally, the clerk will require a bedroom, a sitting room and somewhere to eat. They each require bathroom facilities, and additionally a further room is required for the fax, computer, printing facilities and so on. To find these facilities in a hotel no doubt can be done, but at enormous expense. Where three judges are together it is unlikely that such accommodation can be guaranteed ahead of their arrival. But more particularly, a judge requires privacy. This is not because judges are snobbish, elitist or stand-offish. It is because a great number of the cases with which judges deal have a high profile, particularly in the immediate locality. To try a murder charge in a particular locality and then to wander into a public dining room where all the local journalists are staying is a recipe for disaster. The judge could not possibly discuss any aspects of a case with the other judges in public. The possibility of meeting up with jurors cannot be ignored, and above all the security of the judge is impossible in a public place. Whether staying in an hotel or in a private house there is going to be somebody who will have to do the cooking and somebody who is going to have to wait at table. The use of the words 'cook' and 'butler' no doubt provokes enormous emotion, but it is what a hotel would provide, and many of the lodgings, far from being the Ritz, would not rate more than two or three stars in any hotel guide.

But the idea of judges staying in lodgings is again anathema to the civil servants, who seem determined, if they possibly can, to reduce the judge's status to that of a commercial traveller. It is sad to see this dumbing-down, because it necessarily results in a lack of confidence in the public, and constant criticism in the press does nothing to enhance the quality of justice which the public deserves.

That the judges have come struggling into the twenty-first century is true. Many of the old attitudes have vanished. There is no doubt that the outlook of many of the judges before whom I appeared in the 1950s would no longer be tolerated. A good example was the recent appeal in the case of Craig and Bentley. Lord Goddard's conduct of the trial was robust, to put it mildly. But that was the attitude of the times. The Court of Criminal Appeal recently observed that the standards to be applied are the standards of today and not the standards of yesteryear. How far back that idea can be taken is difficult to know. Guy Fawkes's conviction depended on the confession extracted from him on the rack. Today we would not pay much attention to a confession of that type. No doubt many of the errors of the past need to be corrected, but there is a tendency now for political correctness to become part of judicial thinking and for liberal sentiments to outweigh sensible judgments.

Nowhere is this better illustrated than in our attitude to the prison population. Read any newspaper or any academic report and there will be the allegation that in Great Britain we send more people to prison than in any other country. The fact that that is not strictly true matters not for the moment. Even if it were true, it is a meaningless statistic, as is the allegation that we send more people to prison per head of population. Again, even if it is true, it is meaningless. The reason why it is meaningless is that the number of people sent to prison necessarily depends not only on the number of criminals caught and charged, but also on the number of criminals charged and convicted of an offence that carries a term of imprisonment. Those charged and convicted of a criminal offence which carries a term of imprisonment are not the same, either, as the whole population of the country, as those who are caught, or as those who are charged with an offence which does not carry a term of imprisonment. What the statistician needs to compare is those who are sent to prison in those circumstances with the same category in other countries. No-one has done this comparison, for the obvious reason that it would not bear out the parrot cry of too many people being sent to prison.

There is also a theory that once you have built prisons for X thousand prisoners you should never send anyone else to prison because the prisons won't accommodate them. If there is regularly an annual increase of some 15 per cent in crime, it necessarily follows that there is going to be some, though not necessarily identical, increase in those who get sent to prison. The constant adjuration to the judges to send fewer people to prison is no doubt based on worthy motives. But it wholly fails to take into account that every judge seeks to avoid sending people to prison, and if they do, only send them to prison for the minimum required. Parliament lays down the sanction and the judges merely apply it. No-one has investigated the correlation between passing lenient sentences and the increase in crime. When I first started, a postman who stole a postal package was sent to prison for three years. It was always a very harsh penalty and, while imprisonment may now be the usual tariff, it is for a period very much less than that. Likewise, offences of indecency between men usually attracted a prison sentence. The law has now changed. We were not then concerned with drugs which now constitute one of the major factors in the increase in crime. It is not in dispute that the taking of drugs, and a necessity to acquire money to buy drugs has caused the crime figures to escalate. Legalising any of them is unlikely to stop the search for money with which to buy them. It is not politically correct to say that the more crimes criminals commit, the greater will be the necessity to increase the number of prison places.

The prospect of success at the bar when I started was moot. While it was possible to get into chambers, there was little or no work for the young person, and we had to resort to self-help by giving lectures and finding other means of supporting ourselves. We did not regard the world as owing us a living. Today it is a grossly overcrowded profession with too many people seeking too few places as pupils and too many pupils seeking too few places as tenants. Whereas we paid 100 guineas for the pleasure of being a pupil, the bar is now introducing a scheme whereby all pupils are to be given substantial sums during their pupillage. This sounds like an act of great benevolence by the bar, the members of which are all self-employed and have their own families to bring up. But whether it will be an advantage to prospective barristers in general must remain in doubt. Whereas barristers are perfectly happy to take on a pupil to teach for the benefit of the pupil in particular, and the bar in general, it may well be that subsidising the pupil, who may, in the result, go off into industry, may not encourage a young member of the bar to have pupils. It may have the effect of limiting the number of those who become pupils and thereby restricting the number of potential barristers. As a way of dealing with the overwhelming numbers it may be a useful tool, but of course it is not what was intended. While it is important to encourage those from poorer backgrounds, self-employment differs from employment in that there is no kindly employer sheltering the employee from the rigours of the market. Nor does it necessarily follow that the quality will be improved. I have to say, given the increase in the numbers coming to the bar and the care with which pupils and tenants are chosen, it often surprises me that the quality of advocacy has not markedly improved.

Sport, too, has seen enormous changes and many of them for the worse. Who, 50 years ago, could have contemplated cricketers fixing matches for money? Who could have thought that an independent match referee would be necessary at test matches to ensure good behaviour? Who could have foreseen the sledging which occurs at all levels of the game? And who could have contemplated the constant badgering of umpires and the attempts to claim non-existent catches, which is nothing less than cheating? In our day batsmen walked. If there was a doubt about whether a catch had carried, the fielder would be asked and that answer accepted. At Cambridge we were taught always to walk in that situation – except against Yorkshire and Oxford! It is no surprise that failure to walk has given umpires problems, and it serves batsmen right if they do get bad decisions. I have had so much fun at cricket, in the days when these problems were few and far between. Sadly, like many things in life, some standards have fallen, but I can only look back with pleasure and reflect how lucky I have been in my sporting activities.

I regard my years at the bar and on the bench with enormous pleasure. I remember the fun we all had together, the anxieties about our next case, the problems of being paid, the delights of the victory and the sadness of defeat. These are all matters of nostalgia to be enjoyed. I still remember cases which I lost where I think, if only I had done this or that, how much better it would have turned out. Cases are such personal matters. Only the client and the advocate remember them, but they often leave a mark on both. Surprisingly, such victories as I had have not left the same impression on my mind as did defeats.

23. O.B.P.

Occasionally when I come across an old notebook and read the notes of evidence, the whole case with a picture of the witnesses and the judge comes flooding back. Victories, so few and far between, were that much more enjoyable to savour.

I am sure that my generation were lucky that life at the bar, however hard, and life on the bench, were more agreeable than now. While I am sorry to leave, I am not sorry no longer to be fully involved. And though I have sat from time to time since I retired, I can enjoy mediation and arbitration, having cast off the shackles of Europe, the civil servants and the media. More importantly, I can look forward more fully to enjoying my family and my 12 grandchildren.

'From quiet homes and first beginning,
Out to the undiscovered ends,
there's nothing worth the wear of winning,
but laughter and the love of friends.'

Index